Doing Events Research

Events management is a rapidly expanding discipline with growing student numbers; however, currently there are no specifically focused research methods texts available to serve this growing cohort. Fulfilling the need for a relevant book which reflects the unique characteristics of research in the field, *Doing Events Research* provides students with innovative ideas and inspiration to undertake their own research work, and informs them of the wide diversity of research strategies and contexts that are available.

The content is written from a researcher's point of view and provides a step-by-step guide to accomplishing a project or dissertation in the field of events. The reader is guided right from the beginning in selecting a topic for research; identifying aims, objectives and questions; and then determining which research methods are the most appropriate and practical. They are then shown how to analyse and interpret their data as well as writing up the project.

Whilst many current texts are skewed either towards qualitative or quantitative methods, *Doing Events Research* provides a balanced coverage of both. It incorporates not only traditional research methods, but also contemporary techniques such as using social networking websites and Google analytics. Specific research case studies are integrated to make applications accessible to events students and show the unique characteristics of researching in this field. A range of useful learning aids spur critical thinking and further students' knowledge.

This book is visually accessible, and whilst written in an engaging style it nonetheless maintains academic rigour grounded in research and scholarship. This is essential reading for all events students.

Dorothy Fox is a Lecturer in Events Management in the School of Tourism at Bournemouth University and has a background of mixed methods research. She has experience supervising both undergraduate and postgraduate dissertations and leads the teaching of both the research methods module and the dissertation module for events management students.

Mary Beth Gouthro is Lecturer in Events Management at Bournemouth University and also oversees Graduate and Professional Engagement for the Events and Leisure courses in School of Tourism. She has extensive experience supervising both undergraduate and postgraduate dissertations in the field. Mary Beth's research interests in events span the event experience, volunteering in events and event evaluation. Mary Beth draws from a cross section of professional experience that includes working with charities, corporate organisations and government. She is a member of the International Special Events Society (ISES) and the Association for Events Management Educators (AEME).

Yeganeh Morakabati is a Tourism Risk Analyst (for the Middle East) and Research Methods Specialist. She is currently Senior Lecturer in the School of Tourism at Bournemouth

University. She lectures and supervises undergraduate and postgraduate students in research methodology and marketing.

John Brackstone has undertaken and managed a wide variety of commercially focused event and tourism research projects, including very large visitor surveys and event impact studies. John has managed research for event organisers at a national, regional and local level and advises and supports many organisations in their event research. He has a special interest in the practical applications of e-research.

Doing Events Research

From theory to practice

Dorothy Fox, Mary Beth Gouthro,
Yeganeh Morakabati and John Brackstone

Routledge
Taylor & Francis Group

LONDON AND NEW YORK

First published 2014
by Routledge
2 Park Square, Milton Park, Abingdon, Oxon OX14 4RN

and by Routledge
711 Third Avenue, New York, NY 10017

Routledge is an imprint of the Taylor & Francis Group, an informa business

British Library Cataloguing in Publication Data
A catalogue record for this book is available from the British Library

Library of Congress Cataloging in Publication Data
Fox, Dorothy.
Doing events research : from theory to practice / Dorothy Fox,
Mary Beth Gouthro, John Brackstone.
     pages cm.
     Includes bibliographical references and index.
     1. Special events–Research. I. Title.
GT3405.F685 2013
394.2072–dc23   2013034483

ISBN: 978-0-415-66668-8 (hbk)
ISBN: 978-0-415-66669-5 (pbk)
ISBN: 978-1-315-81508-4 (ebk)

Typeset in Frutiger
by Sunrise Setting Ltd, Paignton, UK
Printed in UK by Ashford Colour Press Ltd

Contents

Contents

Contents

List of illustrations

Tables

Graphs

Figures

Acknowledgements

We thank our families and colleagues for their support and encouragement, the team at Routledge for their input and guidance, and the students at Bournemouth University for their inspiration, and especially the following for their contributions:

Aimee Goodwin
Emma Martin
Emma Needham
Georgia Meshkova
Geraldine Sweetland
Gregory Kapuscinski
Jennifer Butler
Jiehong Wang
Lea Degn Falch
Matthew Martineau
Natasha Ladbury
Rachel Pike
Sarah Warr
Tannaz Amirshahi
Thomas Haywood.

PART I

The context of research

Chapter 1

Introduction

'Beginning at the end'

Chapter learning outcomes

In this chapter we:

- Introduce the contents of the book
- Identify the outputs and outcomes of research
- Outline the role of research in events management.

Paradise is a small island in the South Pacific. The government wants to enhance the economic benefits of tourism, by encouraging events and festivals that international visitors will want to attend. The team in the Department for Economic Development begins to draft details of a tender to engage a research consultancy company to undertake research on the island and in those overseas countries that form its main international tourism markets. However, as they do so, they realise that they are unsure as to what exactly they want the researchers to find out for them. So they begin by exploring the events and festivals which they know about already. The members of the Department agree that there are some very good existing events because they have attended them, including sporting events and some cultural festivals organised by the indigenous population. However, they have no idea of the full extent of the island's events nor could they describe them.

Nonetheless, their local knowledge also confirms that there are several good venues for events, including an excellent conference facility, but they are aware that the venues are not close to the island's hotels. There has been some research carried out by the University of Paradise Tourism Faculty. Their survey found for example, that tourists thought the islanders to be very friendly, but that there are not enough taxi cabs. Perhaps, the team realise, the distance to the hotels coupled with the shortage of cabs could explain why the Paradise Convention Centre cannot attract large international conferences. The former colonial power also has some data, but it is very out of date now, yet there is some interesting current material that they could use from the Paradise Island blog. The Department has been instructed to increase tourism spending, but they cannot predict what the impact will be on the local population and the natural environment. The latter is very special because part of the island is a UNESCO World Heritage Site. In fact, as they continue, they recognise that there is a lot that they will need to know, with very little existing data to draw on.

Introduction

Special events have been a part of human society ever since there have been people to get together for a short time to do something different. More formally, Getz (2012: 40) defines 'planned events' as 'live, social events created to achieve specific outcomes, including those related to business, the economy, culture, society and environment'. He goes on to suggest that 'event planning involves the design and implementation of themes, settings, consumables, services and programmes that suggest, facilitate or constrain experiences for participants, guests, spectators and other stakeholders'. These stakeholders may be other individuals such as volunteers and event employees, or at an organisational level, include community groups or corporate organisations such as sponsors (Hede 2007). We believe that every aspect that Getz refers to cannot be planned without prior knowledge and that comes from either the perceptions of the organisers from their previous experience or the experiences of others, from whom they have obtained information. This we believe is at the core of events research, recognising what one already knows and drawing on the expertise of others. That expertise may be from previous research but can also be from the stakeholders. For example, only the attendees can tell you what the reasons were for them going to the event. We propose that this process not only needs to be systematic but also, like many endeavours, should conform to societal norms – in this instance of the events industry and/or academia, if its value is to be acknowledged. We set out in this book to provide practical guidance for students and industry practitioners in undertaking research in the field of events management that can contribute to enhancing the experience of event stakeholders.

Imagine if a city sought to develop an events strategy with the aim of enhancing the lives of the people who live and work there. What research do you think they would need to carry out to develop a successful, sustainable plan? There are obviously many aspects that they would need to consider, and using Rudyard Kipling's 'six honest serving men' of what, where, when, how, why and who could prompt some initial questions:

- What events already take place in the city?
- Where are there suitable venues for events?
- When would be the best time of the year to have events?
- How could the events be marketed?
- Why does the city want to have an events strategy?
- Who would attend the events?

Perth and Kinross Council developed an events strategy and action plan for 2006–2011 (Perth and Kinross Council c.2003) as part of their 'vision to become one of Scotland's most successful event destinations by 2015'.

Their research evaluated the following aspects and found:

- *The market*: 91 per cent of total trips are made by UK residents, of which 64 per cent are Scottish. They are mainly 'empty nesters' (i.e. couples aged 45+ whose children have left home) and are predominantly on short breaks.
- *Current events*: there are a range of over 700 international, national and regional events each year.
- *Economic impact*: calculated through economic impact assessments.
- *Forthcoming major events*: the opportunity to bid for major events, such as the 2014 Ryder Cup golf tournament at Gleneagles.

Consider how the authors of the report obtained this information: would it already have been collated, and if not, how could the data be obtained? Who would have the expertise, what methods would need to be used and how could the data be analysed? It is questions like these to which this book aims to provide answers.

This chapter introduces the contents of the book. It encourages you to consider from the start of your research what outputs you want from a research project and to appreciate the role that research plays in the events industry. The title of the book is *Doing Events Research: From Theory to Practice*, because we hope you will use this book to apply the theory that you learn in lectures and from other sources to real-life research projects. Whilst the principal audience for this text is undergraduate events management students, we hope that it will also help event practitioners, whether professionals in the events industry or volunteers in the charitable sector, who are undertaking research to enhance their events.

Perhaps one of the most daunting tasks as an undergraduate student is when for the first time you are required to produce a significant piece of independent work as a project or dissertation. This may well be something you have not done in the past and whilst the training you receive during your course will always help, the prospect of undertaking an independent piece of research is challenging and can be quite demanding. You may find that you have to select a topic or an approach to a topic, your research aim and objectives and the type of research methodology you are going to use. Your decision on these matters will affect everything you do in your project or dissertation from the very start!

When we first began thinking about writing a textbook, we asked our students what sort of books they liked and what they would want to see in this one. They told us that they didn't like page after page of text, but did like boxes containing information, such as definitions. So for example:

Definition box

Whilst there is no consensus on a precise definition of *research*, it is usually agreed that it is:

A process of enquiry and investigation
It is systematic and methodical; and
Research increases knowledge.
                    (Wilson 2010: 2)

We will discuss this further in the next chapter.

The students were concerned that there is so much information available now, that they didn't have time to read it all and wanted us to provide a few shortcuts. So we are going to give you further reading and links to the internet sources that we think are the most useful. They told us too that they sometimes thought that they were the only one who had problems with their research project – so we provide you with numerous examples from not only industry and academic experts, but also from events management students to help give you confidence when you are doing your own research. Some of our students at Bournemouth University have kindly written about their own experiences of doing research for dissertations. They tell you what they got right as well as some of the things that didn't go quite to plan (or even disastrously wrong) so that you can learn from their mistakes. We will also give you tips from our experiences, as we too were, of course, once novices. Finally, our students suggested that having examples to kick start their thinking about research would be useful, so we begin each chapter with one.

Identifying the output and outcome of the research

This chapter is called 'Beginning at the end', which may sound counterproductive, but we feel that it is essential because you must identify from the start, the *output* and *outcome* of any research. The output is the product created; this may be in a written format or may be something more active, such as a presentation. The outcome is the consequence of producing that output. Understanding exactly what is required and for whom, is essential if you are to be successful. Academic research requires theoretical underpinning as well as empirical data, whereas industry-based research relies more heavily on factual information alone. Business research provides information to inform specific management decisions and whilst academic research may also support commercial decision-making, it tends to be of a more general nature. There can be other differences too. Baines et al. (2009) suggest that in marketing, academic research tends to be applicable in the long term, whereas marketing practitioners are looking for more short-term relevance. This book concentrates on academic research, but many of the same skills apply in the events industry. Chapter 13 describes in more detail the various forms of output, but at this stage, you just need to consider the various types, so that you know what may be required.

Academic achievement

This may be in the form of an assignment, a dissertation or a thesis. Each of these will require you to deliver a written document in a particular format (the *output*) and the direct *outcome* is that hopefully you will do well and receive a good mark which will contribute towards an academic award. For this type of research, what you may find out may not be as important as your ability to demonstrate that you understand the research process and can undertake and write up your research project well. You will be given criteria that you must achieve to be successful and the originality or value of the research may be less important. Fisher (2007: 3) suggests that a dissertation or thesis gives you the opportunity to learn how to undertake a major project that requires you to:

● Be focused on a complex and important issue
● Undertake effective and competent primary research
● Integrate theory and practice
● Incorporate understanding taken from a critical review of the appropriate literature
● Base your dissertation on sound analysis and arguments, and
● Be sensitive to the requirement of the different audiences for the dissertation.

Book

Much academic research into events is published in *authored* books, such as *Events Management* (Bowdin et al. 2011), or in *edited* books such as the chapter 'Wine tourism events: Apulia, Italy' (Novelli 2004) in *Festival and Events Management: An International Arts and Culture Perspective* which is edited by Ian Yeoman and four colleagues. (The distinction between the two types of books is important for when you reference them – see Chapter 6.) Books may be about events management in general or one specific issue, such as *Human Resource Management for Events: Managing the Event Workforce* (Van der Wagen 2007). Chapters on aspects of events may also appear in texts that are not specific to events management, for example 'Special event motives and behaviour' (Getz and Cheyne 2002) in *The Tourist Experience* edited by Chris Ryan, and there are references to events in other genres of book, such as a biography, e.g. *Secret Millionaire David Jamilly's Party People: How We Make Millions from Having Fun* (Jamilly and Cohen 2010).

Journal

Academic journals are peer-reviewed; this is a process that ensures that the work has been 'assessed by independent, expert reviewers, who ensure that the publication is of the appropriate standard' (Gratton and Jones 2010: 57). Again, these journals may relate specifically to events for example, *Event Management* and the *International Journal of Event and Festival Management*, or you may find reference to aspects of research on events in other titles, such as a paper on residents' perceptions of mega-sporting events (Ritchie et al. 2009) in the *Journal of Sport and Tourism*. Generally when we write about a journal throughout this book, we will be referring to academic journals. However, journals can also be professional/industry/trade journals or popular magazines. An example of the former is *Conference and Incentive Travel*.

Conference

A different output is a conference presentation – for example, at the five Global Events Congresses which have been held around the world, most recently in Stavanger, Norway in June 2012. Sessions at conferences may be in various formats. A keynote presentation is given by a widely recognised leader in the field. They tend to last for 30–45 minutes and will often deliver the core message of the conference. Shorter presentations are given by other academics often in sessions of three or four papers, grouped around a particular theme. After the presentation of a paper it may be published as part of the proceedings in paper format, electronically or in a special edition of a journal.

An alternative format is used in poster sessions – these are particularly popular for work in progress and students presenting their studies. Typically, the researcher creates an A3 poster outlining the key issues of their research. They then stand by the poster answering questions and discussing their research with interested delegates at the conference.

Information for an organisation – professional report

A professional report is a form of research output used in market research or event evaluation for the benefit of organisational stakeholders. These stakeholders may include the event organisers or other groups who might be affected by the event. This type of report could for example, enable the assessment of the outcomes that have been achieved based on the decisions taken. These could include:

- The client's needs
- The mission statement – the context of the event
- The event aim and objectives
- The strategy developed to achieve those aims and objectives
- The practices by which the strategy is implemented
- The resources allocated to those practices – human, physical and financial.

SQW Ltd, who are economic and management consultants, prepared two reports for the evaluation of 'Culture 10', which formed part of the North East of England Regional Festival and Events Framework (SQW Ltd 2006). The first was a detailed monitoring and evaluation guidance report which included the development of a framework for evaluation, and the second an evaluation report which used the Framework to assess performance, draw conclusions and make recommendations.

Reports may also be produced to provide information on policies, planning or forecasting and may be in the form of a position statement, which helps decision-makers to become knowledgeable on a particular subject. This type of research is often undertaken by government agencies and can often be found on their websites.

Information for other stakeholders: statistical reports, exhibition or presentation

Finally, the outcomes of research projects can be made available in other forms; the type of output will depend on the stakeholder. Hede (2007) identified community groups as organisational stakeholders as well as corporate organisations. The National Trust, a heritage conservation organisation in England, used events to communicate with their members and visitors to an ancient farm at Saddlescombe, near Brighton. Acquired in 1995, it had escaped the changes of modern farming, retaining many of its original buildings from the past four centuries (National Trust 2009). In 2007 an exhibition was mounted at an open day, in order to consult with the public and the local community on how to conserve the farm for the long term. Through interviews, visitors were asked what they would like to see incorporated into the plan for the farm. Subsequently the findings of the research were presented at further exhibitions at the site (Fox and Johnston 2009).

The role of research in events management

This book aims to help you undertake research relating to festival and events management, and we will therefore describe key areas of research in our field. The events industry has a long history dating back to religious and other celebratory festivals and events, but it is really only in the latter part of the twentieth century that it has been recognised as an industry in its own right, needing professional management to ensure its success. With professionalism has come the recognition that research is an essential element of the event organiser's role. There are two types of research that can be considered. At one end of the spectrum is *pure research*, which is undertaken only to gain a better understanding of an issue with no other purpose than intellectual curiosity. At the other end of the spectrum is *applied research* (see Chapter 2). This research is undertaken specifically to offer a solution to a practical issue. The following are some of the main aspects being researched in relation to events and festivals.

Getz (2007) defines event studies as 'the academic field devoted to creating knowledge and theory about planned events', whereas events management is 'the applied field of study and area of professional practice that draws upon knowledge and theory from Event Studies' (Getz 2007: 2). Event studies draws on a variety of disciplines and therefore research in this area similarly adopts the methods associated with those disciplines.

Event studies

Student vignette

Postgraduate events management student Sara undertook a study of the rose-water festival in Iran to assess its role in cultural tourism.

I was born in Iran (otherwise known as Persia) a country with a population of over 70 million people and one of the world's oldest continuous civilisations. It is

(Continued)

Student vignette (continued)

a country rich in heritage and culture which it celebrates through a variety of festivals including the rose and rosewater festival (*Jashnvareyegolvagolab*). Each spring, near the city of Kashan, the festival hosts a great number of tourists, particularly domestic tourists. During the festival, almost every family in the area participates in the festival and its related activities.

My undergraduate degree was in tourism and I was interested in how the rosewater festival could attract international tourists to what is quite a unique cultural event. This could bring benefits to the local residents, the region and the country.

The light pink Mohammadi rose used for this purpose is named after the prophet Mohammad, for its 'delightful fragrance'. The flower picking season starts in the middle of the spring, before the first heat of summer, when the flowers are fresh and new. The timing of the festival is therefore based on the weather and usually lasts for about 10–20 days. 'Rosewater, itself a by-product of the production of rose oil for use in perfume, is used to flavour food, as a component in some cosmetic and medical preparations, and for religious purposes throughout Europe and Asia' (*Iran Daily* 2009).

Flower picking starts at dawn and continues until mid morning as the ideal aroma and best quality rosewater is obtained from early morning fresh flowers. For this reason, during the flower picking period, every member of the family goes to help in order to expedite the process. The distillation process must be carried out immediately, with the process taking 4–18 hours, and they say the slower the process the better the quality of rosewater upon condensation (*Iran Daily* 2009). Visitors are taken on tours to the rose gardens and local houses to be shown the traditional process of rosewater extraction.

My findings showed that the festival lacked destination management, with little or no policy or planning, and insufficient infrastructure, such as hotels and tourism facilities, including credit card services and internet access. There was insufficient marketing or promotion of the event to international audiences. Interestingly, some of the local people I interviewed believed that their traditions are more interesting for native visitors rather than foreign tourists. This they thought was because foreigners, especially non-Middle Eastern tourists, do not use rosewater in their lives and/or have no idea about this product, therefore there is no motivation for them to go and participate in such an event.

Market research

Market research (or marketing research) is the 'systematic, objective collection and analysis of data about a particular target market, competition, and/or environment' (DJS Research Ltd 2011). Market research therefore incorporates much more than simply identifying the target market for an event and establishing whether they would want to attend. It also incorporates the effectiveness of any marketing communications and the influences of price and supply (Getz 2007). Wood (2004) identified that the aim and objectives of an event are the starting point for the marketing information needed. Thereafter the focus is on an analysis of the customer, including segmentation and expectations and satisfaction. Considerable research has been undertaken into event segmentation; for example, Fox and Edwards (2009) analysed the socio-demographic and other characteristics of actual and potential visitors to horticultural shows. They collected data from a survey of residents in southern England and found that whilst age is a key demographic variable, a more valuable means of segmenting the population is by their level of enthusiasm for gardening.

A key element of event market research is to forecast attendance for major events. Witt et al. (1995) developed a model for an international conference, based on income, travel cost and the conference fee as three economic variables, together with the place of origin of a delegate and the location of the conference.

Some market research is undertaken to collect data about a sector rather than an individual event. Research like this is often carried out by commercial companies such as Mintel, and organisations (including universities, who make the reports available to their students) are able to purchase the data for a subscription fee. Occasionally the reports can offer apparently conflicting data, so the assumptions made when collecting the data should be read carefully.

Event research in action

Lisa worked for a UK multi-award winning festival which runs each year in July for five days. It has a programme of music, comedy, free workshops, street theatre, spoken word and film. With a limited capacity of 4,000, it is an intimate festival aimed at all ages and has sold out in advance for the past sixteen years. However, ticket bookings for the Festival have slowed over the past few years. Although still a sell-out, the date of the final ticket being sold has moved closer and closer to the event. Therefore the festival organisers decided to run a new data capture campaign at the 2011 festival called 'The Big Survey' and Lisa was allocated the task of managing the process. They designed a survey asking questions, such as age, postcode, type of ticket purchase, how many times the festival attendee had been to the festival, favourite places at the festival and reasons for coming. The data will be invaluable to festival organisers in identifying their key target audience and demographics, why they attend the festival, what they do and don't like at the festival and so forth. The festival hopes that they will be able to use this data to target their marketing campaign previous to the 2012 festival more successfully so that they will notice a higher rate of selling tickets.

Researching venues, contractors, suppliers

Event organisers undertake considerable research at the planning stage into the suppliers for an event. However, little of this research is formally collated and it is rarely published. Selection of venues and contractors is often based on previous experience, personal contacts and the use of trade organisations. In the UK examples include the National Outdoor Events Association and industry media, such as The Main Event which contains an A–Z directory of suppliers for every aspect of an event. Another means is to use internet search engines, but websites are a tool for selling a venue and as Owen and Holliday (1993) recommend a site visit should be made (preferably unannounced) so that through participant observation (see Chapter 8) the ambience, decoration, courtesy of staff, etc. can all be verified prior to any contract being agreed.

Assessing risks

Events are special because they are different; there is always therefore inherent risk in organising one (Laybourn 2004). Additionally, if there was no risk, there would be no competitive advantage (Allen 2000). 'Risk can be defined as the combination of the probability of an event and its consequences' (The Institute of Risk Management 2002:2); and as Tum et al. (2006: 149) state: 'Risk management is the art of being aware of all the things that could go wrong and having plans and contingencies to prevent this, not to remedy the situation as best as possible if things do go wrong'. The process of risk management is therefore to anticipate the risks associated with an event, and this of course requires research. Thereafter the degree to which the risks could impact upon the event need to be assessed and contingency plans developed to avoid or minimise the potential impacts of the risks. Types of risks that can affect events include economic, political, social, technological, environmental, legal and of course health and safety risks.

Various techniques have been developed to help identify risks. Bowdin et al. (2011) list the following:

- A work breakdown structure
- Test events
- Internal/external classification of risks (SWOT analysis – Strengths, Weaknesses, Opportunities and Threats)
- Fault diagram
- Incident reports
- Contingency plan
- Scenario development/tabletop exercises
- Consultation.

Identifying financial elements, including sponsorship, grants and donations

One of the fundamental risks of an event that needs to be managed is the economic risk that arises if the event's costs exceed the income so that the event consequently makes a loss. Identifying and calculating all the likely costs that may be incurred and the predicted income is therefore vital for event success. Sponsorship differs from a grant (which is a form of financial assistance given by an organisation to assist in the achievement of the organisation's aims or programmes) and from a donation (which is given for philanthropic reasons) because it is a marketing investment made for strategic purposes (for example, to increase awareness of a brand).

Appropriate research is needed to identify potential donors and grant-making organisations, but considerably more information is needed at all stages of the development of an event sponsorship plan. Bowdin et al. (2011) suggest that the first step in creating the plan is to profile the event audience, based on the market research referred to previously. A register then needs to be created of the assets of the event which can form part of the event sponsorship portfolio. Assets to be identified include event naming, merchandising, hospitality, services, and public relations opportunities.

Research then needs to be undertaken to match assets to potential sponsors. An essential element of this is identifying the marketing trends of the targeted sponsor through event industry associations, the media, etc.

Event evaluation

There are three key phases of event evaluation:

- The pre-event evaluation – for example, this may evaluate the event concept as part of a feasibility study
- The implementation stage – this is the monitoring and control process which is a standard part of project management
- The post-event evaluation.

Shone and Parry (2010) suggest that shortly after the close-down of an event, the organisers and other interested parties, such as suppliers and sponsors, should meet to evaluate the event. However, they note that often, there is little information (data) collected and that good intentions are forgotten under the pressure of organising the next event. The purpose of evaluating an event is not simply to find out what went wrong so that something can be done differently next time. Evaluation should also look at what went well and could be repeated next time, in the same way if possible, and then what went well but could be improved upon further. Evaluating activities and actions in these ways should then enable the question of whether an event achieved its objectives to be answered.

Stakeholders, such as clients, sponsors and grant administrators, will have their own objectives for an event and it is important that they receive the appropriate data to inform their evaluations too. The information that they will need may vary because their idea of success may be different too. They may need to be assured that money that they have invested was used wisely and not wasted. A client may be interested in the actual number of attendees at an event, whereas the sponsor may be keen to know if the visitors are within the target market for their product or brand. Economic objectives can relate simply to the overall gross or net profit or the financial value of sponsorship attracted. Other measures could be the Return on Investment (ROI); that is the percentage return on the amount of capital invested or maybe the percentage increase in market share. Whilst some objectives can be measured, for example, the increase in media coverage of an event, there are other objectives which may be more intangible, for example a charity's need to increase awareness of its activities.

Customer satisfaction

Assessing the customer's satisfaction with an event is perhaps the most frequently carried out aspect of evaluation. Methods used in visitor surveys include asking attendees to fill in a questionnaire or answer questions in a brief interview at the event. However, this is just the first step in evaluating an event. The data may show that the event attendees were not satisfied with the length of the queues for food. However, knowing how long customers had to wait; when the queues to be served formed; why they happened and who was responsible for the decisions made, may all be necessary details if a full evaluation is to be undertaken effectively and a repeat event is to achieve higher levels of satisfaction.

Assessing the impacts (positive and negative)

In addition to the outcomes sought by the organisers, events can have 'externalities' which Getz (2007) suggests often no-one is willing to consider. These impacts should however, be identified and monitored. Positive impacts may include, for example, increased tourism, community pride, enhanced infrastructure and job creation. However, there can also be negative impacts such as traffic congestion, environmental pollution, feelings of exclusion and loss of amenity. Sadd (2010) discusses the impacts on the host communities of the 1992 Olympic Games held in Barcelona, Spain and the 2000 event held in Sydney, Australia. Having undertaken interviews with stakeholders, she reveals that whilst one impact of these mega events is often described as regeneration (a positive outcome) they should more accurately be described as gentrification (a negative impact on the host community).

The structure of the book

The book is divided into three parts; this first part considers the context of research, the second discusses the methods of collecting data and finally, the third part helps you to analyse the data and present your findings and conclusions. These parts are divided into thirteen chapters. The next four chapters consider the initial planning of a research project. Chapter 2 helps you develop the aim and objectives of your research, whilst Chapter 3 describes some of the factors that may influence your project and which are best considered before you begin. Similarly, Chapter 4 encourages you to identify what resources you may or may not have to carry out the research. Building on the previous chapters, Chapter 5 identifies various research designs, so that you can make an informed decision as to which approach may best suit your project. Chapter 6 then discusses existing sources of knowledge and undertaking a literature review. Then in Part II, Chapter 7 considers who or what should be the subject of the research and Chapters 8 and 9 identify how you can obtain data. Chapter 10 begins Part III of the book by suggesting how this needs to be prepared, ready for analysis, which is described in Chapters 11 and 12. The final chapter (13) advises on writing up and presenting your research.

Scenario

You have recently been appointed as the Head of Events in a city or town with which you are familiar and have been asked to develop an events strategy. Answer the questions, using your personal experience and searching the internet for information.

- What events already take place in the city?
- Where are there suitable venues for events?
- When would be the best time of the year to have events?
- How could the events be marketed?
- Why does the city want to have an events strategy?
- Who would attend the events?

Summary

This opening chapter has highlighted:

- The output is the product created by a research study, which is often, but not always, in a written format.
- The outcome is the consequence of producing that output.
- The role of research in events management; and shown that whilst academic research supports industry professionals, they also depend on various other forms of research in order to undertake events effectively.

Further reading

Journals

Examples of academic research on events and festivals can be found in the following journals:

- *Event Management*
- *International Journal of Event and Festival Management*
- *International Journal of Tourism Research*
- *Journal of Sport and Tourism*
- *Journal of Travel Research*
- *Sport Management Review*
- *Tourism Management.*

This list is not complete – articles about different aspects of events and festivals may also appear in other journals – but it is a good starting point.

Books

The following are all books about events management in general:

Allen, J., O'Toole, W., Harris, R. and McDonnell, I. (2008) *Festival and Special Event Management*, 4th edn. Queensland: John Wiley and Sons Australia, Ltd.

Andrews, H. (2013) *Events and the Social Sciences*. Abingdon: Routledge.

Bladen, C., Kennell, J., Abson, E. and Wilde, N. (2012) *Events Management: An Introduction*. Abingdon: Routledge.

Bowdin, G., Allen, J., O'Toole, W., Harris, R. and McDonnell, I. (2011) *Events Management*, 3rd edn. Oxford: Butterworth-Heinemann.

Getz, D. (2012) *Event Studies: Theory, Research and Policy for Planned Events*, 2nd edn. Abingdon: Routledge.

Goldblatt, J. J. (2008) *Special Events: The Roots and Wings of Celebration*, 5th edn. New York: John Wiley and Sons.

Page, S. and Connell, J. (2011) *The Routledge Handbook of Events*. Abingdon: Routledge. See particularly chapter 29, 'Quantitative and qualitative research tools in events' by R. Shipway, L. Jago and M. Deery.

Quinn, B. (2013) *Key Concepts in Special Events Management*. London: Sage Publications.

Raj, R., Walters, P. and Rashid, T. (2013) *Events Management*, 2nd edn. London: Sage Publications.

Web links

Here are some useful links to event industry journals and associations:

- *Event Design Magazine* (www.eventdesignmag.com/index.asp)
- *The Event Magazine* (www.eventmagazine.co.uk/home/)
- Event Planners Association (www.eventplannersassociation.com/)
- Event Solutions: For Successful Events, Meetings and Incentives (www.event-solutions.com/)
- Exhibition and Event Association of Australasia (www.eeaa.com.au/)
- International Special Events Society (www.ises.com/Home/tabid/36/Default.aspx)
- *The Main Event* (www.themaineventmagazine.co.uk/)
- Meeting Professionals International (www.mpiweb.org/Home)
- National Outdoor Events Association (www.noea.org.uk/default.asp?pageId=47)
- *Special Events Magazine* (http://specialevents.com/)
- *Whatsonwhen* (www.whatsonwhen.com/sisp/index.htm).

Video links

Professor Joe Goldblatt, a leading academic in events management, talks about research on events in Scotland: *Prof Joe Goldblatt: Research* (5.26 minutes). Online. Available HTTP: www.youtube.com/watch?v=q0F-Y5rV2fA&feature=related (accessed 7 April 2013).

Whilst designed for postgraduate students this video will also help undergraduates: *Writing a Dissertation* (21.48 minutes). Online. Available HTTP: www.youtube.com/watch?v=1hVNF_8S6Ok (accessed 7 April 2013).

Chapter 2

The initial planning of a research project

Chapter learning outcomes

In this chapter we:

- Suggest ways of generating a topic for a research project
- Describe different types of research
- Provide help in shaping the aim and objectives of a study.

Rob is in the final semester of his penultimate year of study for an events management degree. He knows that he has to undertake a dissertation in the following year, but can't make his mind up as to what he should do. He knows the output will be a 10,000-word dissertation and he hopes the outcome will be a high grade, but beyond that he's still quite disorganised. He has discussed some possible ideas with his friends, but is still undecided. At university he has enjoyed the lectures and seminars on consumer behaviour, especially the work on event travel careers and particularly Stebbin's theory of 'serious leisure' (Stebbins 2006). However, he wonders if he should consider a topic that is very contemporary such as the major incident involving the crowd at a music festival earlier in the year, which received considerable media coverage. Or perhaps something based on the volunteering he undertook last break – he could do a case study. Finally, he thinks about his weekend hobby of sailing – he'd love to do a dissertation about that. When he talks to his friends about it, he becomes really enthusiastic for one or other of the ideas, but then the next time, he has changed his mind again. It seems that each idea has possibilities, but also drawbacks and he's not sure which are the most important aspects to consider. In the end he decides to read more about the topics and then discuss them with his supervisor at his first meeting next year!

Introduction

In the last chapter we considered the *outcome* of your research and the *output* that would be needed to achieve this successfully. In this chapter we begin by describing the research process in a general way to achieve that outcome. You will discover that the research process does not proceed in a tidy, orderly fashion, with one part finished, so that you can begin the next. Instead you need to be moving back and forth between different activities as your research progresses. It is, however, systematic. You also need to be aware that there is not one correct order of proceeding. Some methodological approaches demand a different order – we discuss those in Chapter 6. For now, we suggest as a guide the following steps (the relevant chapters in this book are shown in brackets):

1 Selection of topic
2 Identifying the aim and objectives and scope of the research (Chapters 2–4)
3 Review of the literature both theoretical and methodological (Chapters 5–6)
4 Collection of data, including a pilot study (Chapters 7–10)
5 Analysis of data (Chapters 11–12)
6 Drawing conclusions (Chapter 13).

Next in this chapter we begin to think about what the topic of the research will be. The outcome required influences this. For example, if you are undertaking a study in industry, the output will be determined by the person or organisation commissioning the research. If however, your study is part of the academic requirements of your course, you may have considerable freedom in choosing your project. This chapter therefore considers ways in which you are able to first generate ideas for topics and then develop finely tuned research *aim(s) and objectives, research questions* and *hypotheses*.

First, if you have the opportunity of determining the subject of your own research study, there are a few considerations to bear in mind before you think about the factors that influence the design of all research projects:

● This is your chance to explore your own ideas, so does the topic really interest you?
● Will the research be interesting to others?

- Do you have the appropriate background knowledge or expertise for example, to take part in an activity in which you need to be a participant observer?
- Would you like the research to benefit an organisation with whom you are associated?
- Will the study be useful for you in terms of career development?

Generating ideas for topics

You may find it difficult at first to identify a topic for your research. Getz (2007) suggests a research agenda for event studies providing themes, key research questions and possible research methods, which may help you. The agenda consists of:

- Planned event experiences and meanings
- Antecedents and choices
- Management, planning, design and operations of events
- Patterns and processes
- Outcomes and the impacted.

Alternatively, students often start with a context, such as an event, type of event or industry organisation with which they are familiar. This may be from working at an events company, volunteering or attending an event. Your institution may keep examples of previous dissertations submitted and you may find an idea for a topic there. Sometimes an issue may be discussed in the media, which may highlight that this is an issue worthy of investigation. For example, the travel section of *The Times* newspaper (Roe 2012) featured the small city of Guimarães, Portugal, which was the 2012 European Capital of Culture. The article describes how the host community was involved in the festival in a way that was different to what had happened in the past in other larger cities. What sorts of research topics does this example suggest?

Another way to be inspired is through past projects, for example, through research in journals. Look back through recent editions of some of the journals listed at the end of Chapter 1 and think about the ideas or theories that interest you. Also, most research articles will give suggestions for further research near the end which can also help. For example, Hvenegaard (2011) suggested at the end of his article on the conservation benefits of wildlife festivals that much research is needed, including:

- More studies should be undertaken to evaluate the economic impact and value of wildlife festivals.
- Does economic impact correspond consistently with economic value?
- Do local people recognise the connection between economic benefits and festival resources?
- Why do some festivals attract tourists, while others attract more local residents?
- Does educating visitors about wildlife and their habitats at the festivals translate into environmentally friendly behaviour?
- Why do people participate in planning and organising wildlife festivals?
- Are festival evaluations conducted and what are the results?
- How are volunteers utilised?

Remember, the originality or value of the research may be less important than the achievement of criteria by which your research is assessed. However, your research can still be original, not by generating new theories, for example, but by using existing ones in an original way. Veal (2011) suggests a number of examples of how you can achieve this:

- *Geographically*. Often issues are studied in particular countries or areas (perhaps because the researchers who have undertaken the research work have connections in those countries). Therefore you could carry out a similar study in your country – you may also then be able to see if you obtain comparable results.
- *Socially*. Some social groups have been studied more than others. Many student dissertations base their studies on fellow students, but you may have access to another social group, for example, through a leisure interest, which may give you the basis for an original study.
- *Temporally*. Societies are rapidly changing, particularly through the advent of the internet and social media. Therefore a theory that was developed in the twentieth century may be less relevant in the twenty-first, and you could collect up-to-date data to see if this is the case.
- *Contextually*. Through your previous studies, you may have learnt a theory in another discipline that could be applied in the area of events and festivals. Similarly you could apply a theory developed to explain one context in another.
- *Methodologically*. As more *qualitative* studies are undertaken, the opportunity to test a theory *quantitatively* is increasing. Therefore you could obtain data that you can test statistically – we discuss this more in this chapter.

Student vignette

Sam used an interest in video games as the focus for research on e-sports events.

Through the continued development of gaming and internet technology, a distinct consumer group, the 'online gamer', has evolved, of which I am one. We play video games with networks of people across the world on local area networks (LANs). From this has developed e-sports tournaments, which were originally small, for example, the first major UK LAN event was held in 1995 and had twenty participants competing in the then popular game Doom 2 (Fletcher 2002). This then led to many successful events that were later named the i-series. In 2009 there were four i-series, the most recent of which was Multiplay's i-38 that attracted several thousand gamers to compete in competitions in most of the popular games available today. As I searched the literature, I discovered that the events are now being researched by academics, for example, Hutchins (2008) looked at the growth of e-sports and specifically the World Cyber Games.

I was aware that this group of avid gamers has received considerable attention over the past decade, most of which focuses upon obsession, social reclusion and the links between gaming and violence. However, I knew that many travelled long distances and paid high prices to participate in these conventions and I wanted to know more. I chose as my theoretical underpinning the Serious Leisure Framework (Stebbins 2007) as DFC Intelligence (2010) suggests that gamers can be grouped into three categories: 'Hard-Core', 'Moderate' and 'Mass Market'.

A study by Delwiche (2006) comments on the popular modern communication tools used by gamers, which includes online discussion forums. It was clear to me from the abundance of active gaming forums available on the internet that they are a particular rich source of material relating to the topic. This provided the inspiration for my methodology, which included analysing data extracted from the forums of a UK based e-sports event.

Different types of research

Before developing your ideas for your study any further, there are important distinctions between different types of research that you need to consider.

Theoretical and empirical research

One type of difference occurs between *theoretical* and *empirical* research. The former generally analyses existing *theory* and explanations to develop new ideas. Your research would therefore be involved in debating between theories and would not include collecting evidence in the form of data. Hede (2007) used stakeholder theory to develop a framework that can help the principles of the Triple Bottom Line (TBL) to be incorporated at the planning stage of an event in order to make it more sustainable. In contrast, *empirical* research does involve collecting data (empirical means based upon measurement or observation). It is therefore evidence-based research rather than theorising alone. However, researchers often collect empirical data and then interpret them using theory, and it is this empirical approach that we recommend for a dissertation and which we discuss throughout the book.

Logic of enquiry – inductive, deductive, retroductive, abductive

Two main forms of empirical research that you will read about are the inductive and deductive. Blaikie (2000) describes four logics of enquiry and we will look at his additional two forms below, but first, *inductive* research. This is an approach which begins with the collection of data from which generalisations are derived using 'inductive' logic to develop a theory or model. This strategy is often useful for answering descriptive questions where there is insufficient knowledge of a topic. *The Times* newspaper deconstructed the medal table for the London 2012 Olympic Games, and examples of the data they provided are used here to explain these four terms (*The Times* 2012). The United States were 'best for athletics', winning twenty-four medals, Russia was 'best for fighting sports', winning eighteen medals, and Great Britain was 'best for sitting down', having won thirty-two medals. As little is known about whether there is anything inherent in British society to explain why the nation's athletes are so good at sports for which you sit down (e.g. rowing and cycling) as opposed to other types of sports, an inductive strategy would be best used to obtain an understanding of this odd aspect of sporting life.

Having collected data inductively, a newly formed theory could then be tested (and perhaps refined) by collecting further data. This is known as *deductive* research and entails the development of an idea from existing theory, which is tested by gathering data. *The Times'* table shows that the number of gold medals won per $1 trillion of Gross Domestic Product (GDP) was UK, 10.9; Australia, 7.6; Russia, 5.4; China, 3.1 and USA, 2.6. There could be a relationship between the GDP of a country and the number of medals won – perhaps because some countries could afford to invest more in sports than others. Data could be collected on GDP, investment in sports and sporting success to test this theory.

Blaikie's third logic of enquiry is a *retroductive* research strategy. This seeks to reveal the underlying structure or mechanism which is responsible for producing some occurrence which can be observed and therefore measured. Because structures are *not* observable they cannot be measured directly; an example is capitalism. However, if appropriate descriptive data cannot be collected, there can be no evidence that the structure is the only relevant factor. Therefore a deductive approach does not suffice. An example from London 2012 is that the democratic countries of the world won 1.5 medals per 10 million of population, whereas athletes from countries ruled by dictatorships won only 0.76 medals. It would not be possible to use a deductive approach to show how a democratic form of government caused more medals to be won, and so a retroductive strategy would need to be used to identify the structures in democratic and non-democratic countries that could have influenced achievement in sport.

Finally, an *abductive* research strategy aims to provide an understanding of the social world of a person or organisation, which can help provide a more systematic explanation of their actions. Blaikie (2000: 25) describes this as 'their way of conceptualizing and giving meaning to their social world, their tacit knowledge'. Our final example from *The Times* is of Hiroshi Hoketsu, aged 71, from Japan, taking part in the equestrian event, the oldest participant at the 2012 Olympics; and the youngest, 13-year-old swimmer Adzo Kpossi from Togo. They each live in different social worlds, because of the differences in their age, gender and nationalities, but beyond their socio-demographic differences there will also be huge variation in their experiences because of their participation in such different sports.

Exploratory, descriptive, explanatory and predictive research

Imagine if you are interested in new forms of social media prevalent in events and festivals. The first type of research you would have to undertake would be *exploratory* research – you could not research a phenomenon that you didn't know anything about. You would want to keep an open mind – with no preconceived ideas. So you would probably start by talking to people who you think might know about social media. They would be able to tell you about existing types and anything they had learnt about any new forms. Having established that a new form exists, next you would want to form a picture of what it is like. This is achieved through *descriptive* research, and you might find out how it works; who is using it; how effective it is, for example. These are both therefore inductive approaches to research.

You might be told that when the new media are used, it seems that more tickets are sold than usual. You could theorise from this, that there is a link between the new social media and increased ticket sales. You would therefore create a *theoretical framework* (see Chapter 6) so that you could establish, first, whether there is a definite link between the two factors, and second, show that the increased sales are caused by the new media and not by any other cause. This is *explanatory* research. Finally, having reached this stage you would want to know how many more tickets might be sold by marketing them in this way – that is, *predictive* research. This type of research asks 'what if' questions; for example, what if we introduce the new media, how many more tickets might we sell? You will have realised that the explanatory and predictive forms of research both use a *deductive* approach.

From this example, you can see that there is a precise order in which each type of research has to be undertaken. It is impossible to make statistical predictions unless *causality*, (sometimes called causation, that is, one phenomenon causes another to happen) has been demonstrated, and you cannot show that one variable has an effect on another before they have been described. Often these earlier stages may have been carried out by other researchers and the results published in journal articles. Sometimes two stages may be embarked on at the same time – this usually occurs with *descriptive* and *explanatory* research where the same survey is used. If this is the case, as we discuss later (see Chapter 13), the descriptive results are given before the explanatory findings, so as to maintain the logical order. We will discuss how these four types of research are carried out in much greater detail throughout the book. For now, just remember the order in which they have to be undertaken – exploratory, descriptive, explanatory and predictive.

Pure and applied research

If we continue with the example above, you may have been interested in new forms of social media simply to gain knowledge about them with no practical purpose in mind, other than to form theory. This would be *pure research*, which is also sometimes referred to as *basic research* (Flick 2011; Saunders et al. 2007; Wilson 2010) and is most prevalent in academia. This form of research is also used to support or refute existing theories and can sometimes produce new ways of thinking about a topic. If, however, you wanted to find out about the media to solve a particular problem or to resolve a practical issue, for example trying to establish if the increased ticket sales were a result of the new form of social media, this would have a practical application and is therefore *applied research*. This approach is therefore most prevalent in the events industry but although it has a practical basis, it is still undertaken in a systematic way.

Primary and secondary research

Primary research generally refers to research that involves the statistical or other analysis of data for the first time. The methodology is described in full and results or findings are given. Whereas *secondary research* usually relates to the whole or part of a study where information is retrieved and presented logically but not formally analysed (for example, information included in the introduction or literature review of a dissertation). Hvenegaard (2011) referred to earlier used economic data from a variety of studies reported in various publications for his primary research, to show the local expenditure resulting from wildlife festivals in Canada and the USA.

Primary data is data that is collected specifically for analysis in a particular study, for example, data that you might collect from surveys or interviews for your dissertation. *Secondary data*, however, has been obtained by you or someone else for a purpose other than your dissertation, but which you are going to analyse or reanalyse for your dissertation. You might be able to obtain data from two similar events and undertake a statistical analysis to show any similarities or differences between them.

Quantitative, qualitative and mixed methods research

A final distinction is often made between quantitative and qualitative research, based on the characteristics of the data collected. *Quantitative* research methods were initially developed for science subjects but are now also used within the social sciences and humanities. As the name suggests, they are primarily concerned with numbers. Quantitative research is interested in information that can be assessed and used numerically and to examine the relationship between variables (for example, the relationship between age and the propensity to attend a music festival). Also it can be used for *hypothesis* testing, however, which is suited to more advanced types of research. A key means of gathering quantitative data is through a survey. Sometimes, however, it is not the responses of people that form the data – it can also be obtained from other sources of numeric data. Financial records are an example of this (and this would be *secondary data*). What should be clear from this is that there is a variety of ways that researchers can obtain quantitative data.

A quantitative method is designed to provide a general view and this makes it a really useful method to use. However, it may lack the ability to address the underlying reasons for the answers obtained. You must also bear in mind that understanding the numbers is essential but not sufficient on its own; you will also need to relate the outputs to existing theories as we described above.

Qualitative research, on the other hand, uses non-numerical data. This is usually in the form of words, but could also be images for example. Its aim is to describe, understand or obtain meaning. The data is therefore less objective, but can be more detailed or 'rich' and provide depth to a study. Approaches used to gather and analyse the data can be more flexible, but just as rigorous as in quantitative research. Smaller samples or 'cases' are used and the context and the background of the researcher themselves are often important in qualitative research.

Hopefully, you may have grasped that qualitative research is often best for *exploratory* and *descriptive* research and is generally *inductive*, whereas quantitative research is usually necessary to be *explanatory* or *predictive* and hence *deductive*.

A final option is to mix quantitative or qualitative methods, although there are differing views among academics and practitioners about *mixed methods* research. We will discuss this further in Chapter 5.

Student vignette

Gemma carried out a study of the relationship between the motivation and satisfaction of Chinese visitors to the Hong Kong Shopping Festival.

Hong Kong is in the south of mainland China and was ruled by Britain for over 100 years before being handed back to China in 1997. Since then there has been a rapid increase in the number of visitors from the mainland. In 2002 the Hong Kong Tourist Board launched the first Hong Kong Shopping Festival, building on the city's established reputation as a shopping paradise. It has continued every year since and lasts for about ten weeks from June to August. Unfortunately in 2003, the outbreak of SARS in Hong Kong led to a sharp drop in the number of both mainland and overseas visitors. In order to help boost Hong Kong's economy some visitors from mainland China were allowed to travel there individually rather than with a tour party. Initially these visas were only available to residents in four cities in neighbouring Guangdong, but the scheme is now extended to forty-nine cities. The festival is not just about shopping; visitors can attend other events including a dragon boat carnival, a book fair and a beerfest.

I collected data from a survey of Chinese visitors to the festival and so my research was *empirical* rather than theoretical. The *primary research* was based on the analysis of *primary data* from the survey and the *secondary research* consisted of the information I included in my literature review. I used two theories, the pull/push theory of motivation (Dann 1997) and the expectancy disconfirmation theory (Oliver 1980) to underpin my research. As I was testing these theories, my study was *deductive* rather than *inductive*. I wanted to see whether there is a link between the motivation of the visitors and their satisfaction with their experience and so my research was *explanatory*, which suited the deductive approach. The survey provided a considerable amount of *quantitative* data which I analysed statistically. My research can be classified as *applied* research as I made recommendations at the end of my dissertation. For example, I suggested that the service quality could be improved by enhancing the language skills of the festival staff. Mainland China's official language is Mandarin Chinese while the official language of Hong Kong is Cantonese Chinese. The difference lies in the grammar and pronunciation, so it can be an obstacle when serving people.

(More details of Gemma's survey can be found in Chapter 9)

Research aims and objectives

Having considered the sections above, you should now be able to select a topic and have an idea of the type of research you would like to carry out. The next stage is to hone these ideas into a set of aims and objectives that you would like your research to achieve – this is the specific outcome that you would like to achieve from your research rather than the general outcome we referred to in Chapter 1. You need to be reading a variety of literature sources in order to do this. We describe writing up the literature review in Chapter 6; for now, you need to read widely, make some notes and *think* about your topic.

Many of our students spend weeks or even months at the beginning of their research debating on a final title. As you will see in Chapter 13, we suggest that you decide on a final title at the very end of your research. This way it can accurately reflect the research you have undertaken, rather than your initial ideas, which may change along the way. At this initial stage you may just have an idea of what you would like to research, for example *volunteering at events*. We suggest that you make sure your topic is focused and specific by starting with a general research question which you use as a *working title*. So our example could be *What motivates people to volunteer at mega-events?*

This working title, however, falls into the trap that many students make – it is much too broad. Who are the people referred to and what sort of mega-events are you talking about? And that is the easy part; much harder are the key terms 'motivation' and 'volunteer'! So you need to be more specific. In the next chapter we consider the *scope* of the research, but for now, some obvious improvements could be made by identifying who we mean by people and referring to a specific mega-event. One way could be to say students and the Olympics, so our working title is now *What motivates students to volunteer at the Olympics?*

Definition box

Research aim   A general statement of the specific outcome the research is intended to accomplish.
Research objectives   Specific statements that identify the individual stages that will be achieved, which together accomplish the research aim.

The *aim* of a study is therefore a statement of intent expressed in general terms. *Objectives* are more specific; they show the specific outcomes of the research. It is important that you state what you want to achieve, not what you are going to do. So the aim is what you want to achieve, and the objective describes how you are going to achieve that aim. At this stage, we suggest you draft your aim and objectives, but remember you may need to improve them as you learn more in later chapters.

You may already be familiar with the acronym 'SMART' when setting objectives for organising an event, which stands for 'Specific, Measurable, Achievable, Relevant and Timed'. Although this is useful, remember not all objectives need to be measurable.

Practical tip box

Objectives, like aims, are always written starting with 'to' and are of three main types:

1   Knowledge-based, e.g. 'To understand … '
2   Measurement-based, e.g. 'To calculate … '
3   Skill-based, e.g. 'To develop a new method of … '

Here are some of the aims and objectives of our students' dissertations:

Aims

To identify the visitors' motivation and satisfaction of the Hong Kong Shopping Festival and examine the relationship between them (Gemma).
To understand effective advertising techniques in order to effectively promote wedding venues to consumers (Becky).

Objectives

To critically evaluate the literature relating to integrated marketing communications (Jon).

To identify the factors that are most important to gamers considering attending e-sports events (Sam).

To critically appraise advertisement designs (Becky).

To provide some specific recommendations for festival organisers to enhance visitors' satisfaction (Gemma).

Research questions and hypotheses

Associated with the development of the aim and objectives of a research project is the formation of research questions or hypotheses. Most research relating to events management is about people and their social behaviour. We therefore carry out social science research, which differs from physical or natural science research because people do not always behave in the same way or predicatively like other subjects of study. Therefore many studies in our field use *research questions*, which explore the relationships between the elements of the research context. Neirotti et al. (2001) identified seven research questions as central to their study of spectator motivation at the 1996 Summer Olympic Games, held in Atlanta, USA. The first three, by way of example, are:

- What is the primary reason or motivation for attendance at the 1996 Summer Olympic Games in Atlanta?
- Does past Olympic Games attendance influence the decision to attend the current Olympic Games?
- When did the temporal decision to attend the Games occur?

(Neirotti et al. 2001: 328)

However, some areas of events research are more similar to the natural sciences and in these studies *hypotheses* are crafted, which are assumptions or suggestions which can be tested. A *hypothesis* is primarily a predicted result, based on the findings of previous studies. For example, there are many studies reported regarding the income of visitors to events and this could suggest the hypothesis, 'Higher income is positively related with more attendance at events.' Research projects also present a *null hypothesis* which suggests that there is no relationship between the two variables (in this case, income and attendance), and it is this null hypothesis which is tested by statistical analysis (see Chapter 12). From this you will see that the use of hypotheses *must* involve the collection of quantitative data and is therefore associated with *deductive* research which is *explanatory* or *predictive*.

Research questions, on the other hand, suit *exploratory* or *descriptive* research undertaken *inductively* through the collection of qualitative data. However, research questions can also be used in association with the collection of quantitative data if the data is being used to explore or describe a phenomenon in an inductive way. The reading you are doing should enable you to be familiar with what is already known about your topic. You should therefore be able to identify the best approach for your study.

Research philosophies

An understanding of research philosophy is useful in clarifying your design (for example, what sort of data you will collect and how it will be analysed). There are numerous different philosophical approaches, but for the purpose of this book and your research, we will discuss just four important ones.

Post-positivism

This philosophical approach has developed in the social sciences from positivism, which is the research philosophy of the natural sciences. A positivist approach is an objective stance where the researcher's beliefs are truly independent from the subject of study. This is simple in the natural sciences, but more complex in the social sciences. So this led to the development of post-positivism, in which it is recognised that the researcher's personal beliefs cannot be truly independent of the study – although they must do their utmost to ensure that they are, as much as possible. Similarly they aim to be as objective as possible. This means that the researcher must put aside their own personal biases and be detached from the research participants.

Like a positivist approach, post-positivism is *empirical* and adopts the same characteristics of science, moving from theory to observation and measurement – that is, a *deductive* approach. The data obtained tends to be quantitative, with the aim of generalising to the whole of a population. Occasionally mixed methods can be used (see Chapter 5).

Interpretivism

In contrast, an *interpretivist approach* tends to be qualitative and subjective, because the researcher recognises that the social world (or context) of the participants cannot be separated from the research itself and nor can they as a researcher. Sometimes they may be a part of that social world, for example, if they are undertaking *participant observation* (see Chapter 8) or they are even the subject of the research (see *autoethnography* in Chapter 5). A social world is always complex and interpretivists recognise that there may be more than one way of understanding it. The research produced is therefore an 'interpretation' of the data and another researcher may reach a different conclusion from the same material. Therefore this form of research is not used to generalise to a whole population, in the way that a post-positivist piece of research could be. This philosophy suits research that moves from observation to theory, that is, an *inductive* approach.

Event research in action

Schulenkorf et al. (2011) undertook research based on an intercommunity sporting event in a divided society to understand how it could act as a means of building social capital. Whilst they hoped that their study would be of practical value to 'assist governments, policy makers, and nongovernmental organizations (NGOs) in advancing policies and practical measures' (2011: 105) it was nonetheless pure or basic research. The study collected primary data with stakeholders at the first International Run for Peace (IR4P), held in Colombo, Sri Lanka in October 2006. Sri Lanka is ethnically divided and includes Sinhalese, Tamil and Muslim communities and until May 2009 was embroiled in civil war. Therefore, at the time when the research was conducted, the island was a divided society. The event, however, was a day of celebration for thousands of spectators as well as 800 national and international runners. They took part in three races; a half-marathon, a 10km 'mini-marathon' and a 5km 'peace move' after which there was a multicultural music festival. At the awards ceremony, 'groups were awarded for their valued participation, performance, social contribution, and personal commitment, rather than identifying winners and losers' (2011: 109).

The research undertaken was qualitative, as data was gathered from in-depth interviews. It was inductive and underpinned by the interpretative paradigm. The researchers argued that this was appropriate because 'interpretive studies aim to understand the context of a phenomenon through the meanings that people assign to it' (2011: 110). The aim of the research 'was to empirically test whether the IR4P as an intercommunity sport event could provide positive sociocultural experiences on a practical level, while enhancing intergroup relations and stocks of social capital between disparate Sinhalese, Tamil, and Muslim communities in Sri Lanka' (2011: 114). The authors found that the positive experiences did contribute to an increase in social capital amongst the community groups. They concluded that whilst sporting events could not affect community relations without political agreement, they could be a catalyst for change. Finally, they made recommendations for future research, suggesting it 'focus on developing strategies to sustain and grow relationships and social capital beyond the sport event lifecycle, and to leverage positive experiences to the wider community' (2011: 117).

Social constructivism

This third philosophical approach is based on the assumption that knowledge is constructed by social scientists rather than 'out there' to be observed and measured as in post-positivism. Therefore there is no single methodology uniquely used in this approach. As an example, think about language as a social construction – each language is developed by groups of people and whilst they may think a word means the same thing to both groups, it may not. In Australia, a thong is a type of sandal with a toe strap; however, it is referred to as a 'flip-flop' in the UK and the USA. A thong in British culture, however, is a pair of very scanty woman's briefs – confusing the two words could therefore be very embarrassing! This should make you consider carefully the wording of questionnaires or interviews – will the person responding to it understand the question in the way you intended?

Critical realism

Another tradition is the realist paradigm. This, or one of its linked positions (e.g. *critical realism*), uses theory to describe structures and mechanisms in society (which they cannot directly observe and therefore measure, as in the positivist or post-positivist tradition), but whose effect they can observe. So for example, they cannot observe or measure 'feminism' directly. However, they can show that it has caused a major impact on the lives of women especially, and this could be measured, for example, by recording the narrowing of the pay gap between men and women in most countries. So like positivists, critical realists believe in the possibility of causal relationships; that is, they can explain a phenomenon.

In the two following chapters, we will consider the scope of the study and the resources that you may have available to you in order to carry out the research. These considerations will help you define your core concepts more precisely, after which you can finalise the wording of your aim and objectives, research questions or hypotheses.

Scenario

An entrepreneur is planning a major new event on his land called 'Arts by the Lake'. The local community are very concerned about the social and environmental impacts this may have; however, the organiser has argued in the local press that 'the economic impacts will far outweigh any problems' the event might cause. A community leader has raised funds to fight the proposal and has asked the commercial research company in which you are a researcher to undertake a study to 'measure the impacts', to see if this assumption is correct.

- Discuss whether you can 'measure the impacts' of an event before it takes place.
- What specific impacts would you identify?
- What impacts could you assess?
- What assumptions would you have to make?
- Now write an aim and four objectives for the proposed study.

Summary

Chapter 2 has highlighted:

- The many ways that a topic for a research project can be generated if it has not been provided by someone else
- That there are different types of research which interconnect
- That the decision as to which approach to use is based on previous knowledge in the public domain
- The difference between an aim and an objective, and outlined how they are written.

Further reading

Journals

Hede, A. (2007) 'Managing special events in the new era of the triple bottom line', *Event Management*, 11: 13–22, is a good example of *theoretical* research investigating special events and the triple bottom line.

Compare this to Dickson, C. and Arcodia, C. (2010) 'Promoting sustainable event practice: The role of professional associations', *International Journal of Hospitality Management*, 29: 236–244, which reports *empirical* research on sustainable event practice.

Books

Myers, M. (2013) *Qualitative Research in Business and Management*, 2nd edn. London: Sage Publications. Chapter 2 provides an overview of qualitative research.

Wisker, G. (2009) *The Undergraduate Research Handbook*. Basingstoke: Palgrave Macmillan. This is a general text on undertaking a dissertation.

Web links

Cardiff Business School (2012) Learning to Think like an Expert Management Researcher. Online. Available HTTP: www.restore.ac.uk/logicofenquiry/logicofenquiry/Pages/Home.html (accessed 7 April 2013). This is a very useful online learning resource which covers a wide range of the skills that you will need in undertaking an academic research project.

Video links

Whilst the subject matter is not relevant to events management, the debate that the two computer generated characters have in this video really helps explain the differences between qualitative and quantitative research:

Qualitative vs Quantitative Research (6.11 minutes). Online. Available HTTP: www.youtube.com/watch?v=ddx9PshVWXI&feature=related (accessed 7 April 2013).

Hypotheses by Peeyush Malhotra Gurdaspuria.wmv (1.52 minutes) describes the formulation of hypotheses. Online. Available HTTP: www.youtube.com/watch?v=_btOsMgASMM (accessed 7 April 2013).

Chapter 3

The scope of the research

Chapter learning outcomes

In this chapter we:

- Discuss the theoretical aspects of your study
- Encourage you to think about the factors that may influence your research project
- Provide guidance on the ethics of research.

Summertown is a coastal resort that wants to involve its community in a major new event for people with disabilities, as they feel that this market is not served sufficiently by existing events. Thomas, the event organiser, talks informally to members of a local club for people with disabilities, both mental and physical, to see what type of event they would like. The members say that they would really like the opportunity to take part in water-based activities, such as surfing, canoeing and sailing. Thomas realises that he has considered the *disabilities* of the members rather than their *abilities* and has underestimated what the event could involve. He decides that he needs to carry out more formal research before he begins drafting his event proposal. Initially, he contemplates the scope of the research in terms of the focus it will have, but then realises that there is much more to consider.

Thomas is already familiar with organising events for the public in the town generally, but recognises that many of the existing practices they use may not be feasible for the new event. For example, he is used to putting up signs to show where the exits are, but then thinks that event participants with a visual impairment would not be able to see them. Then, it occurs to him that some visitors to his other events may have been in a similar situation and he resolves to rethink his practices for these events too in the future. In the meanwhile, he realises that there will be other health and safety issues that he will need to plan for at the event as he considers the various disabilities of the participants and spectators. Suddenly he grasps the fact that it is not just the event that he needs to think about in this way, but also the research he needs to undertake. His previous practice of handing out paper questionnaires won't be appropriate for some of the people he'd like to involve – he'll need to revise his methodology and come up with an appropriate method to best suit them.

Then Thomas wonders about local residents with mental disabilities – he'd like to involve them in the event and so he recognises that they need to be participants in the research too. This he concedes may raise other new issues that he hasn't properly considered before. He has always been careful in ensuring that respondents in previous research he has undertaken have given their *informed consent* to take part, but with his fresh way of thinking about people with disabilities, he realises that he will also need to rethink who can give their consent personally and who may need a carer to provide it on their behalf.

Introduction

In the last chapter we discussed the difference between *theoretical* and *empirical* research and suggested that events management students would usually be undertaking empirical research and industry practitioners, such as Thomas, certainly would. However, that does not mean that *theory* does not play a part in the design of an empirical research study. In this chapter, we consider the scope of the research, including such factors as the focus, the research chronology and the social context, but we begin with theoretical considerations.

Theoretical considerations

Grix (2010: 101) suggests that 'Understanding the meaning and purpose of theory is very important for undergraduates, necessary for postgraduates and crucial for those undertaking doctoral studies'. This is because the theoretical part of a dissertation provides the underpinning to the empirical section, as all research is rooted in some form of theoretical framework. Therefore the actual research and the theoretical section have to be intricately linked – you cannot just include lots of theories – the parts have to be connected.

This can be problematic, though, because there is no consensus on what theory is.

Definition box

A general definition of a *theory* is a formal idea which seeks to explain something.

However, within different research traditions, based on the philosophical approaches we discussed in the previous chapter, theory has different roles. In the positivist paradigm of the natural sciences, theory orders, explains and predicts outcomes; that is, there are replicable relationships between variables, which can be tested and which can be used to predict what happens in a given set of circumstances. In the *post-positivism* of the social sciences, there are not the same 'laws', but the aims of using theory are the same; that is, to be able to show *causality* and to be *predictive*.

In an *interpretivist* approach, researchers view theory as a means of understanding society by describing and interpreting how people live their lives. They tend not to show that one variable causes another, or try to predict what might happen in a given set of circumstances.

This is only a simple outline of research paradigms, and more information can be found in the further reading section at the end of the chapter. The important point here is that when you plan and design your research you must be consistent throughout. So for example, if you want to predict an outcome in your research, you need to use the *post-positivist* approach. Therefore you need to work *deductively*, collect *quantitative* data and test *hypotheses*. If, however, you want to explain why something happens in events management you could use a *critical realist* position. This is also *deductive*, but you develop *research questions* to answer rather than *hypotheses* to test. Your data is most likely to be quantitative but may also be *qualitative*. Finally, you create research questions and work *inductively* in the *interpretivist* tradition if you want to describe or understand some aspect of events management. Here your data is predominantly qualitative.

Event research in action

Choi and Almanza (2012) undertook deductive research 'to investigate the differences in health inspection violations between temporary food services (those found at fairs, festivals and farmers' markets) and restaurants' (2012: 295). It has been demonstrated that there is increased risk from some types of food-borne illnesses when consumed away from home and an outbreak of disease, such as occurred at the Taste of Chicago event when hundreds of visitors became ill with salmonellosis, can affect the success of the event. Choi and Almanza developed two research questions:

R1: Does the number of health inspection violations differ between permanent food service establishments and temporary establishments?
R2: Are the number of critical violations and noncritical violations significantly different between permanent food service establishments and temporary establishments?

Their research used data from a single context, namely health inspection reports from Tippecanoe County, Indiana, USA and was carried out 'after the fact' as the analysis was based on reports from 2008.

In defining the scope of the research, they first had to identify the various forms of establishment that can serve food. They drew on existing classifications to define food service establishments in ten forms of permanent establishments and one group of temporary establishments. The latter they defined using the 2009 FDA Model Food Code (Food and Drug Administration 2009) as 'one that operates for a period of no more than 14 consecutive days in conjunction with a single event or celebration' (Choi and Almanza 2012: 297). They then subdivided this group into fairs and festival events and farmers' market events.

Their results were based on 1,295 inspection reports carried out at 181 temporary establishments (29 of which were farmers' markets) and 553 permanent establishments. The farmers' markets had 2.59 routine inspections on average compared to only one on average at fairs and festivals. In comparison the permanent food-service establishments received 1.92 routine inspections. It was also shown that fairs and festivals had a lower mean number of violations compared to most of the categories of permanent establishments, and also a lower mean than the farmers' markets.

We consider the use of theory further in Chapter 6, when we discuss a literature review (which is where existing theory is presented). First, however, we consider some of the other factors that influence research design.

The focus or context

In the previous chapter we discussed generating ideas and the selection of a research topic, if that option is open to you, or you may be researching an assigned topic. In either case you need to establish the boundaries or 'parameters' of your study.

Morgan (2008) based his research on the event experience on a single event, the 2005 Sidmouth Folk Festival in southwest England. He describes the context of his research, beginning with the start of the Sidmouth Folk Week in 1955 as 'a seaside holiday for folk dance teams' which 'soon developed into a folk song, music, and dance festival' (Morgan 2008: 86). He goes on to show how the event was organised by a professional music promoter and event management company until 2004. That year, bad weather caused the professional organisers to withdraw and its organisation was taken over by 'regional folk music associations, the local town council, and local businesses' (ibid.). This led to the event being held in the town centre and tickets had to be bought for individual events from the town's tourist information office. This context was important to the study, as Morgan (2008: 87) explains:

> The threat to the future of the festival and the changes in organization meant that the respondents were all consciously evaluating the new format and reflecting on their experience of the festival. This makes their insights particularly rich and useful in exploring the underlying issues.

One of the first considerations, therefore, for a research study is whether to base it on a single context (or case) or two or more. A *comparative* design compares two or more groups in relation to a variable or characteristic. Comparisons may be made on a variety of issues, including geographically or over time.

The research chronology

The next consideration is whether the research is to be carried out *ex post facto*, which is 'after the fact'. Most research in events management does fall into this category, but it is essential if you want to show *causality* as we discussed earlier. An exception is *experimental research* (see Chapter 5) where participants are studied as they undertake some action.

Thereafter, you need to think about whether the research is carried out just once or is repeated over a period of time.

Definition box

Cross-sectional research is the study of a phenomenon at a single point in time.

A *cross-sectional* design incorporates data that is collected at a particular point in time, i.e. it provides a 'snapshot'. This may be advantageous for students in that it can be less time-consuming and completed over a relatively short period. However, not all topics are suitable for this type of design. Imagine you wanted to conduct research on an event using new technology. The first event may produce very positive market research, but over a period of years the technology will date and if the organisers do not change the format, the feedback will be less positive.

In contrast to a cross-sectional design a *longitudinal* study may be more effective in some circumstances. This is a study, often of a single case, which is repeated either once or a number of times – often over a period of years. It is used where the aim of the research is to examine change over time. These could be changes in organisations or perhaps an event format and can be brought out by changes that are economic, demographic, social, political, environmental, etc. One of the key decisions in this type of design is whether the exact same participants are to be part of the study. For example, a company may want research undertaken on an experiential event to raise awareness of their brand. The sample could be drawn from attendees at the event and then a multi-stage study (as opposed to a single-stage study) could be carried out over a period of time, perhaps on arrival at the event, immediately after it and then again finally some months later. A problem with this format is that participants may withdraw prior to completion of the research. Alternatively, different people could be asked to participate in each stage of a study over a number of years.

One form of longitudinal design that may be appropriate for students is where a study has already been undertaken by someone else and with their permission, the same method is repeated. For example, the student uses *secondary data* (see Chapter 2) from an original study and then undertakes their own *primary research* using the same survey instrument to make comparisons between the two data sets. Remember that permission to do this must be obtained from the original researchers (see *plagiarism* in Chapter 6), and check with your tutor that this is permissible within your institution's regulations if you are being assessed.

The term *action research* was suggested by the social psychologist Kurt Lewin in 1946 (Wilson 2010). Not only does the researcher take an active role in the research, but also actions as well as a research outcome are produced (see Chapter 5). Action research is often associated with organisational change and can involve a longer time frame than that usually available to a student. Also a student may not be in a position or be able to obtain the authority to instigate changes within an organisation.

Fox and Morrison (2010) used action research to investigate the introduction of a change in the learning and assessment of event management students to see if it enhanced their employability. Data collection was carried out twice within the first academic year, with modifications, highlighted by the research, introduced for the next cohort of students in the following academic year.

The geographic scope or location

One of the problems that tutors most often cite about students' research is that it is 'too broad'. Research projects can be too broad in many ways, but one of the easiest ways to limit this to some extent, is through its geographical scope. Imagine some research was to be undertaken on catering for spectators at rugby league matches. Rugby is played in many countries around the world, and so one of the first ways of limiting the scope is to stipulate that the research will be undertaken in just one country, say South Africa, New Zealand, Argentina or France. All of these countries play rugby and have very different cultural backgrounds and hence different forms of catering for the spectators. Then perhaps you could limit the study further, for example, in South Africa, the game is divided into five provinces and just one could be studied. This has the effect of reducing the number of possible variables as well as making the project more manageable. The practical aspects also matter, with probably the most important factors being where you are living or can visit or whether you can speak a language to gain access. The important point is that you clearly set out the geographic limits of your study from the outset.

Political, economic, environmental contexts

Other considerations can also influence the research design. The *political* context of a research project can have far reaching implications, particularly if the study has policy implications. Consider the social impacts of a major event on a host destination – politicians at a local level may have a very different perspective to that of regional or national politicians, even if they are from the same political party, let alone if they are from opposing parties. Therefore it is important to consider whether the political aspects are relevant to a research project.

The *economic* context is similarly important. One of the frequent suggestions made to students is to avoid undertaking research if possible on the impacts of an economic situation, such as the global economic crisis, which began in 2007. The problem with this sort of research is that because it may be ongoing and unpredictable, the research has no natural end point – except that imposed by an assignment hand-in date. There will always be new literature appearing, particularly in the media, and it can be difficult to finish the project without seeming outdated.

The final context that may have some bearing on the research design is the *natural environment*. This has two influences – first on data collection and second on sustainable research. An event is different from other activities because it is not permanent; it has a finite beginning and end. This can be problematic, therefore, if the event is cancelled or postponed for any reason, and the planning of the design needs to take this into consideration and have a contingency plan in the background. A frequent reason in many countries for an event to be cancelled is the weather (Fox 2012). Even if an event is not cancelled, the weather can still impact on the data collection and in particular the willingness of people to participate in surveys or interviews.

A second factor in thinking about the environment is the sustainability of a research design in terms of environmental impacts. Printed questionnaires sent to households are most likely to end up at best in the recycling bin and at worst in landfill; only a small number will be returned for data entry. Therefore it is worth considering whether an alternative form of data collection could be better. Similarly, organisations might find it more economic as well as saving on carbon emissions to subcontract local interviewers for a project rather than using in-house employees.

Health and safety

An aspect of research that is often overlooked even by experienced researchers is the health and safety of themselves, their participants and other people who may be impacted by the research. The latter for example, could include innocent bystanders tripping over the legs of a camera tripod while recording an event for an observation study. We consider the well-being of participants (in the section on ethics that follows), but the same general duty of care is owed to them as other members of the public.

Most organisations require you to complete a risk assessment. This may be a formal written document or for students an informal discussion with your tutor. Which is required will depend on the methods you will be using to carry out the study. *E-research* (see Chapter 4) will put you at little risk, whereas employing *participant observation* for example, may increase the risks to yourself.

Finally, any researcher needs to check their insurance cover. You need public liability insurance in case you injure (or even kill) someone whilst undertaking your research, such as the person injured by your camera tripod. Students should be covered by their university policy and industry practitioners by their organisation, but you should check, particularly if the research is to be carried out overseas. Whereas many organisations provide personal insurance for their employees, most universities will not insure a student for any harm to themselves, so personal accident insurance and medical cover too should be obtained, depending on where the research is to be carried out. Lastly, remember to check out insurance cover for any personal or business equipment such as laptop computers.

Ethical issues

Ethics must be considered at all stages of a research project and especially in the planning stage. Denscombe (2002: 175) provides a good understanding of what is required.

> At a practical level, it deals with what ought to be done and what ought not to be done. The word 'ought' recurs time and again when ethics comes into consideration and, for researchers, this calls for some change in their approach to the process of research. The problem is no longer one of what it is possible or logical to do, crucial to the rest of the methodology, but one of what ought to be done taking into consideration the rules of conduct that indicate what it is right and proper to do. It calls for a moral perspective on things, rather than a practical perspective.

The main areas in which ethical problems can arise in research are identified by Punch (2000) as:

- Harm
- Consent
- Deception
- Privacy
- Confidentiality.

When considering whether your research could *harm* any of the participants or other people associated with them, you need to think not just of physical harm which could occur in an experiment for example, but also, which may be more difficult to predict, the psychological impact of your research. You do not know what traumatic event a person may have suffered in the past, the memories of which you could inadvertently resurrect. So you must be cautious if researching a possibly sensitive issue.

Consent to participate in a research study should be obtained wherever possible. Ideally it should be in a written and signed form. This consent should be *informed*, that is a participant should know what they are consenting to. If children or vulnerable adults are taking part, the informed consent of a parent or carer should be obtained. Sometimes, there can be ethical dilemmas over whether and how to obtain this consent. For example, if you were undertaking observation of the crowd management at an open air festival, it would be impossible to obtain the consent of everyone whom you might observe. Similarly, your research might involve the observation of how someone behaves in a 'natural setting'. If you told them beforehand that they were being observed, their behaviour might change. If this is the case, you might obtain the consent of their employer, for example, or the event organiser. Wisker (2009: 215) reminds us that 'If you are an insider to the organisation or group from whom you are seeking information they might feel obliged to reveal things to you, and either this could be helpful or it may be an abuse of your position'. *Autoethnographic* research can also create difficulties, as you are an integral part of the research and you may observe or hear about matters that you had not anticipated, and hence would not have obtained prior consent.

Deception is defined by Grix (2010: 146) as a situation 'in which researchers deliberately give false information to respondents in order to elicit a particular response'. Similarly you need to respect a person's *privacy* and *confidentiality*, so if you state that you will not reveal a person, event or organisation's identity, you must ensure that you do not. Sometimes, however, it is necessary to reveal identities if the research is to be of value. An example of this is Fox and Johnston (2009), who published a paper titled 'The contribution of an events programme to sustainable heritage conservation: a study of the National Trust in England'. The National Trust is the leading conservation organisation in England and so it would be not only difficult but also unnecessary to conceal the fact that this case study research was about the organisation. Similarly, the NT's head of sustainability, Rob Jarman, was widely known and his interview responses provided credence to the interview data which was part of the 'evidence' in this study. Again therefore, the researchers judged it best from the outset to plan to reveal his identity, if he were to consent. When the telephone interview was carried out, his consent was recorded at the beginning and confirmed again at the end of the interview. The interviewer also checked that everything said was quotable as sometimes interviewees say things that are 'off the record', but which they feel will help inform the research.

Ethics in e-research

Research carried out online (*e-research* – see Chapter 4) needs to be undertaken with just as much consideration to ethics as if it were face-to-face. Gaiser and Schreiner (2009: 14) list some questions to consider if you are planning an online study:

- Can participant security be guaranteed? Anonymity? Protection of the data?
- Can someone ever really be anonymous online? And if not, how might this impact on the overall study design?
- Can someone 'see' a participant's information, when s/he participates?
- Can someone unassociated with the study access data on a hard drive?
- Should there be informed consent to participate? If so, how might online security issues impact on the informed consent?
- If a study design calls for participant observations, is it okay to 'lurk'? Is it always okay? If not then when? What are the determining factors?
- Is it ever okay to deceive online? What constitutes online deception?

Practical tip box

- All universities and many other organisations (for example, the Marketing Association of Australia and New Zealand) have procedures or a code of ethics to ensure that research is carried out appropriately. Students probably need to complete a form having discussed their research with their tutor. The form will also need to be 'signed off' by someone with the necessary authority and be kept as part of a record. Some research, particularly if it is more contentious, may need to be considered by some form of ethics committee.

If this is the case remember at the planning stage that you have to allow extra time for the committee to meet (see Chapter 4) before you are able to proceed with your study.

- It is not only people that may be damaged by your research; events and organisations can be adversely affected either financially or by harm to their reputation. So everything that applies to a person, equally applies to an event or organisation.

- In many countries there are also legal requirements as well as ethical necessities that the privacy of individuals is protected and/or any data relating to them is stored securely on computers, so that it cannot be accessed by external parties to the research. For example, in Australia the Privacy Amendment (Private Sector) Act 2000 regulates the collection, use and disclosure of personal information; and in the UK the Data Protection Act 1998 details the legal obligations to protect personal information about individuals.

- All participants need to be provided with the necessary information to make *informed consent*. This may be for example, face-to-face in a visitor interview, a paragraph at the beginning of a self-completion questionnaire, or in an email requesting an interview. Essentially they need to be told the purpose of the research, how the data is to be used and whether their contribution is anonymous.

- It may be that ethical issues are not so important in your country, but you need to consider the rules and regulations of where your research is undertaken. Also, ethics can vary across cultures – consider your participants' culture, not just your own. Show respect for different ways of living – even if you may privately disagree with them.

- If you are in any doubt about the ethics of your research, either at the planning stage or at any point throughout the project – seek advice! Talk to your tutor or the person responsible for ethical behaviour in your university or organisation.

Student vignette

Carol felt that the topic of recreational drug use was important in understanding events in night clubs. Here she describes why she changed her methodology at the planning stage.

My original suggestion for a dissertation topic involved collecting data on the use of recreational drugs, commonly used amongst student social groups, namely in the clubbing events scene. I knew the topic was sensitive and that there would be an increased concern with confidentiality, and in order to overcome this issue I suggested I would keep the data collected strictly confidential. However, I had overlooked that the use of the drugs is also illegal, which could put me in a very difficult, if not dangerous, position and my proposal was therefore rejected by my supervisor.

(Continued)

Student vignette (continued)

After the rejection of my research topic based on the sensitive issues involved, my topic had to be altered. My research question developed, taking into account the ethics and health and safety issues, still focusing on clubbing events, but focusing on the motivations to attend. The pull motivations were classified as escapism and conformity, which very generically included the alcohol/recreational drug taking side of socialisation, but in an unspecified way which allowed the topic to be approved.

In order to collect the appropriate data, a health and safety risk assessment also had to be completed. There were minimal health and safety issues to overcome with my revised plans as my data collection method was an online survey which meant I had no physical contact with respondents.

This chapter has considered the scope of a research study and many of the issues that need to be considered before one begins. Research is very similar to organising an event, in that if you change the scope in one way, for example, increase the number of dining tables at a business event, you will affect other aspects, such as the number of waiting staff required, which will impact on the logistics and the finances and so on. This ripple effect is the same in research design, so it is important that decisions are taken at an early stage and the implications of any later modifications are thought through thoroughly before changes are made.

Scenario

You would like to replicate Choi and Almanza's research (described earlier), where you live. Read the journal article and then answer the following questions:

- Can you identify one example of each of the ten forms of permanent food-service establishments in your country?
- Would the FDA definition of a temporary food-service establishment be appropriate where you live?
- Suggest an event that would meet the criteria and one that would not.
- Which organisation undertakes health inspections of the events near you – what geographic area do these cover?

Summary

Chapter 3 has highlighted:

- The importance of theory in research
- How the research chronology is determined by the aim and objectives
- How the geographic scope can be limited
- That the political, economic and environmental contexts of your research need to be considered

- The importance of assessing the risks to the researcher, the participants and other people or organisations that may be impacted by the research
- That the ethics of the research need to be carefully thought out not only at the planning stage but also continuously throughout the research project.

Further reading

Journals

On page 372 of Sutton, R. I. and Shaw, B. M. (1995) 'What theory is not', *Administrative Science Quarterly*, 40: 371–384, they suggest that 'Though there is conflict about what theory is and should be, there is more consensus about what theory is *not*.' They then go on to explain that references, data, variables, diagrams, and hypotheses in journal articles are not theory.

Books

Denscombe, M. (2002) *Ground Rules for Good Research: A Ten-point Guide for Social Researchers*. Buckinghamshire: Open University Press. Chapter 9 contains useful information on ethics in research.

Oliver, P. (2010) *The Student's Guide to Research Ethics*, 2nd edn. Maidenhead: Open University Press.

Saunders, M., Lewis, P. and Thornhill, A. (2007) *Research Methods for Business Students*, 5th edn. Harlow: Pearson Education. This helps provide an understanding of research philosophies in Chapter 4.

Wisker, G. (2009) *The Undergraduate Research Handbook*. Basingstoke: Palgrave Macmillan. This provides good examples of a participation information sheet and a participant consent form on pages 213–215.

Web links

ESOMAR is an organisation 'for encouraging, advancing and elevating market research' and provides extensive guidance on ethical and professional standards in market research at ESOMAR (2012) *Codes and Guidelines*. Online. Available HTTP: www.esomar.org/knowledge-and-standards/codes-and-guidelines.php (accessed 10 April 2013).

Video links

Research Ethics for Undergraduate Students (7.53 minutes) by Dr Phillip Cole offers useful guidance. Online. Available HTTP: www.youtube.com/watch?v=w8ANF9uRejk (accessed 10 April 2013).

In *Research Insights: Personal and Environmental Influences on Research* (3.06 minutes) some more unusual considerations in carrying out observational research are discussed. Online. Available HTTP: www.methodspace.com/video/research-insights-personal-and-environmental-influences-on (accessed 10 April 2013).

Chapter 4

The resources and e-methods available

Chapter learning outcomes

In this chapter we:

- Consider the resources that may be available to you when carrying out a study
- Identify the characteristics of the researcher(s) that may be of benefit
- Evaluate the technology available, both hardware and software
- Discuss *e-research* and how to apply it.

Ali is a member of a Colombian community organisation which is trying to educate the people of his town on the environmental threats facing the local area. The industrial town where he grew up has considerable problems with air and water pollution and the group is interested in having research carried out on how a series of proposed events and festivals could best be used to educate young people in the town about the environmental threats. The group has many volunteers who are happy to help with the research, especially the data collection, although they have no experience in designing a study or analysing the data. One member, however, is very interested in the latest technology and has offered to help; he wants to use a technological approach to data collection. Ali must decide not only which resources are of most benefit to the study (both in terms of physical and human resources) but also which are in tune with the group's environmental ethos. This consideration extends to the potential environmental impact of traditional methods of data gathering in comparison to the data quality issues that can be a problem with more technology driven techniques.

Introduction

In the last chapter we discussed the theoretical aspects of your study, encouraged you to think about the factors that may influence your research project and provided guidance on the ethics of research. In this chapter we want you to think about the resources that may or may not be available to you in carrying out your research project. These include the characteristics of you and any other people who are involved and other resources such as hardware, software and *e-research* resources. It is at the design stage of the project that these need to be thought about. If a resource is not already available or cannot be easily acquired, it may be best if the method is rethought.

Definition box

E-research (can also be written as eResearch) is the use of information technology to support research. Therefore e-research is a general description given to any type of information technology driven technique and covers everything from the classic online survey 'can you spare 5 minutes to tell us what you think about ... ' through to ecosystem modelling. It goes beyond how the basic data can be gathered, shared and understood to touch the very nature of connectivity between humans.

The researchers

Whatever kind of research is carried out, the people who make the decisions, do the field work, analysis and writing up are paramount to the success of the project. So we begin by considering the *human capital*.

Definition box

Human capital: the skills, knowledge and experience available; in short it is the sum of all the human talent you have access to.

Individual or team

For student assessments, research is frequently carried out by individuals, often supported by a supervisor, but in industry or academia, research is usually undertaken by a team of people, including research managers, field workers, data entry staff and analysts. We begin by considering you, the researcher, what your strengths and weaknesses are, and what will be your role in the research.

Outsider or insider

Consider the context of a research project; is it one that is familiar to you? If you were undertaking research on the employability of events management students, you may consider that you know what it is like to be a student. What about if you were looking at the experiences of women and you are a man, or vice versa; or how about if you are a Muslim and your participants are Christians? Perhaps you may have worked in a company where you were undertaking interviews or perhaps you have not. Whether you are an insider or outsider will therefore be important. As an insider you may have important contextual knowledge which will help your research, but there are also advantages in being an outsider, as you may come to the project with 'fresh eyes'. Your view of the research is inevitably influenced by your own cultural background, however much you try to be objective. So it is important to recognise this rather than pretend it is not the case.

Existing skills and those needing to be learnt

Undertaking research requires numerous specific skills – which we hope this book will help you learn. However, there are also skills and abilities that you may have already learnt such as searching the literature, dealing with complex matters and developing your own ways of thinking about the literature. You will need to be critical in an academic way and perhaps challenge ideas that you have previously taken for granted. At this stage reflect on your learning and you will probably be surprised by how much you can already do. Where there are gaps in your abilities, try to learn as early as possible how to overcome them – your university will have support in place that you can draw on. When you work as part of a team in industry, it can be useful to find colleagues whose abilities complement yours rather than replicate them, as the 'whole' can be greater than the 'parts'.

Additional learning support (ALS) and disability

Consider too areas where you may need additional support. Students with dyspraxia may choose to avoid statistical analysis (although some are determined to rise to the challenge). Similarly a researcher with dyslexia can seek help with transcribing. A student with a disability should not feel disadvantaged, but rather should identify their advantages. For example, a visually impaired researcher can often be a better listener, which is an essential requirement in qualitative interviewing. Often too students may change the way that they are used to working to achieve success.

Student vignette

Joanna was interested in volunteering at charity events and so she investigated the impact the volunteers had.

I was found to have dyslexia in my fourth year of university. I had always struggled with my grammar, spelling and maths throughout my education, but put it down to missing school through illness when I was younger. Since learning I have dyslexia it has made me feel better about the grades and feedback I was receiving from tutors, and instead of wondering why some aspects of my assignments I wasn't doing well in, e.g. my structure and grammar, I understand that this is related to my dyslexia.

For my dissertation I have had to adapt the way in which I researched for my literature review. As there is so much to read I struggled with sitting down and working my way through the journals. To tackle this I time managed my week; this meant that instead of sitting in the library for hours trying to get through them I set a certain amount of hours a day so they would still be read but the task was manageable, and due to my lack of concentration levels also meant that I was more productive. By setting myself tasks for each day it also meant that I kept on top of all my other units and didn't just focus on one subject.

When writing my literature review I also realised that what I thought sounded good when writing it, didn't when reading it back afterwards. To make sure that what I had written made sense, flowed and was grammatically correct, each section I wrote I would leave for a day or so then go back to it. I would then read it back to myself out loud, so when I read it I would know if it sounded right. Both of these methods, although only small changes to how I usually studied, helped me keep up with my dissertation so I didn't fall behind and made sure that what I wrote was of a good standard.

Cultural awareness

Events are global phenomena and you may be undertaking research in a culture which is not your own. Similarly, you may be studying in a country that is not the one from which you originate. Whichever context you may find yourself in, it is important that you recognise that there may be cultural differences and understand how these may impact on you and your research. This cultural sensitivity goes beyond the ethical issues discussed in the previous chapter and into an area of adjusting to cultural norms and thinking about the implication of each and every action. Different countries have different learning expectations and practices, which can add confusion when told to reference, think critically or work independently for example. In some cultures, there is a requirement of deference to authority, whereas in others you will be expected to question, critique or debate with that authority. Whichever system you are used to, it can be difficult to make the adjustment to the cultural norm of where you are studying. Make sure that you discuss your previous learning experiences with your research supervisor, so that they can support you appropriately. They are then much more likely to understand if you get the balance wrong, than if you leave them in the dark.

Writing styles are also different across the world. Carroll and Ryan suggest that in some cultures 'The writing process takes a more circuitous approach, where the reader is gradually taken along the journey in the argument, the main thesis only appears at the very end' (Carroll and Ryan 2005: 105). Whereas, in most Western cultures, it is usual to establish first the main aim and objectives and then the issues and argument, using evidence from the literature in support of your argument. Again it is best to discuss this with your supervisor and ask them to review a small piece of your writing to see if you are expressing yourself in the appropriate way for the dissertation. Another issue may arise through the referencing of work. In Western cultures you are expected to fully reference your work, often in a particular style, such as that known as Harvard referencing or parenthetical referencing. This is a style in which the citation is enclosed within parentheses (or curved brackets) and is the system that you are familiar with from this book.

Student vignette

Danish student Anne carried out research on how corporate event venues are promoting customer loyalty on their websites.

Since the ninth grade the Danish school system has prepared me towards writing a B.A. level dissertation, by slowly providing me with tools and knowledge of how to structure, formulate and build an academic piece of work from introduction to conclusion. Every year, the size and depth of the aims and objectives were increased and the picture of how to do the future dissertation made more and more clear. Then I decided to change the angle of my B.A. degree, by going to the UK for the final year and attending a course that does not currently exist in Denmark. My pre-arrival thought was that language would be the main issue, and as I have already lived and worked in several English speaking countries, this challenge did not seem that frightening.

Looking back, the challenges of being an international student, making a direct entry to the fourth year of a B.A. (Hons) degree, were a lot bigger than expected, and the language was not the major one. Instead mentality, culture and academic approach were the big differences.

I quickly realized that my knowledge of how to build bigger assignments and reports was different from the approach that was expected of me at Bournemouth University. Where I had spent my whole school life arguing my own opinion I had to learn how to argue opinions already expressed by others, which changes the way of writing a lot. And due to just attending the final year in the British system, the assignment I got to practice this new way of thinking on was the dissertation itself. Deciding the approach and methodology for the dissertation without knowing any of the suggested theories made it difficult and extremely time consuming, and put me in several situations where I just took a chance and hoped that my approach would work.

Writing a dissertation in England made me more insecure and dependent on my tutor than I have ever experienced before in a school situation, which sounds foolish as the final year of a degree is all about being independent while trusting and using your skills gained from the previous university years. However, my dissertation was a success and I have a feeling that this experience will make me stand even more strong and independent back home than I did before coming to the UK.

Other resources

Time

The first of the other resources you need to consider is the amount of time that you have available to undertake the research and what other demands are being made on your time. In our experience novice researchers often underestimate the amount of time required for the various activities that you will need to accomplish in order to achieve a successful outcome to your research. When students are conducting research as part of their studies, inevitably they are trying to balance the research with the rest of their course commitments, possibly paid work and/or volunteering, not to mention a personal life. It is important therefore that you plan for the time it takes to conduct your research. The areas where you will spend considerable amounts of time include:

- Fine tuning your research aim and objectives (note: this could take as little as an hour, or go on for weeks on end! Turn to your supervisor for help so valuable time isn't lost here)
- Searching sources
- Scanning resources
- Reading resources
- Writing draft content
- Rewriting drafts
- Building literature review chapters.

And this is only the first stage of conducting research. From here, you will need to also spend time deciding on a methodological approach and related methods of data collection.

Practical tip box

Here are some examples of the amount of time some activities may need (Gratton and Jones 2010).

- Using an online database to find relevant literature – at least a day
- Reading a journal article – at least an hour
- Piloting an initial questionnaire – may take several weeks.

Saunders et al. (2007: 41–42) provide a good example of a student's research timescale in tabular form and then one based on a Gantt chart. The latter shows the activities that make up the research project plotted against a time line, in the same way that many event managers plan their events. The difference between the two is that for the

Gantt chart, you need to assign a period of time in which an activity will be completed. This may be reasonably straightforward for a deductive study (see Chapter 2) where tasks are usually sequential, but may be more problematic for an inductive study for which you may be working iteratively (see Chapter 3). Additionally for novice researchers there can be problems in estimating how long each task may take to complete. However, whichever format you use, remember to not only consider the activities of your research, but also other demands on your time. For those in industry, the need to undertake just one project at a time is rare and planning and prioritising is therefore required. For students, considerations may include assignments, paid and voluntary work and key social activities, such as holidays and birthdays. In Chapter 2, we gave an outline of the research process which can form the basis of your planning. However, one key factor that you must consider is whether your data collection is based on a particular event. If you are intending to carry out a survey of participants at an event, that is an unchangeable period of time. You will need to have completed your literature review and piloted the questionnaire before you can collect the data. The topic of your research can also influence the collection time. It is clearly best to ask respondents what is motivating them to attend an event, prior to their attendance; and similarly, you cannot assess their satisfaction until during or after the event. Some universities or tutors offer a suggested timescale for you to follow. This is based on much experience and you would be foolish to ignore it, except in exceptional circumstances that you discuss with your tutor.

Another aspect of this is time management. Try and be realistic about how much time you will need to undertake the research. If you are unrealistic you may put yourself under too much stress to achieve what you want. Remember you need to work well and not just for a long time. Spending hours at the computer doesn't always equate to the quantity or quality of work produced (especially if that time is spent on Facebook, Freecell or reading emails!). Think about how you can work smartly. For example, what aspects require more time and those for which can you use a short cut (we give some useful ideas for these in Chapter 13 on writing up). Avoid rushing at the beginning especially – redoing something always takes much longer than doing it right the first time, and there are some mistakes where there are no second chances. For example, consider it is too late to change a question in a survey once the questionnaires have been printed and handed out. Consider also which aspects of the study can be carried out at any time and which need to be prioritised.

Sometimes it can be hard to start writing (even as I sit and type this sentence, I think of the many times that has happened to me – so don't think you are alone in this!). The first sentence is often the hardest to write; particularly if it is the introduction to a chapter. So don't waste time staring at the screen, write the next section first and then come back to the introduction. You will be surprised how often this works. If not, stop trying to write and do something else on the project. Reading some more literature can often get you going, or even formatting your references will be time well spent, just don't give up altogether.

Similarly, there can be 'deadtime' on a project – perhaps, for example, you are waiting for your supervisor to read a section of writing. However, you shouldn't think of it as wasted time but as an opportunity to prepare for the next task. Another form of 'deadtime' is when you are doing something else such as going to the library. Remember, you usually think best when you are relaxed and this may be when you are walking, washing up, listening to music, swimming, etc.

Event managers are used to contingency planning for live events and it is exactly the same when it comes to doing research about events. For example, if it poured with rain, an event might be cancelled and any planned data collection could not be undertaken. An alternative date or venue would therefore be needed. So always allow for contingency time when planning your research.Finally, remember deadlines, these may be academic, such as assignment hand-in times, or commercial. Many projects in industry have dates by which the finished research must be presented.

Finance

As a student you must consider whether you can afford to undertake the method that you propose, including travel costs, printing, etc. You need to be clear what costs your institution may contribute to and whether there are any other sources that might contribute, such as a case study company (see Chapter 5) or a grant giving organisation.

Event research in action

When undertaking research within an organisation or commercially for profit, Saunders et al. (2007: 42) state very succinctly that 'Conducting research costs money'. Consideration needs to be given to not only how much the research may cost, but who is paying. When the costs are to be met by a client, they will need careful calculation in the planning stage, if an organisation is to be successful in bidding for the research project. If the quoted costs are too high, an organisation may be undercut by a competitor and lose the business. If too low, they will be operating at a loss, which is not sustainable. As in any commercial operation indirect costs, (such as estate costs and national insurance payments), need to be included, as well as the direct costs of interviewers, data entry, etc. Remember too, an organisation will not be paid until everyone is happy with the research, which may affect cash flow.

Academic support

The main source of guidance for most dissertations is the research supervisor (who is often referred to as a tutor). They will either be allocated to you or in some institutions you may be able to suggest a tutor who you would like to supervise your research. Remember there are various issues you may want to consider if the latter case applies to you. Selecting a tutor with whom you already have a good student/tutor relationship may be understandable, but you may also want to consider tutors who are less familiar to you, but may have the appropriate detailed knowledge in the area of events management that you are planning to investigate. Another matter you may want to consider is whether their expertise is in qualitative or quantitative research and whether they are prepared to supervise more novel methodologies in events management such as experiments or research using images, if this what you are planning. Finally, you may want to find out how much management of your research they will carry out. A dissertation is designed to test your ability to undertake an independent piece of research, and different institutions have different guidelines as to how proactive supervisors may be. Also within institutions there may be considerable variation between tutors. Some may give very clear instructions as to the time line for your research and expect you to adhere strictly to it. Others may hold the view that this is your research and you know best what other commitments you have to meet and when you have time to work on your research. They may be less controlling, which may suit you better. However, if you recognise yourself as the type of student who needs someone else pushing you to work, then the former style of supervision may suit you better.

Other support

In addition to your supervisor, you may be able to obtain support from another lecturer who specialises in the area or context of your research. Just be careful to ensure that your supervisor is happy for you to approach them and that the boundaries of each of their roles are clear. Subject librarians are also a useful source of help, particularly in finding literature, for example, or sometimes with study skills and referencing too.

Remember that many university libraries are open to people who are not employed or studying there. For example, some universities have a reciprocal arrangement with other further and higher education establishments in the local area, whereby students and researchers can borrow library materials (in the UK and Ireland ask about Sconul access). Members of the general public may be able to have reference-only membership at many institutions and some offer subscription memberships to the public and companies or other corporate bodies, which may be valuable to event industry researchers.

Equipment

Hardware: computers, telephones, mobile phones – the sliding scale of technology

The use of technology is all about presenting potential respondents with a survey in a more efficient way or gathering more data from them, thus allowing a more complete picture to be built.

But technology needs to be the servant, not the master, and so it should only be used where it brings real benefit and risks, such as non-response bias, can be controlled.

There are some inherent risks when using technology. For example, it might be that responses are biased towards those who are more familiar with technology. Or the technology itself might become a toy and the answers given not as serious as they might be. But once these are overcome the benefits of using technology in research can be realised.

Paper questionnaires

The simplest way to produce a questionnaire is to design it and print it onto paper; a paper questionnaire can be completed by the respondent, by the interviewer or handed out for later completion and returned in a freepost envelope.

An effective paper questionnaire can be designed with either word-processing software (such as Microsoft Word) or with spreadsheet software (such as Microsoft Excel). Which one you choose will probably be about the piece of software you are most comfortable and familiar with, and the amount of time spent making the questionnaire look appealing depends on how you will be using it. For example, if you're doing the interviews face-to-face yourself then the questionnaire only needs to be a tidy way to record the answers. However, if you're handing them out for respondents to complete later, then time needs to be spent making the questionnaire look as good as possible.

There are advantages and disadvantages to both types of software, so choosing the one you are most at home with is usually the best approach. If you decide to design your questionnaire in some form of word processor then using tables can really help. For example you can use the table to align your questions and responses, but don't forget to hide the gridlines before you print. Figures 4.1 and 4.2 show how you can include boxes for the respondent or the interviewer to tick.

A paper questionnaire allows flexibility in its application but requires data entry to be undertaken subsequently. The next step on from this is using a scanner to machine-read the responses that have been added to the paper questionnaire. However, this is a reasonably specialist activity and requires skill and resources that go beyond the scope of most student research projects. It is used widely in commercial research settings as a way of bringing technological cost saving into traditional research methods.

Technology basics

These days we carry an amazing array of technology in our pockets, all packed into a mobile phone. These tools can be incredibly useful when it comes to research. The key items are the

- Voice recorder: built into most phones (it is in the utilities folder on most iPhones) and ideal for interviews or even at a push recording a focus group (Figure 4.3). The high quality microphones built into most new phones allow small focus groups to be captured adequately. Just make sure you've got enough battery life, memory space (an iPhone uses about 0.5MB per minute so a 10-minute recording is about 5MB, which is usually fine, but some older phones may struggle to record longer sessions) and of course that it is switched to airplane mode.
- Film camera: with permission, focus groups or interviews can be filmed on a mobile phone camera, which can also be used for observation studies. But filming is resource-intensive, emptying batteries fast and using around 4–8GB an hour or 70 and 140MB a minute of memory on an iPhone. Again, ensure that you have both battery and memory space and that airplane mode is on.

Qx. What time did you arrive at the event?			
9am ☐	10am ☐	11am ☐	12pm ☐

Figure 4.1 Tables can include response boxes that have been inserted as symbols

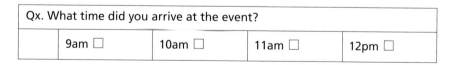

Figure 4.2 Response boxes built into the table

Figure 4.3 Standard iPhone voice recorder

Booth interviews

You have probably seen a computer booth at an event; it is usually a stainless steel stand with the computer inside. The computer runs simple questionnaire software allowing respondents to enter their data directly into the system. This has the obvious advantage of eliminating the data entry phase, which results from paper questionnaires. More-over, questionnaires can be easily produced in full colour, have more space between questions, use images or animations and intelligently ensure that all essential questions have been answered and that priority order and other complex questions have been completed correctly. The system also does not require an operator, and so unlike paper questionnaires, several booths can be put into place and data gathered without further input from the researcher. The specialist software can either store the information locally or transfer it to a central location wirelessly or by an ethernet connection. Once the data has been transferred it can be analysed using traditional methods.

However, there are some serious issues with using booth interviews. These include problems with the technology, either the hardware or software failing of its own accord or being broken by respondents, data being lost or corrupted, and of course theft of the unit! Moreover, respondents using the booth are generally totally self-selecting and not all respondents take the data gathering phase as seriously as they might, leaving the researcher to attempt to decide which responses are genuine and which have been added by people simply playing with the booth. As computers have become old tech-nology and no longer exert a draw of their own, the proportion of people simply play-ing with the booth has dropped over time, but a new wave of technology is replacing the cumbersome, unsightly and expensive technology of computer booths.

This new technology is built around touch screen tablets such as the iPad, and uti-lises floor standing kiosks or lecterns. They have similar advantages and disadvantages to computer booths but take up much less space, are less expensive, look more modern and can be deployed in locations without mains power as they are portable and will run on internal batteries for as long as 10 hours (with the wireless turned off and the screen brightness turned down). The increased use of tablets and the hugely reduced cost of specialist survey software, for example those available in the App Store including Questionnaire by iApps Ltd, has brought tablets within reach of the student researcher. However, the cost of lectern or kiosk stands remains high and application of the tablet technology may be limited to PDA interviews as outlined below.

The decision over whether a booth is appropriate generally comes down to the cost and availability of the technology and the nature of the audience. Only one person at a time can use a booth, therefore it requires a regular steady flow of potential respondents to work. If people are rushing into or out of an event it simply will not work, but if visitors are onsite all day then it has potential.

PDA interviews

Historically, PDA (Personal Digital Assistant) interviews were undertaken using a palmtop computer that was about the size of an iPhone, but as technology has moved forward they are much more likely to be undertaken using similar hardware and software to booth interviews but without the kiosk or lectern stand. Thus the iPad or similar tablet has taken the role of PDA, and software on the tablet can often be used either in a kiosk or by an interviewer. This method of data gathering is often seen on the high street: an interviewer with a tablet, asking questions and jotting responses directly into the system.

As outlined above, the falling cost of tablets and in particular the reduced price of software has brought the use of this technology into everyone's reach. PDA interviews have some clear advantages; these include eliminating the data entry phase caused by paper questionnaires, a reduction in issues around self-selection of respondents seen with booths, and a greatly reduced theft risk. But they do require the interviewer to be present for the duration and cannot be handed out for later completion the way paper questionnaires can be.

Post-event telephone or e-research

Most event research requires responses to be gathered at the time of the event, or at least for the questionnaires to be distributed at the time of the event. However, if a list of attendees and their contact information is available then it is possible to undertake research after the event. Usually this would take the form of a telephone call to interview visitors to the event utilising a structured questionnaire or an email sent to visitors either containing the questionnaire or directing them to a website where the questionnaire is hosted. Although a questionnaire embedded in an email may be easier to respond to, some mail clients may produce problems and it is often more reliable to direct respondents to a website where you have complete control over the formatting and display. Telephone interviewing can be done reasonably simply by using a printed paper questionnaire which is completed by the interviewer during the conversation, or using a script and recording the interview for subsequent transcription. Web questionnaires can be created using a variety of online tools (for example the Bristol Online Tool, www.survey.bris.ac.uk/, or Survey Monkey, www.surveymonkey.com/, or specialist software such as Snap, www.snapsurveys.com).

It is important to look at the limitations of any online tools that you use. For example, Survey Monkey's basic function is free to use but has a limit of 10 questions per survey and 100 responses per survey. This is unlikely to provide a sample large enough to show statistical significance, and therefore a pay service allowing more responses may have to be used. The Bristol Online Tool generally has to be paid for; however, if you are part of a university they may already have an account that you can use.

Online questionnaires have some specific advantages: respondents have experienced the whole event (including travelling home) and have had time for their opinions to 'set' rather than being driven by a minor but recent positive or negative incident. Non-response bias can be controlled to a certain extent by following up with individuals who have not completed their questionnaire. The event experience is not negatively impacted by the questionnaire process and researchers do not need to be on the ground at the time of the event. And finally, if correctly managed a post-event web survey can yield a very high volume of respondents.

That said, it can be difficult to gather a complete or representative list of those who have attended the event, and there are also some data protection implications (although there is an exemption for pure research), and response rates from web surveys can be very poor.

Social media

The internet has become an important tool for the researcher (Flick 2011) and as an element of this social media are growing in usefulness. This can be especially the case in web surveys that do not claim to be representative of a population or web surveys with no limitation on who is expected to take part. Thus if you wanted to gather comments, a variety of views or suggestions for improvement, it would be possible to *snowball* your questions out in a social media forum to a wide audience.

Observation of social media can provide an interesting insight into perceptions of an event. This can either be passive, observing what others put into the social media environment, or active, based on the researcher posting content and observing comments made about it. For more on this topic see the video link at the end of this chapter which deals with undertaking market research within Twitter.

Audience response systems

Audience response systems can be utilised if you have a static audience to give instant feedback, either on a topic, a presenter, or the event in general. Results do not need to be published instantly on the screen but some software offers this option. This is particularly useful if an audience response system is being used at the event anyway and wireless or other keypads are available. The system can simply be utilised when it's not undertaking its primary function to provide feedback on the event. For example, in a break during a conference where an audience response system is in use, questions can be put onto the screen and participants asked to vote using their audience response system.

RFID and other tracking

Radio Frequency Identification (RFID) technology has a wide variety of applications from retail through monitoring pets to use in passports and road toll systems. RFID is simply a way of universal identification, like the bar code on almost everything you buy, but it works wirelessly. Thus when an RFID chip comes within range of a reader it can be identified, and if required reference can be made to a database for more information. For example, when you purchase a can of baked beans the scanner at the checkout reads the Universal Product Code (UPC) or barcode on the can, looks up what that code means and adds the price of the beans to your bill; with RFID the process is the same but the code is read wirelessly.

At an event RFID technology can be embedded into wristbands or badges through the use of a small chip; this may then be used to track individuals without reference to a database, thus the individuals can remain anonymous, or it can be linked to a name, address or any other detail required.

RFID and other tracking techniques take observational research to a new level; they allow organisers to follow participants around the event, observing dwell time and interest in specific elements of the event in detail. The data from this observational element can be combined with data gathered utilising more traditional techniques such as questionnaires to build a comprehensive picture of a visitor's interests and experience.

At events such as trade fairs and similar where space is sold to businesses, the value of specific pitches can be monitored and assigned using RFID as the number of people who have passed the pitch can be identified. Similarly, the value of food zones can be monitored and appropriate pitch fees charged.

In addition to evaluating visitor experience, RFID can be used to all but eliminate counterfeit pass/ticket problems, authenticate attendees, streamline registration and manage restricted areas access. In the future it seems likely that the use of RFID will become commonplace at festivals and large events.

Event apps/mobile phone polling systems and questionnaires

Mobile phones can be used to send very short questionnaires via text message, or longer questionnaires can be hosted online in a mobile-friendly format for visitors to use their own smartphone. The design of questionnaire is similar to that used for post-event web surveys, but they are optimised for use at smartphone screen resolutions. The results can then be instantly collated and displayed online, sent in a text message, or simply stored for future analysis.

If an event-specific app is being created, then an evaluation element can be built into this using the techniques outlined for questionnaire design. Event-specific apps are commonly created from a purchased framework, but they will still need to go through an approval process irrespective of which platform they are designed for; to facilitate this process the use of external professionals is recommended. As more events have event-specific apps, this method of data gathering will surely grow, and researchers will need to be involved in the design phase of the app to ensure that research questions are answered.

Technology and focus groups

When considering technology within a focus group there is the basic level of technology that can be utilised if the group is face-to-face; this includes a digital voice recorder or digital camcorder. However, the whole group session can occur online; within this there are two key types of group: synchronous (real time) or asynchronous (non-real time). With a synchronous group all participants are online at the same time and use either a chat room or specialist conferencing software (a paid subscription to Skype can be used or there is more specialist software such as Cisco WebEx Meetings). An asynchronous group may also occur in a chat room with respondents able to add their comments on a variety of topics over a longer period of time.

The advantages of running a focus group online are the potential for reduced time and cost, both in relation to organising the event, travel and transcription. However, technical problems and changes in respondent behaviour resulting from online anonymity may present some problems.

Data analysis software

Finally, consideration needs to be given to the type of software that can be used to analyse data. For qualitative data there are packages such as:

- Atlas ti (www.atlasti.com/index.html)
- NVivo (www.qsrinternational.com/products_nvivo.aspx)
- MAXQDA (www.maxqda.com/products/what-is-maxqda).

Quantitative software packages include:

- Statistical Analysis Software (SAS/STAT) (www.sas.com/technologies/analytics/statistics/stat/)
- Minitab (www.minitab.com/en-US/products/minitab/default.aspx)
- IBM SPSS (originally this was called the Statistical Package for the Social Sciences) (http://www-03.ibm.com/software/products/gb/en/spss-stats-standard)

In this book we describe how to use the latter as it is widely used by students across the world. However, even if your organisation uses a different package many of the processes remain the same.

Scenario

You have seen an advertisement for a researcher in a major events management company. Complete the application form answering the following questions:

1 What experience of events management do you have? (*Hint – think about voluntary as well as paid roles*).
2 What research projects have you undertaken in the past? (*Hint – think about research you may have undertaken at school in science lessons, for example*).
3 What relevant skills do you have? (*Hint – think about communication skills, IT skills, etc.*).
4 What relevant attributes do you have? (*Hint – think about whether you work better alone or as part of a team, or, for example, whether you learn new skills quickly*).

Having listed the answers, consider which types of research are you better suited to *now*, and which types you could be good at if you learnt a new skill. Finally, how could you learn that new skill?

Summary

This chapter has highlighted:

- The social and technical resources that may or may not be available to you to carry out a study
- The characteristics of you as a researcher
- Technological resources that organisations can draw on to enhance their research capabilities.

Further reading

Books

Bryman, A. (2008) *Social Research Methods*, 3rd edn. Oxford: Oxford University Press. Provides a much fuller discussion of email and web surveys; in particular see pages 646–650 if you need further help with elements of e-research.

Flick, U. (2011) *Introducing Research Methodology: A Beginner's Guide to Doing a Research Project*. London: Sage Publications. Chapter 9 provides an excellent guide to all elements of e-research. This comprehensive guide gives in-depth detail for even the most comprehensive of studies.

Gratton, C. and Jones, I. (2010) *Research Methods for Sports Studies*, 2nd edn. Abingdon: Routledge. Pages 277–280 give some very useful answers to frequently asked questions on dissertation tutors and their role.

Wisker, G. (2009) *The Undergraduate Research Handbook*. Basingstoke: Palgrave Macmillan. Chapter 15 guides you on managing your tutor or supervisor.

Web links

ESOMAR is an organisation 'for encouraging, advancing and elevating market research' and provides extensive guidance on ethical and professional standards in market research at: ESOMAR (2012) *Guidelines for Online Research*. Online. Available HTTP: www.esomar.org/knowledge-and-standards/codes-and-guidelines/guideline-for-online-research/ethical-issues.php (accessed 29 June 2013).

A design, hosting and analysis tool for online questionnaires can be found at either: Survey Monkey, www.surveymonkey.com/ (accessed 29 June 2013); or Bristol Online Surveys, www.survey.bris.ac.uk/ (accessed 29 June 2013). Questionnaire design software is available at www.snapsurveys.com (accessed 29 June 2013).

Video links

How to use Google Trends and the Google Keyword tool to do market research are explained in *How to Do Market Research with Google Trends* (9.43 minutes) by Luis Teixeira. Online. Available HTTP: www.youtube.com/watch?v=5fSxsWtrf58 (accessed 29 June 2013).

How to Market Research on Twitter (14.59 minutes) by Matt Mansfield. Conducting market research on Twitter is a great way to discover the topics about which your current and potential customers are asking questions. Online. Available HTTP: www.youtube.com/watch?v=EAthblL1gc0 (accessed 29 June 2013).

Chapter 5

Research designs for studying events

Chapter learning outcomes

In this chapter we:

- Discuss the nature of knowledge in research
- Outline various research designs.

Andy had been a palaeontologist for many years when he was asked to organise an exhibition of fossils for young children. The funding body wanted him to create an enjoyable experience and demanded that he carry out research to show that the children had indeed had 'fun' at the exhibition or else he wouldn't get any future funding. As a scientist, Andy thought that he could be objective in all things; that he could identify cause and effect and that he could establish the truth about everything. In short he had a positivist outlook on the world. When he began organising the exhibition, he started to think about what would be fun for the young children and how he could measure the amount of fun that they were having at the event.

Andy had a young daughter and he began by asking her what she would like to play with and soon had a list of activities that she would enjoy. Then he thought he could ask her on a scale of 1–10 how enjoyable a time she was having and the research seemed very simple. Subsequently, however, he had several nieces and nephews visit and his daughter told them all about her dad's fossil exhibition. As she described what she would be doing, one of the children burst into tears and said that he wouldn't want to go and see the fossils because he was frightened, and then another said that it all sounded boring. Andy realised that he could no longer be absolutely certain as to what 'fun' is; in fact all the children seemed to understand something different by the term. Consequently, whilst he could study his fossils scientifically, ascertaining the views of the children would require a social science perspective and a different way of viewing the world.

Introduction

Building on previous chapters, this one enables you to make informed decisions as to a research design, whether the basis for the design elements are chosen pragmatically, philosophically or through using a specific research approach, such as ethnography or mixed methods.

Although, as we observed in Chapter 1, extensive academic research in events management is a relatively new phenomenon, it is undertaken in the same way as research in other areas of the social sciences. This means that it has adopted the research traditions of other disciplines. The aim of any research is to advance our *knowledge* of a subject, but over the centuries, exactly what knowledge is has been debated. Two particular terms used when talking about research and which some students have difficulties in differentiating are *ontology* (what is *it* that we want to know about) and *epistemology* (how and what can we know about *it*). That is, *ontology* is the study of the philosophy of knowledge, whilst *epistemology* is the philosophical study of how knowledge is acquired. One might imagine that such philosophical issues were resolved and agreed upon a long time ago. However, that is not the case and therefore you need to be aware of the debates about these areas that are still ongoing. Gratton and Jones (2010) suggest that this is important for three reasons:

1 There are various assumptions inherent in different types of research, which you need to understand to help you when you read other research.
2 You also need this understanding in deciding on the most appropriate design to achieve your aim and objectives.
3 You may wish to focus your aim and objectives in a way which suits your own ontological and epistemological preferences.

Ontological assumptions are those you make about the social reality under investigation. We have contrasting ways of understanding how societies are made up, how we interpret language, symbols, customs, etc. For example, a red traffic light to law-abiding citizens is a signal to stop and allow other traffic to pass. For other thrill-seeking drivers, it may symbolise a *challenge* to cross the traffic.

Greetham (2009: 26) lists ontological assumptions as:

1   What is the nature of the reality we're investigating?
2   How is it made up?
3   How do its parts interact?

And epistemological assumptions as:

1   The sort of evidence that would count as an answer
2   How are we to find it?

There are obviously interconnections between these assumptions and these have coalesced into general approaches to the nature of knowledge. There are numerous variations in these approaches and new ones are developing as knowledge expands. Here we will briefly outline some of these 'research paradigms' as they are known, an understanding of which, we think, are of most benefit to you in carrying out your research. In the further reading section at the end of the chapter more examples are given.

Approaches to the nature of knowledge

We suggest that one way of understanding the differences between these approaches, is to think of them as being a continuum from the most objective to the most subjective (see Figure 5.1).

Positivism is an approach that understands knowledge as having only one 'true' form. It is scientific and the principles and methods of the natural sciences are used. The research is therefore objective and measurable. The researcher has no influence on the results and they are therefore exactly replicable. This form of research is therefore always quantitative and uses hypotheses (see Chapter 2).

However, as we have noted earlier, social behaviour is different to other areas of knowledge and therefore a *post-positive* approach has developed in the social sciences. This recognises that it is not possible to achieve an absolutely objective understanding

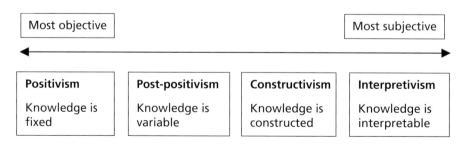

Figure 5.1 A continuum of objectivity

through measurement or observation. The results establish *probable* facts. These may be supplanted by new facts in the future providing a better explanation of a phenomenon in contrast to the scientific laws of positivism. Therefore post-positive approaches recognise a greater variety of methods, including quantitative, qualitative and mixed methods.

The limitations of positivism and post-positivism have supported the development of more subjective approaches. *Constructivism* has as its basis that people construct their own views of reality. One form, *social constructivism*, holds that people in a society co-construct their views of reality. An *interpretative* approach, however, believes that people (and that includes the researcher) provide their own accounts or explanations of society. These approaches allow the researcher to discover explanations rather than deduce them from measurements of variables. The subjectivity of interpreting people's behaviour, thoughts and words can lead to doubts over the reliability and generalisability of the findings – however, we will deal with these issues in later chapters. Researchers usually adopt qualitative methods, as they would argue that the concepts are too multifaceted to be reduced to numbers.

One other means of deciding on the most appropriate methods for your research is a philosophical approach known as *pragmatism*. As the name suggests, it is centred on the linking of theory and practice and is often used in action research and mixed methods research.

Like many authors of research methods books we have not gone into great detail of the philosophical debates appertaining to methodologies. What we suggest is that you decide where on the continuum in Figure 5.1 on p. 62, your beliefs about the social world and the type of research you want to undertake is situated. Thereafter ensure that your methods, vocabulary and claims are all consistent with that approach.

In the remainder of the chapter we look at some specific research designs which you could adopt if appropriate to your research topic. We suggest that you think of these in the same way as you would a recipe when cooking. You can make very minor changes to suit circumstances (but be clear about this when writing up your methodology) but you cannot change the fundamental basis on which these designs are based. Keeping to the cooking analogy, you may vary the brand of chocolate used in a recipe for chocolate brownies, but you cannot leave chocolate out altogether or substitute coffee and still call it a chocolate brownie. However, although less flexible, these research designs often provide a structure which novice students welcome.

Specific approaches to research

As we saw in Chapter 2, the central premise of qualitative research adopted by some methods of data collection differs from those adopted by quantitative methods. Quantitative methods lend well to cause and effect relationships, yet are harder to apply in more complex subject-specific settings found in everyday phenomenon. Objects are not simply reduced to single variables as is sometimes a characteristic of quantitative studies. Rather, with a qualitative approach, subjects are studied in their entirety and in their complex settings.

What follows are some methodological approaches that lend well to qualitative inquiry. The depth and scope of some of these methods, along with their roots in certain disciplines, is something that is debated in wider academia. In any case, many of these are widely practised in contemporary contexts across social science disciplines.

Ethnography

Ethnography is a qualitative approach that has its roots grounded in anthropological studies.

> ## Definition box
>
> *Ethnographic research*: the description of individual human societies; exploring and understanding cultural phenomena in order to describe cultures.

It is generally undertaken by applying an insider perspective to the research findings, whereby the researcher embeds themselves physically in a particular environment to study a subject in more depth. It relies less on perspectives of those told by a third party, but in essence combines the researcher's observations with that of the subjects involved to come to conclusions about findings. Ethnography therefore investigates a phenomenon by collecting a large amount of data from being immersed in an environment for a prolonged period of time.

Ethnography is one of those research approaches that is contested in the literature in terms of its meaning and practice. Social scientists alike still dispute its qualities and attributes. In its truest form, it is claimed that 'ethnography is a work of describing a culture. The essential core of this activity aims to understand another way of life from the native point of view' (Spradley 1979: 3). There are other authors who equate ethnography with participant observation and suggest it is written accounts of observations (Warren and Karner 2005).

An adaptive and equally valid contemporary variation of research that incorporates elements of the above can be said to be research that adopts and applies an ethnographic style. By doing so, cultural anthropologists can remain true to its original intent, and by evolving methods of research is able to be flexible in its labels, i.e. ethnographic style – a method that adopts participant observation within the data collection from participants within a setting, for a prolonged period of time. Ethnographic approaches are typically applied in settings in which a deeper understanding of 'what is going on' is sought. Outside of its originating roots in cultural anthropological contexts, an ethnographic approach has been found to be applied in tourist settings (e.g. islands, cruises); organisational settings (e.g. corporate environments) as well as events and festivals, so as to capture an in-depth perspective of a phenomenon. Ethnographic style is thus considered a valid research approach, and the areas where it could therefore be practised is widespread.

As Berg (2007) has pointed out, the most important part of launching into this style of research method is in fact to gain permission and access to the 'field'. If, for example, you are an employee of a particular company that you would like to engage in ethnographic research, then you may be in a position of being able to undertake the research simply by asking or gaining permission (and supported in writing) from your line manager or director of a company. In a sense, you are already 'in'. If, however, you wish to research the behaviour of inmates during meal times in a prison setting, gaining access can become problematic if you don't already work there or have contacts. If it is this sort of research you wish to undertake, it need not be impossible, but you will need to go through a lot more effort and steps to gain access to the field you wish to study, and in this case a prison is a good example. Another example might be something like an airport; it might be easier, say, if you wish to study the arrival behaviour of travellers and their greeters at a particular international airport. Something like that may mean you take steps to gain permission, but of course there are no guarantees.

If you wish to apply an ethnographic style in your data collection, you must be prepared to spend enough time 'in the field', or least be exposed to it to collect enough data. Social scientists will never agree on 'how much time is enough', but your research supervisor is a good first stop for advice. For example, if you wanted to study the festive behaviour of groups at a 4-day music festival, you could do so by adopting the ethnographic style and being a participant yourself in the same setting. The data collection would be similar to recording data via participant observation and what others around you say or discuss. By comparison, if you wanted to record ethnographically the sales success of reps selling tickets to the same festival in the lead up to this, you would need to follow those reps around for the days that they engage in direct sales for the tickets. It may seem cumbersome, but it is not impossible and some insightful trends may come out of such efforts, e.g. the response the rep receives from different groups of people, and what behaviours might result in a positive – or negative – sales result. For example, does the sales rep have good experience of doing this? Is there anything they should change or does the market have particular qualities? In the end, it depends on the objectives of particular pieces of research. Nonetheless, the point is that an ethnographic approach to research allows a researcher to use in-depth methods of data collection.

Skills to possess/exercise are: the ablity to watch and listen to things around you attentively; being sensitive to the environment in that you don't provoke or instigate action that disrupts the normal flow of that environment; and being ready to engage with potential informants in the area, or who have come into the area.

Event research in action

Research on the co-creation of value at festivals has been undertaken by examining the social practices of festival goers (Rihova et al. 2013). In order to collect this empirical evidence as primary data, the researcher adopted an ethnographic approach. This involved both observing and interviewing attendees at the festival. As such, she attended the festival for the duration (4 days) and camped onsite. She observed and talked to friends, families and the odd solo festival goer about the value of attending the festival. This meant that she was completely immersed in the site and 'went native' in the environment. Being an attendee with the others meant that trust was obtained, so approaching people for their contribution to the study presented fewer barriers. A festival environment provided a captive audience as attendees were there morning, afternoon and night. This allowed for a true ethnographic approach as she remained in the field for an extended period of time to collect data, both in interview form and via recording notes on behaviours of attendees whilst there, e.g. chatting, laughing, singing and chilling out with family and friends. Follow-up interviews also helped reveal the value of these social practices as motivators at the festival.

Netnography

Netnography is a modern innovation that uses the internet to carry out ethnographic research.

Definition box

Netnography is the application of ethnographic research techniques in the social arena of the internet. For example, netnography can be used to understand the culture that exists within a social media environment.

The internet can be a tool for research, for example by posting online surveys or hosting focus groups (see Chapter 4). However, the internet can also be a place or way of being; in this case you can study the internet as a culture or lifestyle. Individuals may develop specific identities and forms of communication or culturally specific behaviours. With this in mind *ethnographic* techniques can be transferred to the internet as a way of understanding the behaviour and the individuals. An academic example is Morgan (2008), where he used netnography to understand the event experience at a folk festival. His data was obtained from internet message boards. He suggested that 'it is the fact that the respondents were motivated to comment on and discuss the festival in a public forum that gives their views validity' (Morgan 2008: 87).

Grounded theory

Grounded theory is a method by which qualitative analysis can be approached. It is most often attributed to the work of Glaser and Strauss (1967); Glaser (1978, 1992); and Strauss (1987). It could be said that the original inception of this research approach is inductive in nature, in that the data itself helps to develop a theory, as opposed to informing or testing existing theories. In essence, such an approach was in part put forward by those authors who posited an alternative approach to knowledge creation in the formulation of theory from data, whereas traditional quantitative approaches to research typically are deductive in nature, i.e. they test existing theories alongside of set hypotheses.

The debate in grounded theory, as with other strands of methodology, also has a way of moving on. The origins are what they are, but perspectives developed since (e.g. Strauss and Corbin 1990; Charmaz 2006) are based on interpretive and socially constructed research accounts that are often rooted in a societal-based inquiry into a particular phenomenon, and then seek to uncover new 'grounded' knowledge, i.e. theory, that can be learned by such an approach. Grounded theory as a qualitative approach to research can be found applied in many different social science disciplines. In essence, the premise maintains that theoretical ideas are induced from the data, again as opposed to testing new theories. It is also common, therefore, to have data collection and concurrent analysis happen alongside of one another, before incorporating the perspective of 'new' literature. This is so as not to taint the existing knowledge, which is the data.

In applying a basic grounded theory approach to events research, you might decide to undertake a study in which you collect data from attendees on their motivations to participate in a team building event. First, you make no assumptions about their motivations to participate. You begin by investigating their reasons behind their participation, and let theories evolve from this. This is different from other methodological approaches to research by which you might research motivation theory first and then apply it to the findings you uncover from the team building participants. A grounded theory approach to such an events research project might uncover high levels of competitiveness among those participants in the team building event, thus allowing you to propose a new theory on that premise due to having allowed the data to inform your findings, rather than applying findings to existing theory.

It is important to note that existing theory is not discounted completely; rather, it is considered after the fact and comparisons made later in the study. This type of methodological approach is not the most common in events research, but does have a place in building new knowledge in the field. If you think the grounded theory approach is of interest to you in your events research, the first step would be to discuss it with a supervisor who is informed on the approach to help you scope out your ideas. The more reading you do on the topic in advance, the better equipped you will be in deciding whether this approach will be useful to apply to the study of your choice.

Phenomenology

To take a *phenomenological* approach to qualitative research is very much to adopt a particular paradigm for the research inquiry and how findings are reported. Theoretically speaking, phenomenology is linked to a subjective approach to qualitative research, whereby findings are grounded in the reflections of experience that are reported by the subjects under study.

Phenomenology is then, in the first instance a philosophical stance that acts as a foundation for a particular research enquiry. It can be, and is, a very illuminating way of investigating an everyday world phenomenon. Some researchers will tell you to steer clear of this approach as it is not clearly understood, and this is partly true. To that end, there is not one universal approach that applies to this line of enquiry, as it has a number of theoretical applications (philosophical, psychological, archaeological, etc.). In essence, to appreciate its theoretical underpinning, phenomenology has its philosophical roots in the work of Husserl and then later his student Heidegger. Indeed, as Husserl (1931: 43) maintains, phenomenology invites us to put 'aside all previous habits of thought, see through and break down the mental barriers which these habits have set along the horizons of our thinking ... to learn to see what stands before our eyes'. What emerges then, is an attempt to understand, describe and maintain the subjective experiences of your participants. It is, in a sense, also attempting to put you as researcher in the place of your participants.

'It stresses the "inter-subjective" nature of human interaction – we constantly work with models of the minds of others – good, bad, complex, simple but never complete models' (Yates 2004). Similarly, Schutz (1967 in Yates 2004: 157) considers that 'the constructs that people use in order to render the world meaningful and intelligible to them [should be] the key focus of a phenomenologically grounded social science'. It is, in essence, a deep enquiry with a subject on what a person's life-world is like for them, and having them share an explicit perspective on that. Phenomenology then, and its philosophical approach to research, would therefore dictate that this approach is highly reliant on the interpretations of the researcher. It can be a colourful and rich way to tackle particular topics of events research enquiry and their related data collection.

Event research in action

Event research provides fertile ground for studies to be conducted by adopting a phenomenological approach. Take for example the complexity of emotions that festival goers may encounter at a gathering such as the Burning Man Festival (www.burningman.com). The whole concept of this event is freedom, self-expression and independence. For those attending the festival, an in-depth phenomenological study has the ability to examine the scope, range and emotions of human behaviour at such festivals. It would be harder to fit such a study into the positivist framework mentioned earlier in the chapter, that is either 'good' or 'bad' as research on emotions will be embedded in subjectivist perspectives, and in effect attendees are encouraged to act and feel 'freely' so good and bad feelings are equally accepted at such a gathering. In addition, a phenomenological piece of research in the field of events into the complexity of emotions at such festivals does help to inform cases of social science and related consumer behaviour as part of our wider understanding of human nature and the relevance of events. If this has inspired you to undertake research by adopting this theoretical underpinning, talk to your supervisor first about where to start.

Case studies

Case study research involves the intensive study of one particular case. For example, this could include such things as a festival, an organisation, a corporation, a specific event. The case study approach allows you to study the contextual elements that are relevant to a particular scenario, such as those listed above. Benefits include being able to describe attributes that are unique to the setting, and thus expand what is known about a particular phenomenon at play in certain environments. It does involve an intense study of a focused scope and can apply multiple methods of data collection in the process. In essence, seeking to define a case study approach at the outset and in a formal way might make you feel like you are closing off the scope of a study, instead of opening it up. However, case studies can be beneficial in the sense that they take a distinct, in-depth look at a particular problem or phenomenon, so as to shed more light on what can be learned or known.

As mentioned earlier, a number of methods may and could be deployed (i.e. justified) in undertaking a case study approach. You could engage in both quantitative and qualitative data collection to get the information that you seek. If you look at the venue booking agency example, some sources of information your study may need will come from monthly sales data (per person and across the organisation). You may also wish to discuss the venue sales service with past and present clients of the venue booking agency. A discussion (or interview) may also be in order with senior staff to get an understanding from them of why their venue sales officers are successful (or not).

On the surface case study research would appear to resemble other quantitative and qualitative approaches on both methodological and methods grounds, and it does. It is most important, however, to qualify differences in the case study approach at least in one way – as advocates have contended (Rose 1991), case study research is a judgement more about the representativeness of the findings uncovered specific to the case, as opposed to seeking more generalised findings often derived from accessing a representative sample from a broader population. Case studies are found in all sorts of applications, the 'how' and 'why' typically being the underlying focus of a 'case'. They can be found to be used in all sorts of different disciplines including that of sociology, anthropology, political science, education, nursing, social work, and, yes, they make for a good approach in the field of events management too.

Yin (2009) maintains that a case study is an empirical enquiry that investigates in-depth a contemporary phenomenon within the everyday context. In addition, he attributes the following parameters to case study inquiry scenarios:

- Copes with the technically distinctive situation in which there will be many more variables of interest than data points, and as one result
- Relies on multiple sources of evidence, with data needing to converge in a triangulating fashion, and as another result
- Benefits from the prior development of theoretical propositions to guide data collection and analysis.

(Yin 2009:18)

In terms of a research approach, a case study can be based on an exploratory, explanatory or descriptive premise of inquiry. Equally, case studies if desired can be embedded within a particular epistemological foundation (i.e. within a methodology), for example the constructionist, phenomenological, post-structuralist, or even feminist perspective. The latter theoretical perspectives are often found in higher level degree studies at master's and/or Ph.D. level, but they need not be scarce in undergraduate studies. If you think you'd like to embed this particular approach in a study, then the first thing to do is discuss the possibilities with your research supervisor.

A former student, for example, wanted to enquire into why it was that some event industry venue suppliers were able to weather the dark doldrums of the late 2000s recession relatively well, while others were not. Subjecting the study to a case scenario, the student retrieved sales records; interviewed senior figures inside and outside of the organisation and their sales people; and asked existing and new clients why it was they chose to continue to do business with the company whilst functioning in a more competitive environment where cost saving measures were put in place by many. Due to retrieving information from multiple sources, the researcher was able to conclude that the strength of the company's brand, alongside maintained professionalism and reasonable costs, was the key influence on the company's competitive position and sustained growth throughout that difficult period.

A good example of another events case study of one organisation is that of Crowther (2010). He sought to gain an in-depth understanding of the entire event management process of a Higher Education Institute (HEI). His interview questions focused on the HEI's brand and marketing policy, how the events contributed to these activities and how the events could be improved.

Action research

Action research is a method by which research findings are collected and then re-applied directly back into the environments being studied. As the data is fed back into the research process, the aim is to adopt an increased understanding of the environment. Action research is a cyclical process whereby the evolution of data continues to evolve new sources of data. Its emphasis is placed on the fact that the environment under study (e.g. a company or organisation) works in continual collaboration with the researcher in a practical setting in tackling context-specific dilemmas with mutual benefit being the desire of both.

Student vignette

Gillian wanted to learn how an online analytical tool could assist her placement company.

I wanted to assess whether, and how, website hits on our boutique wedding planner site converted into actual sales referrals. In order to do so, I decided to adopt an action research approach as this methodology allowed me to undertake an analysis of website activity, apply the analysis tool (i.e. Google Analytics) and see if changes were effective. Instead of having 'one go at it', I undertook the primary data collection using successive rounds of website data statistics and related analysis by the online web tool. Due to the cyclical nature of the process, my study adopted and made use of an 'action research' approach to the data collection and proved valuable in learning more about the website traffic and how our wedding planning service could improve its website presence, navigation and usability.

Dahlberg and McCaig (2010: 97) provide guidance on action research as a methodology:

- Action research is meant to be practical and accessible
- It can be done by anyone
- It may or may not involve more than one person
- Reflection, research and action form its basis
- Action research aims to change practice
- The research is problem driven
- It involves participation and is cyclical.

Hermeneutics

This approach has its roots in the study of meaning found in texts. It has, however, evolved recently to include the analysis in other forms such as visual objects (art and photography) and that of speech, e.g. conversation. In keeping with views on its original purpose, hermeneutics is thought to vary from three different text explanations that include: the detailed analysis, the sequential analysis and a full interpretation of the objective social data (Reichertz 2004).

It could be said that narrative approaches of enquiry to research have their roots in hermeneutics. In its simplest and most historic form, 'Hermeneutics was, and is, the science of biblical interpretation' (Crotty 1998: 87). Language then, and hence the written word, is what is being studied here. However, that is not to say that it is just text that is being examined – early forms also take into consideration elements of human practice, what the writer truly 'meant': the related situations in which a text was written were also taken into further consideration alongside of the written word per se.

To go back to the roots of hermeneutics is to appreciate its function and purpose as a line of enquiry centuries ago. That is to say, in modern society in many cultures, words, i.e. language, are taken at face value. In essence, people mean exactly what they say or write. It does have a function in today's society and can be investigated by a narrative enquiry, but again to reflect on the roots of hermeneutics is to appreciate that in medieval times, philosophers were of the mind that a text and its true meaning could only be contextualised in a wider scope, in that the way the world was and was then perceived, then gets expressed by 'words'. In today's society, modern language can dictate the opposite premise.

An exception to a research approach grounded in more historic origins of hermeneutics is that of 'objective hermeneutics' (Flick 2009), in which the thoughts, beliefs and hopes of the writer are kept out of the 'objective' analysis of the text. In essence, however, in more traditional versions of hermeneutics, which are therefore interpretive in nature, the aim of hermeneutic theory derives 'from the view that in large measure authors' meanings and intentions remain implicit and go unrecognised by the authors themselves' (Crotty 1998: 91). Hermeneutic inquiry goes further, then, to make interpretations of the underlying meanings of a particular author's words, be it a script, diary, memoir or life history. In essence, from a qualitative perspective such an approach to events management research would serve to uncover hidden meanings and contexts to very contemporary and timely scenarios in the field.

An example of the use of hermeneutics as a research approach is the work of Warnes (2004). His study was entitled, 'Heidegger and the festival of being: from the bridal festival to the round dance'. In this, he begins by considering the derivation of the words holiday and festival:

> First, *feria* (pl. *feriae*) which means abstinence from work in honour of the gods, and is semantically nearer to the English holy-day (Hebrew Shabbat). Second, *festum* (pl. *festa*) meaning shared joy, revelry, or feasting, and which is closer to 'festival.' These roots carry over into the German *Feier und Fest*, Spanish *ferias y fiesta*, Italian *feria e festa*. (2004: 3)

He notes that words deriving from *festa* are more positive than those deriving from *feria* and concludes that a holiday festival is 'thus empty time versus fulfilled time' (2004: 4).

In any case, it becomes evident that this methodological approach to research is embedded in different historical contexts and thus applications over time, as we also saw above with the journey that phenomenological applications to research have taken.

Next we look at two methods that use quantitative data.

Surveys

You have, at some time, probably been asked to take part in a survey. Many surveys drop through the mailbox, or you may have received phone calls, texts, or had requests to complete an online survey in your email in-box. You often see people standing in the town centres or at events holding their clipboards waiting for the right type of person – their next 'data victim' – to come along.

Grunwell et al. (2008) carried out a survey of attendees at the Asheville Film Festival in North Carolina, USA. They developed a twenty-two-question audience questionnaire which was given to attendees as they entered four venues, and collected from them as they left. The questionnaires included demographic, economic and film festival related questions, and to encourage participation they offered respondents the chance to enter a draw for free tickets to the closing night reception. In order to capture variations in visiting, the survey was undertaken during eight film slots, both in the afternoon and the evening.

Experiments

Two forms of experiment are generally described: the first, with a control group, is the one familiar from science or medical research. It includes two experimental groups, to which the participants are randomly allocated. The researcher then manipulates the independent variable which is the object of study. The second is the pre-post design experiment, in which a pre-test measurement is made in both groups, an intervention is made to the study group and then both groups are again measured post-test. There can be considerable ethical issues (see Chapter 3) involved in these types of research and the design needs very careful consideration. A third simpler form of experiment is where all the participants are measured pre-test and post-test, with all receiving the intervention. In Becky's experiment below, this was the method used, with the participants exposed to various forms of advertising and their opinions surveyed before and afterwards.

Student vignette

Becky undertook a specially constructed experiment in a study of the effectiveness of advertising designs for a wedding venue. Unfortunately it did not always go as planned.

I designed my experiment based on the work of Pieters et al. (2010), with six designs based on newspaper advertisements and six based on the front pages of the venue website. The first step was to decide on a selection of photographs to include on the designs, along with the chosen text that was previously used in the venue's advertisements. My aim was to gain a minimum of 150 completed questionnaires in which respondents would identify the effectiveness of the different designs. My initial plan was to access the chosen sample through open days whereby engaged couples have the opportunity to visit the venue before any agreement is made. The experiment consisted of two A1-sized boards with each design presented to the sample, who were then asked to complete a questionnaire. Unfortunately once the experiment was underway, I was told that only one open day was available for the experiment to take place, leading to only twelve responses being collected.

I therefore decided to focus on reaching the sample through electronic mail using the venue's mailing list. The questionnaire was sent as an attachment to the email alongside the twelve different advertisements. Respondents were asked to complete the questionnaire and return it by email. Once again, I only received twelve completed questionnaires. There was obviously still an issue with the number of responses, so I changed to using an online electronic software program. However, a mistake was made in relying on the venue staff to distribute the email and there was a further delay of six days. I only received a total of ten completed questionnaires by this method, totalling thirty-four completed questionnaires for analysis. Nonetheless, my results suggested that the newspaper advertisements were most effective when they had a simple design, but there appeared to be little difference between the web pages. On a positive note, although I had problems with the experiment, I was able to write a very good section on the limitations of my research!

Mixed or multiple methods

We first mentioned mixed methods in Chapter 2 when discussing qualitative and quantitative forms of research. Tashakkori and Teddlie (2003) argue that using mixed methods, rather than a single approach, has three advantages:

- Mixed methods research can answer research questions that the other methodologies cannot.
- Mixed methods research provides better (stronger) conclusions.
- Mixed methods provide the opportunity for presenting a greater diversity of divergent views.

(Tashakkori and Teddlie 2003: 14–15)

Other arguments in support of mixed methods include those of Bryman (2004), who suggests that quantitative research can tend to produce a static view of a phenomenon, whereas qualitative research can reveal processes. Obtaining a static view can be valuable in uncovering regularities, which may allow an analysis of a process to then take place. Similarly, qualitative data can help in explaining the relationships between quantitative variables and in identifying intervening variables. However, the main argument in support of a mixed method is usually cited as 'triangulation'. This refers to 'the practice of employing several research tools within the same research design' (Sarantakos 2005: 145). This approach enables the researcher to consider the subject of a study from more than one perspective, allowing an enrichment of knowledge and/or to test the reliability of the research. Murphy and Carmichael (1991), for example, wanted to estimate the direct spending of tourists to the 1989 British Columbia Winter Games in Canada. They used two independent surveys to calculate an estimate of tourist numbers, with the expectation that they would provide a more accurate number than a single estimate.

Practical tip box

As there are various forms of mixed methods it is necessary to decide on a strategy. Creswell et al. (2003) suggest that there are four main criteria to consider:

- The implementation sequence
- The priority between data types
- The stage at which the data types are integrated
- And whether a theoretical perspective guides the entire design.

Scenario

For each of the following research questions, identify the most appropriate research approach to adopt:

1 How much waste was recycled at a music festival?
2 Did the job description for volunteers properly explain their role and did they understand what was required of them?
3 Have changes to the amount of money spent on advertising the festival been effective in widening participation? Which change was the most effective?
4 What was it like to be the person who had to clean the toilets?

Summary

This chapter has highlighted that:

- There are different views amongst academics as to what we mean by knowledge, and this may influence the design of your research project.
- There are numerous specific research designs which achieve different outcomes, one of which may suit your aim and objectives.

Further reading

Journals

There are several journals which publish articles about particular approaches, for example:

Qualitative Inquiry
Qualitative Market Research: An International Journal
International Journal of Qualitative Methods
Qualitative Research in Organizations and Management: An International Journal
Quantitative Marketing and Economics.

A good article on ethnography is Elliott, R. and Jankel-Elliott, N. (2003) 'Using ethnography in strategic consumer research', *Qualitative Market Research: An International Journal*, 6: 215–223.

Johnson, R. B. and Onwuegbuzie, A. J. (2004) 'Mixed methods research: A research paradigm whose time has come', *Educational Researcher*, 33: 14–26. Online. Available HTTP: www.tc.umn.edu/~dillon/CI%208148%20Qual%20Research/Session%2014/ Johnson%20&%20Onwuegbuzie%20PDF.pdf (accessed 14 August 2013) discusses some of the issues relating to using mixed methods.

Books

Similarly, there are books that specialise in different methods. Some useful ones are:

Berg, B. L. (2007) *Qualitative Research Methods for the Social Sciences*, 6th edn. London: Pearson.

Keegan, S. (2009) *Qualitative Research: Good Decision Making through Understanding People, Cultures and Markets*. London: Kogan Page.

Sarantakos, S. (2005) *Foundations of Social Research*, 3rd edn. London: Palgrave Macmillan.

Silverman, D. (ed.) (2004) *Qualitative Research: Theory, Method and Practice*. London: Sage Publications.

Spradley, J. P. (1979) *The Ethnographic Interview*. New York: Holt, Rinehart & Winston.

Warren, C. A. B. and Karner, T. X. (2005) *Discovering Qualitative Methods: Field Research, Interviews, and Analysis*. Los Angeles, CA: Roxbury.

Web links

Galt, K. (2008) 'An introduction to mixed methods research'. Online. Available HTTP: http://spahp2.creighton.edu/OfficeOfResearch/share/sharedfiles/UserFiles/file/Galt_ MM_slides_CU_092309.pdf (accessed 14 August 2013) helps explain the philosophical issues arising from using mixed methods.

Video links

Further details of two of the methods discussed in this chapter can be found at:

Ethnographic Methods (2.13 minutes). Online. Available HTTP: www.youtube.com/ watch?v=XAYPdCO_inY&feature=related (accessed 14 August 2013).

Grounded Theorists and Some Critiques of Grounded Theory (7.52 minutes). Online. Available HTTP: www.youtube.com/watch?v=hik-NKtI_vY (accessed 14 August 2013).

Chapter 6

Using existing knowledge in a research project

Chapter learning outcomes

In this chapter we:

- Consider the knowledge that the researcher may have gained from previous experience
- Discuss the purpose of literature in research
- Outline the writing of a research proposal
- Discuss the writing of a literature review
- Provide guidance on referencing sources
- Consider the development of a conceptual framework.

Marie graduated several years ago in events management and is now employed by an international hotel chain that is in the process of constructing a new resort on an island archipelago. As well as accommodation, the resort has an eighteen-hole golf course, spa, swimming pool and conference facilities. The complex is surrounded by a national park, but there is considerable land within the development that can be planted and used for corporate entertainment. Marie has been tasked with undertaking a consultancy project to research how the land should best be planted to enhance the guests' experience and maximise the opportunities for corporate events.

She starts to plan the research and realises that many decisions are outside her control. Clearly the study is *applied research* and the budget, timescale, resources, etc. have all been agreed at a higher management level and she must work within their limitations. Her boss has also stipulated that he would like her to use qualitative as well as quantitative methods 'because he doesn't understand statistics!' Beyond that she must decide how best to proceed with the project. Marie begins by thinking about what she already knows about the topic. She has worked for the company since graduating and visited several of their existing resorts, so she has a good idea of what they have done before. However, the climate at those venues was different and there was no golf course, so she wonders if the target market for the new development is the same. Luckily, the company keeps good records and she knows if she contacts head office she'll be able to access documents that may provide some detailed information on the other resorts. The trade press too, may feature some articles on her company's competitors operating in the same country, which might be useful. As the new hotel is situated within the boundaries of the National Park, she should be able to access some official documentation from when the Park was created, which should give her a better idea about the type of plants that are indigenous to the area. Finally, she is grateful that she has kept her assignments from her undergraduate study – one of those, she remembers, could be really useful when she needs to decide which aspects she should concentrate on.

Introduction

In Chapter 2 we discussed the initial planning of your research project and we assume that you began by thinking about the issues that you were already familiar with from the literature, and that you then perhaps read some more as you started to develop your aim and objectives. Maybe something stood out in your memory because you had read about it in the media or maybe it was because of your personal experience at an event. In subsequent chapters we considered different approaches to research and the resources that you can draw on. Now we discuss existing or background knowledge. No research starts from a blank sheet; it always builds on what is already known. So in this chapter, we look at how you can draw on this knowledge and use it to good effect in your research.

Personal experience

Always start with what you already know. You may be surprised by how much that is. If you were an astronaut, you might not have much previous experience to draw on, but it is easier in events management because you have probably attended a considerable number of different events. You may have also volunteered at an event or worked in the events industry, which could give you a different perspective. Whilst you cannot simply write down all you know about events, these experiences can give you an insight into the topic that you may not have had when learning about other subjects. Compared to other disciplines, the study of events is fairly new to academia and there are many areas that are still waiting to be researched. Therefore, your experience may be a valuable asset, so don't dismiss it out of hand. However, avoid the temptation of giving your *opinions* – you are not an expert and therefore what you think is not appropriate in a research project until the very end when you have data to draw on (see Chapter 13).

Next we consider more formal sources of information that you need to use. These sources are usually referred to generically as literature, although images, maps and unpublished sources may occasionally also be included. We are going to assume that you have basic academic skills, such as library skills, when using the literature, but if you need additional support, some suggestions are made at the end of the chapter as to where you can find help.

Primary and secondary literature sources

In Chapter 2, we considered the difference between primary and secondary *research*. In this chapter we concentrate on primary and secondary *sources*. Finally, in Chapter 8, we will look at primary and secondary *data*. It is important that you distinguish between each of these terms and be clear about the differences between them, as each is used differently from the other.

Flick (2011) gives three very good examples of each type of source in order to distinguish between them. *Primary sources* include autobiographies; an article which gives the empirical results of a piece of research; and an original document which, in our context, could include, for example, an event programme. *Secondary sources* are often summaries or the information has been reworked in some way. So a biography (which is written by a third person); a textbook which gives an overview of an area of research, a conceptual paper or an official statistic summarising the number of attendees at an event are all secondary sources. Aim to use primary sources predominantly, as these are more reliable than secondary sources, but depending on your topic, using a secondary source may also be beneficial.

Student vignette

Sara undertook a study of the rosewater festival in Iran to assess its role in cultural tourism.

I used over seventy different sources for my dissertation research. Primary sources included a paper by McKercher et al. (2006) titled 'Are short duration festivals tourist attractions?' This was a primary source because it provided empirical research on three festivals in Hong Kong, which I used in discussing the role of the host community and its attitudes towards festival visitors.

A secondary source, in contrast, was the textbook on festivals and events management by Yeoman et al. (2004). This I found useful because it discussed the different impacts on the host community, such as economic, socio-cultural and environmental effects.

Searching the literature

The literature search helps you:

- To source initial ideas for a research project (see Chapter 2)
- To obtain ideas on theoretical approaches to your topic (see Chapter 2)
- To place the research in context (see Chapter 3)
- To help you identify what the key issues are
- To establish the crucial questions you should be thinking about
- To identify any contradictory results of findings in the empirical literature
- To undertake original research and avoid duplication
- To identify theories in order to create a theoretical or conceptual framework for deductive research that you will subsequently test
- To gain sufficient knowledge to undertake inductive research competently
- To learn about methodological approaches
- To compare your findings with previous work.

There are several occasions when you search for literature.

1 *The broad scan.* This is the first phase and probably started when you were still deciding what topic to pursue as it helps you to develop an overview of the topic area. It is at this stage that your previous experience may be of most use, as it helps guide you in starting to search. This scan should reveal whether there is already a substantial body of literature on the topic you are interested in. It also shows what types of literature are available, for example whether there are academic sources or those from the events industry.

2 *The initial 'literature review'.* This stage may be when you are preparing a research proposal or seeking funding. You should be identifying who are the key authors that are relevant to your topic and what the major issues are that have been identified by them. You may start to identify a 'gap' in the literature, that is, an area that is new or has so far been overlooked. You use the literature to provide the rationale for your own study.

3 *The literature review.* In this phase you answer focused questions and have identified any ongoing debates or contradictions. To do this you weigh up the relevance of each piece and think about it in a critical way. You need to ensure that you have sought out sufficient primary sources as well as secondary sources. If you are undertaking *deductive* research, it is at this stage that the search must be complete as it forms the basis for your *conceptual framework* which determines the questions you want answered.

4 *The methodological literature.* In this stage you identify the literature that you can use to justify your choices of research methodology.

5 *The final review.* If you are undertaking *inductive* research your participants may provide new insights that you have not previously considered, so it may be appropriate at this stage to search the literature again in related areas for any additional sources that enable comparisons to be made. If you are undertaking *deductive* research, you should make a final search for any new literature that has been published whilst your data has been collected and analysed.

Defining the parameters and identifying key words

The parameters of your research can be thought of as the boundaries. Obviously you cannot research everything that has ever been written about events and events management, so you need to decide what is relevant and what is not. One way to do this is to develop key words relevant to your topic. If you are not to waste your time repeating the same searches or miss something out that is important, you also need to be methodical and keep records of your searches.

Your library staff or virtual learning environment should be able to provide help on searching the various databases, but a good place to start is with a general search engine such as Google, which has a very useful application called Google Scholar. When searching it is a good idea to include the key word 'festival' as well as 'event', as the latter is used in many other disciplines as well as ours. Also, if you know your topic has a great deal of literature available, it is good to include the year or the previous year for which you are reading (e.g. 2014) in the key words. This means that you start reading the current literature, which directs you to what is current rather than what has become obsolete. Alternatively, use the advanced search facility, if available, and order the search findings in date order, commencing with the most recent.

Available sources of literature

There is a wide range of sources available as described in Chapter 1, so look back to refresh your memory. It is good practice to use a variety of them, bearing in mind the advantages and disadvantages that the different types have. Additionally, contextual information may be found in newspapers, magazines and internet websites. A word of caution about the latter – you need to consider carefully the reliability of the web-based source. Whilst many academics warn you not to use Wikipedia, for example, we suggest that it is used thoughtfully in the early stages of your literature search. Do not rely on or quote any of the information given; but it can help by providing a number of useful references that you can use to begin your search.

Be a little cautious too about using dictionaries, although of course, they do not have the reliability problems of web pages. Many students use a dictionary to define the key terms in their research, but it is much better to use an academic source, as this gives a specific events focus rather than the general definition of a dictionary.

Remember, whenever you are searching you are looking for three types of literature:

● Theoretical, which underpins the topic of your study
● Empirical, which discusses existing research in your study area
● Methodological, which helps you justify the methods chosen.

Criteria for evaluating empirical studies

● What was the aim of the research being undertaken? Is it clearly stated?
● When was the data collected? Is it still current or might there be more recent data available (for example a later census)?
● What is the expertise of the individuals or organisations undertaking the research?
● Is the research fair or biased in any way?
● Was the research undertaken deductively or inductively?
● What was the methodology – did the researchers create hypotheses or research questions?

- Were the ethics of the study considered?
- What were the key issues or variables identified?
- What sampling technique was used, and what was the size of the sample? (see Chapter 7)
- What was the response rate? (see Chapter 7)
- What methods were used to collect the data? (see Chapters 8–10)
- What methods were used to analyse the data? (see Chapters 11–12)
- Have the results been discussed and generalised, if appropriate? (see Chapter 13)
- How dependable is the data? Is it reliable, credible, valid and trustworthy? (see Chapter 13)
- What limitations (see Chapter 13) did the authors identify and can you see any others?

Reading and making notes

Start by reading the abstract (if there is one) and then read through the whole piece of literature to get a sense of it and ensure its relevance. Whilst you are reading and making notes remember that you are going to be writing a discussion about the topic and so don't make notes on a source-by-source or article-by-article basis. You may find it easier to use mind maps instead of linear notes, either using software or on paper. Whichever method you use, try and think about what you are reading and make the connections and links between the pieces as you read them. Summarise the main points and consider the authors' conclusions carefully. Highlight any quotes that you think may be useful. Add the reference to your bibliography list – write it in full and remember to note the date accessed if it is an online source. It is important that you always cite the source of your work so that you do not plagiarise the original author's work. Finally, look at the references the authors have used for further reading.

Undertaking a literature search can be time consuming, so avoid trying to read everything as you will never finish. Part of the skill of a literature review is to identify the relevance and significance of the literature you are using. You will know when you can stop searching as you will be seeing the same authors you have already read. Rarely, a student may say that they can't find any literature on their topic. This usually means that they have been looking in the wrong place or their key words are too specific. As we have said earlier, events management is a relatively new area, so the literature (especially theoretical literature) may be found in other disciplines, such as psychology, or in other areas such as leisure or business studies. Finally, other problems are reading but not thinking, and thinking but not writing; and worst of all, procrastination!

In the next part of this chapter we discuss three outputs from undertaking the literature search; first, a *research proposal*, second a *literature review*, and third a *conceptual framework*.

The research proposal

The proposal is a crucial part of any research project. In industry, you need to justify the cost of the research and demonstrate that there will be an appropriate return on investment (although this may not be a direct economic return). Alternatively, if you are providing research for a commercial client, it is necessary to submit a proposal to them, and this can be part of the contract between your organisation and theirs as to exactly what will be done, by what date, at what cost, etc. In academia, it is necessary if you are applying for research funding, and for students it is often a vital part of the dissertation process (although it may be assessed or unassessed depending on your institution). Whether or not it is formally assessed, the feedback you receive will hope-fully give reassurance that you are on the right path – although of course, that is no guarantee of success. Your tutor will be able to give you specific guidance on the fea-sibility of your intended project before you commit too many resources to it. Most importantly of all, it will make you start actually writing and this is the best way of clarifying your thoughts. There is software that can assist in preparing research propos-als, particularly for peer review, namely Peer Review Emulator (The Idea Works 2011).

The content of a proposal can vary but Saunders et al. (2007) suggest that for a student dissertation it will consist of:

- Title
- Background
- Research questions and objectives
- Method
- Timescale
- Resources
- References.

For industry and academic purposes the contents may vary but the following is a good guide, whether the proposal is for economic or assessment purposes.

The title

For researchers who are either seeking funds or are bidding to undertake research, a title guides the reader and therefore must be explicit about the study. However, for students, it can be a working title at this stage and can therefore usually be worded as a question rather than in a finished title format. Using a question rather than a state-ment often helps you to focus more easily. Whichever you use, it should accurately reflect the content of your proposal, but do be flexible and recognise that the title may change before the final dissertation is submitted (see Chapter 13). Wilson (2010) sug-gests that a title should not exceed twelve words in length.

Background

This is a key section of the proposal and justifies why the research is worth undertak-ing. In an assignment, you may have identified a problem that needs solving or an aspect of events management that excites you. In industry, the problem is presented to you and if you are bidding for funding, you are probably constrained by the 'call', which sets out the type of project that will be funded. It is in this section that you show your knowledge of the literature and demonstrate the links between what is already known and what you hope to find out.

Research aim and objectives

Having completed the background section you should be able to lead into your aim and objectives. These should be clearly set out with objectives perhaps listed in bullet points for ease of reading (see Chapter 2).

Method

In this section you set out how you intend to achieve the aim and objectives that you have developed. You also need to justify why these are the most appropriate methods to use. This justification should be based not only on the aim and objectives, but also on the practical issues involved. If your methods are not viable, the proposal will obviously be rejected. It can sometimes be hard for students to recognise the realities of research, especially when you are considering the participants. In the next chapter we discuss the sample for your research in detail and look at the practicalities of accessing and receiving the support of participants in your research. It may be appropriate at this stage to include confirmation from organisations with whom you may be working, that you have their support.

Timescale

This is another key aspect in considering the feasibility of your research project, and you should refer back to Chapter 4 for guidance.

Financial aspects

Even student projects are likely to incur some costs, and you should identify these at this stage and show how they are to be met. For a commercial proposal, it is necessary to set out in a table all the expenses that will be incurred or the costs that will need to be recouped.

Appendices

In the appendices, students should attach a bibliography of the references (see below), whilst in an industry proposal, CVs of the principal investigator and any other researchers involved in the project should be included.

Saunders et al. (2007: 43) suggest that the viability of the proposal rests on the answer to the question, *'Can this research be carried out satisfactorily within the timescale and with available resources?'*

The literature review

The second way of using the literature you have found is in the production of a literature review. For students, this is likely to carry a substantial proportion of the marks available, demonstrating its importance in the dissertation process.

Definition box

Literature review: the selection of available documents (both published and unpublished) on the topic, which contain information, ideas, data, and evidence written from a particular standpoint to fulfil certain aims or express certain views on the nature of the topic and how it is to be investigated, and the effective evaluation of these documents in relation to the research being proposed.

(Hart 1998: 13)

The purpose of a literature review

Students from some cultures may find it difficult to understand why a literature review is necessary or the reasons for it being in a particular format. They may find it an unfamiliar process as they are used to writing in a style that demonstrates their knowledge but that does not reference the sources of that knowledge. However, in addition to showing that you have library skills, the literature review also:

- Demonstrates awareness of the *existing work* already undertaken in the area of study
- Identifies for the reader what the *gaps* are in the current state of knowledge
- And provides signposts for the reader about where the research is coming from – that is, what theories and principles are influential in shaping the approach that is being adopted for the study.

Writing the literature review

If you have undertaken your literature search effectively and made notes as you have proceeded, the literature should be reasonably manageable. Don't expect to write a finished literature review in one go; it is likely to take several drafts, with much 'cutting and pasting'. Also you may be able to incorporate amendments made by a tutor, suggestions from a colleague or additional literature, when you realise your own oversights.

Begin by considering how you can organise the literature into a general structure. Begin with basic definitions, but remember as we suggested earlier, using academic definitions rather than those from a dictionary. Write from the general to the specific and ensure that the level of detail increases accordingly, in order to have sufficient breadth and depth. Similarly, write from the theoretical to the practical. So when you are writing in general at the beginning you will give less detail, but by the end of the literature review you will be writing in as much detail as possible about the specific area of your research. Chapter 13 gives some tips on writing up that may be useful at this stage.

Also aim for:

- Clarity
- Brevity
- Rigour
- Consistency.

You should have read numerous journal articles by this point, so if you are still not sure about the layout, have another detailed look at how their literature has been set out.

Critical evaluation

One of the problems students often face is the critical evaluation of the literature. 'You need to be more critical', they are told by their tutor and yet they are not really sure what this means. They often think of criticism, which is different, because, it is usually absolute and negative. For example, if you went shopping for new clothes and a friend said when you tried on some trousers, 'you look awful' – that would be criticism. If, however, they said, 'the trousers are nice, but they're too big on you, try and find a smaller size', that would be critique, as it is not dogmatic. One way of practising to become more critical is to look at the critique of the research methodology that the authors themselves make – except they will not refer to it as critique, but as the 'limitations to the study'.

For example, in Crowther's (2010) journal article entitled 'Strategic application of events', the final section is headed 'Limitations and suggested future research'. In this section Crowther acknowledges that the research was only carried out in one institution (because the research was *exploratory*). The paper could therefore be critiqued on that basis and if in future, further research was carried out in other institutions or perhaps in other countries, the same findings may be made, confirming Crowther's work, or possibly different findings, which will add to the body of knowledge in this subject area.

A good example of how to write in a critical way is given in the literature review where Crowther critiques an earlier study – note the sections we've emphasised in italics.

> Ravald and Gronoos (1996) highlighted that the core of what an organisation is producing is fundamental, *but it may not ultimately be the reason for purchasing from a given organisation*. Ravald and Gronoos stress the importance of the relationship a company establishes and maintain with customers and clients, and wider stakeholders. This perspective illuminates the relational qualities of events. *It should, however, be noted that practitioners also invest in events as a tactical, sales generation strategy, in addition to more specific brand building activities, such as public relations events* (Gupta, 2003).
>
> (Crowther 2010: 228–229)

Now have another look at some of the journal articles you are using and see how the authors critically review the literature. Then consider how you could critique their work – using other authors' writing.

Subsections of the literature review

The introduction

This acts as a guide to the reader as to what the chapter contains. Remember, like the entire chapter, it is written in the present tense and *not* what you *will* be writing about. It outlines the main topics.

The main section

Group the literature into themes and use headings and subheadings to show the separate parts (see Chapter 13). If relevant show the historical development of the ideas you are presenting, but this is not always the best way, if sometimes the most logical. Ensure you compare and contrast the different views presented and evaluate the contributions. Highlight areas of theoretical and empirical weaknesses. If there are a number of studies in your area of interest, it can be effective to summarise the studies in a table format.

Conclusion

Provide a brief summary of the contents of the chapter and confirm which literature is the most important contribution to your study. Show any weakness in the current state of knowledge and the 'gaps' you have identified. At this stage your conceptual framework and hypotheses and research questions should naturally flow from what you have already written, leading into the methodological chapter.

Student vignette

Claire conducted an examination of the importance of global event companies understanding divergent cultures.

The aim of my literature review chapter was to provide an understanding of existing cultural theories, adjustment theories and cross cultural communication competences. I critically analysed current and past research and stressed the strengths and weaknesses of existing models and theories, to verify gaps in the research for the event industry. The conclusion of the review formed a basis for the primary research. I began by defining culture using a definition by Tayeb (2003: 10) as 'historically evolved values, attitudes and meanings that are learned and shared by the members of a community and which influence their material and non-material way of life'. I then discussed several cultural models, including Hofstede's Five Dimensions of Culture (Hofstede 2001). I discussed the critique by Copeland and Schuster (2008) of Hofstede's model which led to their development of the Global Business Practices Model. Next I considered various adjustment theories, including the classic U Curve Model (Oberg 1960) and the current research such as Maude (2011) which questioned its reliability. Finally, I discussed cross cultural communication competencies. This review of the literature showed that there was a need for a better understanding of how cross cultural training aimed at enhancing cross cultural awareness and cross cultural communication competences, affects the adjustment process of short term assignments abroad and how this could affect event success. Ultimately, I produced a new cross cultural adjustment model incorporating pre-departure training for short-term assignments.

When you have finished drafting your literature review, always reread your aim and objectives, to ensure that one supports the other and that you have not 'wandered off' in a different direction.

Referencing and plagiarism

We stated above that you are not an expert in the topic, so do not give your opinions, but you should provide arguments, provided they are supported by a *reference*. So for example do not claim that in your experience most planned events are small. Instead suggest that probably most planned events are small and give the reference (Getz 2012) or quote the reference: 'Probably the vast majority of planned events are small' (Getz 2012: 48). Professor Donald Getz is one of the leading academics in event studies and *is* an expert and so his view that most planned events are small has authority.

It is extremely important that every piece of material (and that includes online sources and television programmes) must be correctly referenced in the text and in a list (called the bibliography) at the end of the report, dissertation or assignment. This is for all work, whether you quote, paraphrase or summarise. There are specialist software programs which allow you to store your search results and references, such as Microsoft OneNote and 'citeulike' or you can simply keep them in a text document.

If you think about the purposes of having the references in the text and the list it will help remind you to enter them correctly. In the text, the name(s) and year show first that you are acknowledging the work of others. This may be their findings, idea, opinions or their argument from which you may have developed your own thoughts. If you do not do this you are guilty of *plagiarism*, which has become a very serious issue in recent years, particularly because of the availability of material online. Plagiarism is the use of someone else's work and presenting it as though it is one's own. Not only is it unfair, it is also illegal in many countries. Universities use increasingly sophisticated software (such as 'turnitin') to detect cases of plagiarism. In many texts more than two authors are shown with the first author's name and then *et al.* (meaning 'and others'). Note that it is an abbreviation of the Latin *et alia* and must therefore have the full stop (period) at the end. Do ensure that you only use 'anon.' (that is, the work is anonymous) if it really is! An example would be a local nursery rhyme which has not been included in any published form. Anything online will be uploaded by a person, people or organisation as the publisher of the website and they should be referenced appropriately, if no other source can be identified. The year is given to show the age of the source and to distinguish between pieces written by the same author and published in different years.

Practical tip box

- If an exact year is unknown, it is usually acceptable to use an abbreviated form of *circa* (which means 'about'), for example 'ca.1950'.
- When citing a web page either use the copyright date if one is shown (usually at the bottom of the page) or the year in which it was accessed.
- When an author(s) publishes more than one output in any one year, the letters a, b, c, etc. are placed after the year. The first reference used in the text is shown as Smith and Jones 2010a and the second referred to is Smith and Jones 2010b, etc. The same lettering is used in the reference list (bibliography) at the end to distinguish between them.
- If you quote an author's words directly, you must show this either by enclosing the extract in quotation marks or by indenting it (if it is a longer passage) and giving the page or pages on which it is found.

Here are some examples from Rittichainuwat and Mair's (2012) article on the motivations of visitors to consumer travel exhibitions in Thailand:

- For instance, Kozak (2006) found that the major motivations of exhibitors ...
- As Kerin and Cron (1997) note ...
- ... empirical research on motivations is lacking (Lee et al. 2010).

The list at the end of the article or publication is to enable readers to identify and find the material; it is therefore important that the references are given accurately and listed strictly in alphabetical order. Different publishers and institutions use different formats for referencing (e.g. Harvard style), and this is why you may see some variations, for example, the year given in brackets or not in brackets.

Here are the examples from above as they appeared in the references at the end of the journal article:

Kerin, R. A., & Cron, W. L. (1987). Assessing trade show functions and performance: an exploratory study. *Journal of Marketing*, 51(3), 87–94.

Kozak, N. (2006). The expectations of exhibitors in tourism, hospitality and the travel industry. *Journal of Convention and Event Toursim*, 7: 99–116.

Lee, M. J., Yeung, S., & Dewald, B. (2010). An exploratory study examining the determinants of attendance motivations as perceived by attendees at Hong Kong exhibitions. *Journal of Convention and Event Tourism*, 11, 195–208.

Always ensure that you are consistent in your referencing and that it follows *exactly* your organisation's guidelines, including capital letters, full stops (periods) and semi-colons. Sometimes referencing may involve the use of footnotes rather than a list at the end. If materials are not in the public domain, for example an email communication sent to you, this only appears in the text and not in the list. So when Professor Erica McWilliams, in a keynote speech at the Event Education Forum 2012 in Sydney, described plagiarism as 'dumb borrowing', her speech is appropriately acknowledged here in the text, but does not appear in the bibliography at the end of this book. Incidentally, a better alternative, she said, is 'smart borrowing', when you don't imitate without referencing appropriately, but take the essence and use it to add value to what you are doing – which is of course, what we have done here.

Conceptual framework

A conceptual framework is used mainly in *deductive* research (see Chapter 2), but can also be used in *inductive* research.

Definition box

The *conceptual framework* 'explains either graphically, or in narrative form, the main things to be studied – the key factors, concepts or variables' (Miles and Huberman 1994: 18). It not only identifies the concepts to be used in a study, but also describes them and their relationship to each other and how they are to be measured (in quantitative research).

Gratton and Jones (2010: 82) define a concept as 'a representation of an object, a property, or behaviour'. Examples could include weight, age and intelligence. From these definitions it should be clear to you that you need to have completed your literature search before you are able to identify all the relevant concepts. You also use the literature to establish what the relationship between the concepts is. So for example, weight might initially increase with age and then decrease. Having identified your concepts, you then need to operationalise them, that is, transform them into items

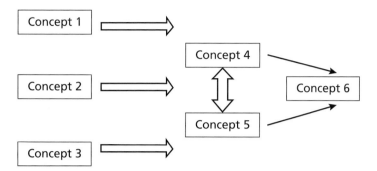

Figure 6.1 A simple conceptual framework

that can be measured or observed. Weight can be measured on an informal basis, such as light, average or heavy, but is better measured precisely by formal means such as kilograms or grams. Again the empirical literature that you have found helps you to know how best to do this. Once you have operationalised a concept it is known as a variable. Two key types of variable you will read about are independent and dependent variables. Independent variables are presumed to cause the effect, so in the example above, age is the independent variable. Weight is the dependent variable because it can be explained by the independent variable. This example shows why it is important that you identify the variables correctly, or else your results could be worthless, such as suggesting that weight causes us to age. Whilst concepts can be listed, many researchers like to also show the relationships between the concepts and so use graphics to illustrate them, as in the example in Figure 6.1.

In qualitative research, the conceptual framework can either be developed as a tentative framework based on what you might already know or have read about the topic (Miles and Huberman 1994) or as the data is collected and analysed (see Chapter 11).

Once a conceptual framework has been established in quantitative research, precise hypotheses or research questions can be developed.

Event research in action

Lee et al. (2013) undertook research at three multicultural festivals in South Korea to explore 'the effect of community attachment on cultural festival visitors' satisfaction and future intentions'. This title immediately gives you a specific understanding of what the research is about. The key words given by the authors are: 'community attachment, cultural festival, visitor satisfaction, future intention and Korea'. From reading just these two short parts of the journal article, you can have an idea of whether it is of relevance to you and whether to read more. If you are searching for literature for your methodology section, a quick glance at the abstract tells you that '420 valid questionnaires ... were collected'. From this you know that the research is empirical, deductive, quantitative, etc. A quick scan of the article reveals further details.

(Continued)

Event research in action (continued)

At the end of the introduction section, the aim of the research is set out, namely 'to shed light on the effect of community attachment on cultural festival visitors, using a case of multicultural festivals in South Korea (hereafter Korea), and to investigate the influence of community attachment on satisfaction and future intention'. Three hypotheses were generated from the literature:

H1: Community attachment is a significant predictor of satisfaction.
H2: Community attachment is a significant predictor of intention to revisit.
H3: Community attachment is a significant predictor of positive word-of-mouth (WOM).

Important variables which could be linked with community attachment and could influence the study were also identified from the literature, namely, age, gender and past visits.

Data was collected in 2010 (see the section in the article headed 'Data collection') and so is contemporary and there is unlikely to have been more recent data published. The results showed first that 'community attachment has a significant effect on the intention to revisit and positive WOM', and second, 'people who are attached to an ethnic minority community are more likely to revisit and spread positive WOM than people who are not attached'. This agreed with findings from a previous study, as visitors to a festival who are celebrating their cultural traditions are more likely to be engaged with it and hence support it. Furthermore, they found that the gender of respondents influenced their intention to revisit and positive WOM, but not their age or previous experience of visiting, which contradicted results from other types of events. The authors discussed these results in terms of their practical use to event organisers and then their contribution to knowledge for festival studies. Finally, they discussed the limitations of the study, including the need to produce the questionnaire in more than one language.

Scenario

In the left-hand column of the following table are five topics, and in the right-hand column, five types of events. Pick one topic from the left-hand column and one event from the right-hand. Then:

- Identify the key words that you would use to search the literature.
- Consider which sources (for example, journal article, textbook, industry report) may provide relevant information and categorise them as primary or secondary sources.
- Undertake the literature search, making notes on the topic.

- Count how many pieces of literature of each you have – check that you have more primary sources (including empirical journal articles) than secondary sources.
- Check that you have appropriate literature to provide a definition(s), theory and context.
- Using bullet points, list the main points you would make about the topic, using the correct referencing.
- Identify a 'gap' in the literature.
- Consider the order of the bullet points: could they be reordered to better effect?
- Finally, consider how hard it was to find literature relevant to the chosen topic and event – try another combination; is this easier or more difficult?

Motivation for attending …	a sporting event
Satisfaction with attending …	a music festival
Cultural issues relating to …	a community event
The marketing of …	a product launch
The economic impacts of …	an agricultural show

Summary

Chapter 6 has highlighted:

- The differences between primary and secondary sources
- The purpose of a literature search
- The purpose and writing of a research proposal
- Some tips on writing a literature review
- Some general guidance on referencing literature sources
- The development of a conceptual framework.

Further reading

Journals

Laing, J. and Frost, W. (2010) 'How green was my festival: Exploring challenges and opportunities associated with staging green events', *International Journal of Hospitality Management*, 29: 261–267, is a good example of a conceptual paper.

Books

Chapter 13 of Greetham, B. (2009) *How to Write Your Undergraduate Dissertation*, Basingstoke: Palgrave Macmillan, discusses in detail the writing of a research proposal.

Hart, C. (2001) *Doing a Literature Search*, London: Sage Publications; and Hart, C. (1998) *Doing a Literature Review*, London: Sage Publications, are both useful.

A worked example of a student research proposal can be found in in Chapter 2 of Saunders, M., Lewis, P. and Thornhill, A. (2007) *Research Methods for Business Students*, 4th edn, Harlow: Pearson Education. They also discuss in Chapter 3 what tutors mean when they say you need to be critical about the literature rather than simply descriptive.

Clough, P. and Nutbrown, C. (2012) *A Student's Guide to Methodology*, 3rd edn, London: Sage Publications, gives a useful audit form and completed example on pages 180–186 which could help you check that you have considered all the aspects of your research design.

Web links

UsingMindMaps.com (2013) 'How to mind map a text book'. Online. Available HTTP: www.usingmindmaps.com/how-to-mind-map-a-text-book.html (accessed 21 June 2013) has a good web page on creating mind maps of a book.

Video links

Further help with writing a research proposal can be found in *The Research Proposal* (13.51 minutes). Online. Available HTTP: www.youtube.com/watch?v=zJ8Vfx4721M& feature=relmfu (accessed 21 June 2013); and *How to Write a Literature Review* (25.06 minutes) Online. Available HTTP: www.youtube.com/watch?v=jKL2pdRmwc4 (accessed 21 June 2013) is similarly helpful.

PART II

Data collection

Chapter 7

The research population

Chapter learning outcomes

In this chapter we:

- Explain sampling
- Evaluate different types of samples
- Discuss sampling size and response rate
- Evaluate research with sensitive groups.

Johnny goes to a football match and asks people about which football team is their favourite, and they all say they support either team X or team Y. From this Johnny concludes that all people in this country (of your choice) support team X or Y – what would you say? True, you might say, no I don't support team X or Y, I support team C. The fact is, his respondents were either fans of team X or team Y and therefore Johnny's result is not 'representative' of the whole population. This means that Johnny's findings are not valid nor reliable, because his sample size was not representative of the whole population.

Introduction

Sampling is the process of selecting subjects or objects from the population of interest. Sampling can determine 'how much' or 'how well' researchers can generalise their findings (Garson 2012). In the example above Johnny cannot generalise anything and relate it to the whole population; he might only be able to say that his sample size were either fans of team X or team Y. It is indeed very difficult to generalise from the results of most studies and sampling is one of the major reasons for this. You might now ask 'how can we generalise from the findings of our research?' The answer is, that without a census where everyone in the population is asked questions, no one can be 100 per cent certain that the findings of their study apply to the whole population, but there are studies that can be used to generalise to some extent.

Types of sampling

There are two main types of sampling (see Figure 7.1 on p. 97), *random* or *probability sampling* and *non-random* or *non-probability sampling*. Random sampling tries to give an equal chance of the respondent being selected from the whole population. Random sampling is the assumption that provides the foundation for inferential statistics (Garson 2012). What does this mean? With inferential statistics, you are trying to reach conclusions that extend beyond 'the immediate data alone', in other words you are trying to generalise your findings and apply them to a wider population. Interestingly, most undergraduate or even postgraduate dissertations tend to fail on this assumption largely because of either inadequate sample size or inappropriate sampling methods. So, if we know the type of sampling we should undertake and the correct sample size that will help us generalise from the findings of the study, why do many students fail to do it? The answer to this is that it is often costly and time consuming (and in some cases impossible) in many studies. In fact government agencies use mixed sampling methods and different types of software and acquire very large data sets, and yet there are still limitations to their findings. Justifying your sampling is a critical task and often a very difficult one, especially when the sample size is small.

There are five types of random sampling (see Figure 7.1). *Simple random sampling* is when the researcher has a sampling frame that contains the whole population and then draws a sample from that population in a random manner. For example, if you want to survey school pupils, from a particular school, to find out what their favourite event is in the Olympics and have a data set that contains all pupils in that school, you can randomly select your targets from that data set. Simple random sampling tends to happen when the sampling frame is small.

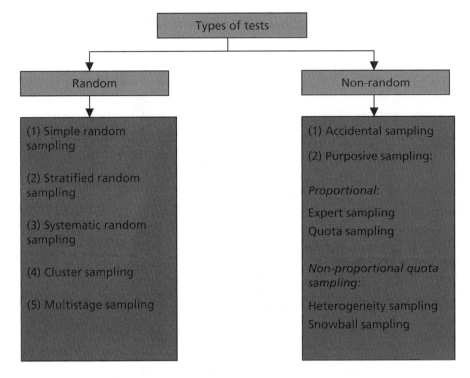

Figure 7.1 Types of sampling

Systematic random sampling is similar to simple random sampling, but you pick every nth term within that population. In other words, you might choose every fifth person from within the sampling frame.

Stratified random sampling is when you take a simple random sample from each stratum of population. A stratum means dividing the population into homogeneous subgroups and then taking a simple random sample from each of the subgroups. An example would be to divide the students in a lecture theatre by their place of residence and then choose a random sample from each category of residence. This method helps represent the overall population and also provides the opportunity to compare or analyse the subgroups. It tends to be more precise than random sampling (Trochim 2006).

Cluster sampling. This tends to be used when a population extends across a large geographical area. In this case researchers might first use simple random sampling to choose or select some of the states/counties, etc., and then draw their samples from the chosen areas. This method has its limitations because some of the areas or counties will not be included in the selection. This might mean that some of the poorer or richer counties are not included in the study and this may bias the results.

Finally, *multi-stage sampling* is a combination of some or all of the above random sampling methods. In the real world, for example when the research involves the whole population of a country, it is more complicated and the researcher might need to combine these methods to be able draw any conclusions.

In *non-random sampling*, a random selection is not included. Strictly speaking, non-random sampling tends to be used for qualitative studies, where perhaps the sampling is more purposeful and the target is smaller. However, random sampling is expensive and time consuming and therefore non-random sampling is widely used in quantitative studies of an explanatory nature. Some argue that the findings of research utilising non-random sampling could be down to pure chance. The reality is that tests of significance for non-random samples are not applicable (Garson 2012).

Accidental or convenience sampling is the most common non-probability sampling used. This means that the researcher asks anyone who happens to be within their arm's reach. A significant number of university students tend to survey their peers when doing the research for their dissertations; the most obvious limitation with this method is the absence of representativeness. Also, qualitative research methods tend to be based on relatively small samples and again, if one confines their interviews to a sample of, say, ten people, this is hardly representative of a population. You might ask, so why do people use them? The simplest answer is because sometimes other types of sampling are not feasible and this way the researcher might get a feel about population. In the case of undergraduate dissertations, it is more the fact that the student demonstrates that they understand how the sampling should take place and the limitations associated with their research rather than achieving statistical significance, but not all academics will agree with this view.

In *purposive sampling*, as implied by its name, selection will take place with a specific purpose in mind. Purposive sampling could be based on some particular demographic background. For example, some specific age bracket in which the researcher is interested, or gender, religion, ethnicity, profession, age, etc. Purposive sampling can take on a variety of forms (see Figure 7.1).

Expert sampling means choosing those who have expertise in a particular area. For example, if one wants to find out the possible outcomes of a certain effect such as climate change on future beach festivals, then they might sample a group of experts on climate change and events management. The Delphi technique is one of the types of data collection that uses expert sampling. Expert sampling provides enhanced validity for your findings by gathering data from a sample size of people who have specific expertise.

Quota sampling is another type of purposive sampling. It is still a form of non-probability sampling but it takes strata into account. An example might be where a researcher samples even numbers of males and females for interviews; this method is a fairly common method of data collection.

There is also *non-proportional quota sampling,* which still comes under the umbrella of purposive sampling but with fewer restrictions. For example, in *snowball sampling*, a researcher will find the first group of people to be their sample and ask them to identify subsequent respondents. They may even be asked to disseminate the questionnaire to people they know.

Definition box

Snowball: a type of data gathering that rapidly grows by being passed from potential respondent to potential respondent.

Snowball sampling, if it is undertaken, should be done so in a well organised and structured manner so that the researcher can understand the structure of the respondent groups and identify/correct for any apparent imbalances that may occur. In such forms of data collection, the sample size might or might not be representative and more likely will not be representative. For example, the survey might end up having too many respondents from one particular age group or particular gender. Finally, we might use a technique known as *heterogeneity sampling*, when we are more concerned with getting a wide range of views and ideas rather than trying to achieve some form of representativeness. What is actually taking place in this type of sampling is the sampling of ideas rather than the sampling of respondents. For example, brainstorming is a form of heterogeneity sampling, or a town council might want to find the range of opinions regarding certain development issues in an attempt to deal with a broad range of opinions.

Size of the sample

The size of the sample depends on the type of research method, and particularly whether the data collection is qualitative or quantitative. The sample size is much larger in quantitative research, where the findings are assessed numerically, based on the size of the population. When you decide on the size of a sample, there is usually a compromise to be made between considerations of time and costs and the need for precision. As sample size increases, sampling error decreases, and usually an error of $\pm$ 5 per cent is acceptable. Based on the assumption that the variables within your questionnaire are normally distributed within the population, and as a guide Yamane (1967) calculates that for a population of about 400,000 the size of the sample should be 400. However, for a student dissertation a smaller sample may be acceptable – this is something you should discuss with your supervisor.

Example

Johnny is planning to compare the opinions of different nationalities attending a music festival in the UK. He plans to collect 150 questionnaires for his dissertation. Once he starts to analyse his finding to compare opinions of different nationalities, his tutor questions sample sufficiency in his survey, pointing out that he has 15 different nationalities and a different numbers of responses in each group including 50 British, 35 American, 8 German, 2 Australian, 2 French, and 1 Dutch. Statistically, although he has collected a reasonable number of completed questionnaires given it is an undergraduate dissertation, the sample in each group cannot justify comparison between the groups. For example 2 Australians cannot be representative of this nationality compared to 50 Britons, therefore, Johnny's sample is challenged in terms of validity and reliability.

Johnny's tutor's reasoning for this is that if a data analysis attempts to make a comparison between the groups, in this case different nationalities, then Johnny needs a statistically sufficient number in each group: this means Johnny might need to collect 300 questionnaires and sufficient numbers of each nationality.

Question

What other factors do you think need to be taken into consideration when Johnny decides how many people he surveys in each nationality group?

True, Johnny also might need to know total numbers of each nationality at that festival and take 5 per cent of total attendance for each nationality; of course a rule of thumb may apply and if two respondents represent 5 per cent of French attendance then one might need to reconsider grouping, etc.

Student vignette

Tom has undertaken research into terrorism and the media.

I have come into contact with sampling in research throughout my studies at UK universities. As an undergraduate student I learnt about the principles and practice of research methodology through class contact and my own reading, and later, through applying this knowledge to my first research project. Sampling is a crucial element of any research project, and often one of the key indicators of its value. While understanding the importance of this process can be stressful, it is above all an exciting experience. After all, through the choices I made as a researcher in designing and executing my first sampling strategy, my ideas about the phenomena I was interested in came to life through contact with the sample of respondents.

This knowledge base and early research experiences gave me the confidence and interest in developing as a student and a researcher. Now in postgraduate studies, I design and execute more elaborate sampling strategies. My current research involves a three-step data collection, based on a nationally representative sample of British leisure tourists using a simple random sampling technique, and Postcode Address Finder as a database.

Response rates

A *response rate* is the percentage of people who respond to a survey. This can be calculated by taking the number of people who completed the survey, dividing it by the number of people contacted, and multiplying by one hundred.

If you asked 280 people at an event to complete a survey and 164 agreed, the response rate would be 164/280 × 100 or 59 per cent. For the research to be accurate a good response rate must be achieved.

However, it is broadly accepted that response rates have fallen over time (Dillman et al. 2009). This raises two key issues: those around non-response bias, and those relating to an increased cost and difficulty when collecting data.

Non-response bias can take two forms, either unit non-response bias where a randomly selected individual does not take part in the survey, or item non-response bias where certain questions are not answered. Non-response bias is a notable problem because it creates a difference between the results of the survey and the true opinion of all of the event attendees, if that could be measured. Non-response bias can have a serious and unpredictable impact on the quality of data. For example it may be found that only the most satisfied and the least satisfied take the time to complete the survey while the 'reasonably satisfied middle' are not sufficiently interested to complete the survey. Or those who are making the most of the event and enjoying it the most do not have the time to complete the survey. Non-response bias cannot usually be avoided but consideration should be given to maximising response rates in both the planning and execution phases.

In relation to undertaking research at an event, response rate is especially critical as the researcher does not get a second chance to gather data. The event has quite simply been and gone, unless of course there is a useable database of those who attended the event.

Table 7.1 shows various methods of gathering data and the potential response rates that might be achieved. Response rates are affected by numerous factors and as such these indications are rough guidelines only.

A potential respondent's decision to complete or decline the survey is generally taken in the first few moments of interaction with an interviewer or the physical questionnaire (Groves and Couper 1996). With this in mind it is the questionnaire design or interviewer that the researcher can have most control over in terms of improving response rate. Therefore good quality questionnaire design, including keeping the questionnaire short, a personal explanation of the value of the research, appropriate distribution (at a point that leads people to see the value of the research or at a time when they're engaged and interested but not busy with the core features of the event), and enthusiastic and interested researchers distributing the questionnaire or undertaking the interviews, are key to improving response rates. In addition to this an appropriate incentive could also be used to help enhance these factors.

Qualitative sampling

Whilst sampling is always associated with quantitative research, it is equally important for qualitative methods, although it does not always seem to the best term to use. Nonetheless, people or cases or places or events or documents or whatever, have to be

Table 7.1 Potential response rates

	Poor	Average	Good
Research undertaken during events			
Distribution of self-complete questionnaires and freepost envelopes with other event related material (such as programmes or maps)	1%	5%	8%
Personal distribution of self-complete questionnaires to event attendees with freepost envelopes	15%	20%	30%
Personal distribution of self-complete questionnaires to event attendees with return boxes onsite	5%	12%	20%
Face-to-face interviews undertaken with event attendees	50%	60%	75%
Research undertaken after events			
Emailing of electronic questionnaires to event attendees after the event has occurred	5%	15%	30%
Posting of paper questionnaires to event attendees with freepost return envelopes after the event has occurred	25%	35%	45%
Telephone interviews with event attendees (subject to the number of calls to each individual and other factors)	30%	40%	55%

selected. Purposive sampling was discussed earlier in the chapter, but here we want to consider some additional forms. Patton (2002) and Flick (2008) suggest:

- Extreme or deviant cases
- Typical cases
- Maximal variation – i.e. as different as possible
- Intensity of the interesting feature
- Critical cases – this could include experts in their field
- Sensitive cases
- Convenience – but this is obviously the least preferable choice.

As we have said before, your choice will depend on your aim and objectives. However, there is one important difference between qualitative sampling and quantitative sampling. In the latter, you must decide your sample from the outset, but in qualitative research it is acceptable to have several stages of sampling or even to adapt your sample as you proceed. For example, you may select a festival, and then several events that form part of the festival, and then the people who may be best able to help you within the event organising team. Alternatively, it may be that having interviewed a sensitive case, you realise that it would aid understanding of your topic if you sought the views of experts in the field, or perhaps other participants who have had very different experiences. In selecting the sample of people for a focus group (which we discuss in more detail in the next chapter) you might want to approach people based on their age or gender, but you might also want to select participants by other characteristics, such as their experiences. We discussed snowball sampling earlier, and an important element of this type of sampling may be identifying 'gatekeepers'. These are participants who can give you access to others whom you might not be able to contact directly.

In qualitative research the sample is therefore much smaller than in quantitative research, and for an undergraduate dissertation could mean as little as 6–10 in-depth interviews or five focus groups with 5–10 participants in each group.

Practical tip box

Whenever we are asked how many semi-structured or unstructured interviews are necessary, the answer is usually always 'it depends', which we know isn't actually very helpful. But it *does* depend on both the skill of the interviewer and the interviewees. If you have an interviewer who is very good at asking questions, prompting, encouraging, etc. (see Chapter 8) and an interviewee who is happy to talk, is knowledgeable and reflective, more information may be obtained in just one interview than can be gained from several interviews with a poor interviewer and/or interviewees who respond minimally to each question. One answer to this is to keep undertaking interviews until you can find out nothing new – this is known as 'saturation'. However, you may run out of time, finances or possibly interviewees before this happens. The important thing is that you can report a range of responses and describe fully how the sample was selected.

Finally, sampling may also apply to secondary data (which we also discuss in the next chapter) such as documents or photographs. Flick (2008) describes a collection of these materials as an archive or corpus: 'we take existing materials, which we select in order to analyze them. Thus, the sequence is turned around – first the material, then the selection, then the use of methods' (Flick 2008: 32).

The researcher as subject

Sometimes, you the researcher are the subject of a study. It could be that you engage in an auto-ethnographic study, whereby you record what is happening to you and around you in a certain situation. For example, if you had volunteered as a 'games maker' volunteer in the London 2012 Olympic Games, you might wish to research your specific experience of being a volunteer in a global event. There is much in the events literature in terms of the value, challenges and management of volunteering at major events, so it could be that you engage in evaluating your own experience alongside of existing knowledge or perspectives, as known or published in the literature.

If you think that you might like to take such an approach to a piece of events research, discuss it and the ways that you can be the subject of the research itself with your supervisor. You can also give thought to the methods you deploy in the process of being subject and creator of the research. For example, you may wish to create a daily diary of your thoughts and observations. Also, you may wish to take photographs to help you contextualise a diary and your memory of events. In any case, the methods are the means by which you go about collecting data for your research focus. It is the combination of all of these sources that you can subject to an in-depth analysis so that you may have the basis for some interesting research findings!

Researching with children

Conducting research with children as respondents can be illuminating and rewarding. Equally it can be challenging and fraught with obstacles. Nonetheless, children, like adults, have a voice, so if we seek their views or opinions, ideally they can be captured for the purposes of research. There is the common issue, however, that ethical standards in many environments such as schools and research councils strictly limit the amount of research that can be conducted with children, for reasons usually concerning safety on moral grounds at a minimum. In any case, data obtained from children can be very illuminating and honest, whereas adults may be more reserved and not completely truthful about their views. Can you imagine asking dozens of school age children their thoughts on the latest Disney movie as they come out of a cinema – what would the range of reactions be? It would be a bit chaotic, as some would be very animated and want to tell you absolutely everything about the film, while others who may not have liked it for whatever reason may begin to cry – or maybe they are scared of you! So you will have some who are willing to speak to you and probably others who are not. A bit like adults really, except you can rest assured the children will be more animated and entertaining to engage in such a discussion with!

Event research in action

In their study of children aged 5 who engage in reading at home outside of school work, Nutbrown and Hannon (2003), the researchers, unveiled some interesting findings yet equally they took account of the research considerations they undertook beforehand. Among these was that parental permission for the children was needed, all children were told in advance why they were being asked questions and were given the opportunity not to participate, or stop an interview whenever they wished; interviewers were accompanied by teachers in the process and proper legal checks were done in relation to current child protection legislation. Finally, children were interviewed in their usual and familiar surroundings so they were comfortable.

Interestingly, experts in early childhood have raised a few concerns in relation to children's reaction to questions, such as: 'they may give you the answers they think you want'; 'they may not understand the questions'; 'they may feel overwhelmed by the situation' (Greig et al. 2012: 202). One can reflect that the same can also happen when interviewing adults! In any case, this research team proceeded to put questions to the children about reading at home, with whom and what. The study also noted that

> five-year-olds can be much better at saying 'no' than many adults, should they not wish to proceed. It was concluded that children would know they were being asked questions and that interviewers could put them at ease, just as they would if the interviewees were adults.
>
> (2012: 203)

In the context of events and festivals you might be interested to know how children have enjoyed a particular event so you might measure or evaluate their interest as part of a research project; let's say the event is a pirate-ship themed family fun day. Their views in essence would be valuable to organisers for discovering what aspects worked best and perhaps what might be lacking in a programme of events. However, it may be difficult to interview the children. In such circumstances, provided you have permission from an organising body, you could possibly approach the parents to ask their impressions of the children's enjoyment of such a particular event. Provided it is soon after the event or even during the event, parents can very likely provide you with an accurate account of the children's experience, for example whether or not they liked face painting, playing in a bouncy castle, being with their friends, or having their photo taken with a 'real' pirate!

In essence, there are ways to go about collecting data on or about children for the purposes of events research. You may rest assured that the first port of call in such cases is indeed your research supervisor, and behind them will be an ethical standards checklist that must also be adhered to. Once that is covered, you will have a better idea of the parameters you have in using children as research subjects or participants.

'At risk' groups including vulnerable adults

Some of the necessary ethical and moral considerations described above concerning interviews with children can apply to vulnerable adults. Views vary considerably in terms of how these are identified; however, we can consider vulnerable adults to be those who are more dependent on assistance from others for some of their typical everyday functions. You can imagine that the health care field and charities often deal with vulnerable adults, for example those who suffer from disease, disability, homelessness, and so forth.

In terms of examples, those who are reliant on aid, such as a blind person wishing to visit the shops, may depend on a guide dog to get around. In the case of charities, there are those that wish to help homeless people out of living on the street. In both of these scenarios, you are dealing with people who may need to gain a bit more trust in you before engaging in research and/or dialogue. Of course, those in all walks of life, young and old and of varying ability, physically and mentally, have value when you are undertaking research for any number of purposes. The point remains, however, that care and attention must be taken when giving thorough consideration to the subjects you wish to engage in your research. As per above with children, your first port of call will be discussing your research ideas in full with your research supervisor. Equally, most institutions and research councils have comprehensive checklists that you can consult so that every eventuality is considered when recruiting vulnerable adults for your research project, and the necessary steps can be taken, for example security clearance checks, or special access permission for individuals and/or certain sites.

Scenario

You are approached by an event company to do a market research project for them to find out what other types of activities visitors to an air festival would like to see alongside the air show. This is to increase participation and therefore increase revenue for the organisers and accordingly, for the region.

- What sampling method would you recommend the company use?
- Give your reasons.
- How many responses do they need to collect?
- Justify your answer.

Summary

This chapter has:

- Explained sampling and evaluated different types of sampling
- Discussed sampling size and response rates
- Evaluated research with sensitive groups.

Sampling is one of the most important elements in a project; it's the fundamental part, which means if your sampling has not got logical reasoning to it, it will affect your findings. Sampling is also challenging in terms of access points. Many good ideas simply never get to be assessed because of access issues. Many managers and policy makers within the industry are simply out of touch with research methodology. This means that doing research in general and dissertations in particular needs to take into consideration the appropriate sampling required. Remember, if your sampling is not good, neither will be your research findings.

Further reading

Journals

Onwuegbuzi, A. J. and Collins, K. M. T. (2007) 'A typology of mixed methods sampling designs in social science research'. *The Qualitative Report*, 12: 281–316.

Books

Malhotra, N. and Birks, D. F. (2006) *Marketing Research: An Applied Approach*, 3rd edn. Harlow: Prentice Hall. Chapters 14 and 15 discuss sample design, including determining an initial sample size.

Greig, A. D., Taylor, J. and MacKay, T. (2012) *Doing Research with Children: A Practical Guide*, 3rd edn. London: Sage Publications.

Web links

Shaw, C., Brady, L. and Davey (2011) *Guidelines for Research with Children and Young People*. London: NCB Research Centre. Online. Available HTTP: www.ncb.org.uk/media/434791/guidelines_for_research_with_cyp.pdf (accessed 18 July 2013) is a useful guide if your respondents are children or young adults, and includes some case studies.

Trochim, W. M. K. (2006) 'Sampling'. *Research Methods Knowledge Base*, Online. Available HTTP: www.socialresearchmethods.net/kb/sampling.php (accessed 18 July 2013), considers the key terms in sampling.

Baker, S. E. and Edwards, R. (undated) 'How many qualitative interviews is enough?' *National Centre for Research Methods*. Online. Available HTTP: http://eprints.ncrm.ac.uk/2273/4/how_many_interviews.pdf (accessed 11 August 2013). This includes expert voices and early career reflections on sampling in qualitative research, which although designed for Ph.D. researchers, may be helpful.

Video links

Samples (6.11 minutes) Online. Available HTTP: www.youtube.com/watch?v=n3n-8PP0Sk5U (accessed 18 July 2013). This video considers the distinction between populations, samples, and groups in social science research.

Chapter 8

Obtaining research material (1)

Chapter learning outcomes

In this chapter we:

- Consider the use of secondary data for primary research
- Identify research material that is directly accessible to the senses of the researcher through observation
- Discuss the three forms of interview undertaken with individuals: structured, semi-structured and unstructured
- Introduce obtaining qualitative data from a group of participants
- Provide advice on designing questions for interview schedules
- Discuss using images as data.

An annual wine and cheese festival is held in Tuscany, Italy. After realising that interest in attending has been dropping over the last couple of years, the organisers want to know what visitors like about the current festival, and ways they could possibly improve things. They know that they can design and distribute a questionnaire to festival visitors, but they would also like to obtain an in-depth appreciation for visitor preferences and perceptions. They decide that semi-structured interviews would be best. Although a questionnaire might be useful, the researchers can also control who they interview by ensuring that they haven't had too much to drink, which might be harder to control with a questionnaire. An interview researcher team of five people got together and decided on an interview schedule. This is a set list of guiding questions used with willing participants in a short interview of say 10–20 minutes.

The interview team's goal is to target particular attendees of the festival late in the afternoon, as this appears to be a good time for those who are not rushed and are relaxed (and thus more open to being asked interview questions than those who are just arriving or ready to leave). They ask attendees questions about their likes and dislikes of the festival in an open question format and are able to collate a wide range of responses from them and analyse these for the organisers. Questionnaires typically offer a selection of responses to choose from, whereas the interviews are meant to encourage the attendees to be as open as possible about their thoughts. The interview process was thorough and allowed organisers a wide scope of factors to review, everything from the quality of loos onsite to expanding the wine choices to more global selections, for example tasters from Argentina and Chile. This semi-structured interview approach therefore fed a robust data set of variables and factors for festival organisers to consider improving on in the future.

Introduction

In this chapter we begin by considering how you can use existing data as research material. Next, we discuss collecting data that is directly accessible to the senses of the researcher – through *observation*. Then we look at data that you obtain by asking other people questions – it is therefore socially mediated data. So for example, you could observe the activities that people take part in at a community event or you could ask them what activities they are doing. Either method may be equally effective. However, if you just observe them, you cannot know *why* they might want to take part in that activity; it may not become obvious just by watching them. However, on the other hand, if you ask them why they are taking part, participants may not always tell you the truth (perhaps they may be embarrassed) or not the whole truth, or they may not even be aware of why they are doing something. Therefore there are strengths and weaknesses in both approaches.

Taking your research aim and objectives as your starting point (see Chapter 2), presuming the objectives are expressed properly, this can inform you about the most appropriate research methodology you should use for your dissertation. For example, if you wish to do research that helps to identify people's perceptions of a music festival, such as Glastonbury, England (welly boots and mud!) you may think of developing a survey instrument (questionnaire) and distributing it to festival goers to collect information using a quantitative methods approach. However, you may also want to examine what the organisers have done to minimise damage to the land and improve facilities for visitors. Thus, you may need to undertake some interviews with them.

In both cases you will be asking questions, but the form of the questions will differ. We want to ensure that it is at *this* stage that you design your questions correctly to provide the type of answer that will meet your objectives.

Primary research using secondary data sources

Alongside your literature review sources, you may wish to engage with *secondary data* sources in another way in your research study. In Chapters 2 and 6, we distinguished between primary and secondary research and primary and secondary data. In this section, we consider how you can use secondary data – which is data that you have not collected especially for the study – and analyse it. This is therefore primary research using secondary data.

For example, if you are doing research into the growing market for wedding venues then you might wish to consult secondary sources of data to help you with information. In the developed world and Christian traditions (found in the UK, America, Europe and Australia) church weddings were the most common type until the 1970s and 1980s. After that time, people started getting married in all sorts of places, for example shops, beaches, or historic properties. Can you imagine getting married underwater or in a coal mine? People have!

So in this instance, you could find secondary data from sources such as national archives or census data. In the UK for example, figures can be found that show the number of marriages and second marriages citizens have had over time. You could also obtain data on how many weddings people have had based on a religious ceremony or a civil ceremony, in churches, town halls, etc. This data could then be analysed statistically (see Chapter 12).

Depending on the scope and research of your study, you may also wish to consult local/regional, national, European or global bodies for statistical information, i.e. secondary data, to help your study. Perhaps you wish to research the amount of tourist visitors to a region, city, country or even international area. Provided these records are kept by public bodies in (arguably most cases but not always) democratic countries, it is data that you can obtain, for example Canada's national visitor statistics are recorded annually and kept by the Canadian Tourism Commission. The WTO (World Tourism Organization) keeps periodic statistics of tourism visitors for many countries around the world. If you are interested in what records your own city or town keeps, visit your local council office and/or website to find out how these records are kept and what figures they are able to share with you. All of this information can be considered secondary data to support a study, and what you use depends on the focus of your research.

Your library is often a more valuable source of secondary data than you may realise. You may wish to spend time with a library tutor or subject specialist so that you can fully appreciate places where you can obtain data. Many students are reliant on 'books on the shelf' (n.b.: a growing number are available as e-books) or even a few key journal articles to play a role in secondary research. Although it is a critical part of your literature search, the library is often a goldmine of valuable data through other channels to help make the most out of obtaining supporting information such as secondary data. University libraries often pay a lot of money to obtain market intelligence information not typically accessible or affordable for everyday traders or businesses, yet it is at your fingertips at a higher or further education library. For example, have a look at your library's database resources or spend some time with the staff so that they can explain to you where you can find information on special reserve collections of old regional archives, census data, or market intelligence (e.g. broadcasting data and TV viewing figures).

Event research in action

Jones et al. (2006) undertook a case study in Canada to identify the implications of climate change for outdoor event planning. Their research was based on three major events, namely Winterlude, 'one of the largest winter festivals in North America' (Jones et al. 2006: 66); the Canadian Tulip Festival; and Canada Day celebrations. A change in climate could, first, impact on Winterlude if the organisers could not maintain ice-based attractions (ice skating on the Rideau Canal Skateway being a key event); second, cause the tulips to flower at a different time to the festival, and third, increase the need for more heating during Canada Day.

The researchers used secondary data from the nearest Meteorological Service of Canada climate station to give them temperature and precipitation information. They also used climate change scenarios 'developed from monthly global climate models (GCM) available from the Canadian Climate Impacts and Scenarios (CCIS) Project' (Jones et al. 2006: 68). However, using secondary data is not without its problems. For example, in the case of the Winterlude festival, data could be obtained for the period 1970/71 to 2003/04, which provided the number of days the Skateway was open for skating (i.e. the length of the season) and the calendar date for the official opening of the Skateway for public skating. However, the method used to calculate season length changed in the mid-1990s. Prior to 1994/95, the season length included days in which the Skateway was closed due to poor ice conditions after it had officially opened, whereas after 1994/95 the season length excluded those days. Furthermore, when the researchers tried to calculate the relationship between climate and the day each year that the Skateway opened, they found that a robust model could not be developed, which they attributed to changes in safety standards, which might have influenced the decisions made over the years as to when it was safe to open the Skateway.

In the age of the internet and the web, there are also wedding venue blogs, discussion boards, Twitter, and other social media that can reveal a trend into the thoughts, perspectives and choices for wedding venues, as we discussed earlier. All of this takes time, effort and creativity in terms of where you would look for secondary data, but your supervisor should be able to help. It is good practice to get into the habit of looking for information 'outside of the box'. The internet provides a wealth of information, but remember it is harder to screen the content for quality. I once watched a group research presentation on the Olympic Games of 1986, complete with video footage the group had found online. When I pointed out the fact that there were no Olympics Games in 1986 (rather in 1984 and 1988) they were aghast that someone posted footage online that claimed that! If in doubt, ask around and/or a tutor. Using secondary data for primary research requires that you not only consider the reliability of the data but also the ethics (see Chapter 3) of using it. However, it can be a much more cost effective means of obtaining data and can often save valuable amounts of time.

Next, we turn to another method of obtaining data, one that is directly accessible to the senses of the researcher, namely observation. We begin with this because this is probably the earliest form of research we undertake. As children, we learn through our senses and we only ask questions if we don't understand and want more information. (If as a child you always wanted to find out what's happening and *why* – you've probably grown up to be a very good researcher!)

Observation and participant observation

Observation and participant observation are closely related to ethnographic methods of collecting data (see Chapter 5). However, that doesn't mean observation and participant observation need to sit within ethnography to be considered a valid approach to research methods.

Qualitative methods

Observation

This approach to data collection means that you will engage in using your senses – seeing, hearing, touching, smelling and possibly tasting – to observe a scene/situation under study.

Definition box

Observation 'consists of gathering impressions of the surrounding world through all relevant human faculties' (Adler and Adler 1994: 378).

It is commonplace to record field notes to aid in data collection. Depending on the environment and the permissions gained, these can be anything from handwritten notes, photos, film or electronic capture via smartphone as discussed later in this chapter. In essence, there are five dimensions generally applicable to observation:

- *Covert vs. overt observation*: how far is the observation revealed to those who are observed?
- *Non-participant vs. participant observation*: how far does the observer have to go to become an active part of the observed field?
- *Systematic vs. unsystematic observation*: is a more or less standardised observation scheme applied or does the observation remain flexible and responsive to the processes themselves?
- *Observation in natural vs. artificial situations*: are observations done in the field of interest or are interactions 'moved' to a special place (e.g. a laboratory) to make them more systematically observable?
- *Self-observation vs. observing others*: mostly other people are observed, so how much attention is paid to the researcher's reflexive self-observation for further grounding the interpretation of the observed?

(Flick 2009: 222)

An important distinction between *non-participant observation* and *participant observation* is that the former does not make any meaningful intervention into the scene/situation that is being observed. Adler and Adler (1998: 81) point out that 'Simple observers follow the flow of events. Behavior and interaction continue as they would without the presence of a researcher, uninterrupted by intrusion'. In contrast, participant observation generally means that the observer is integrated into the scene, and actively experiences and/or observes elements along the way.

In *non-participant observation*, you need to be able to identify the setting in which you wish to observe. Using the example of an exhibition floor, one events management student observed the paths of attendees on the show floor. Her information was able to determine a pattern of movement with these individuals, which proved useful in identifying those exhibition booths that were inviting and appealing to attendees. The true observer is able to distance themselves from the area and/or subjects being observed so that they do not influence movement or judgement of the participants.

Participant observation differs in that the observer is overt and known to those in the setting, participating in an appropriate way. This will often mean that they have been granted access or permission to the setting by means of association (e.g. an employer, or a social group such as sports team) or have an official invitation (special occasion, anniversary party or similar).

Spradley (1980) captures three phases of participant observation, and how you might focus your related data collection:

1 *Descriptive observation*, at the beginning, serves to provide the researcher with an orientation to the field under study. It provides non-specific descriptions and is used to grasp the complexity of the field as far as possible and to develop (at the same time) more concrete research questions and lines of vision.
2 *Focused observation* narrows your perspective on those processes and problems which are most essential for your research question.
3 *Selective observation*, toward the end of the data collection, is focused on finding further evidence and examples of types of practices and processes found in the second step.

(Spradley 1980: 34)

It is important, whether you are engaging in participant or non-participant observation, to be able to reflect meaningfully on your research questions and your efforts in observation. For example, if you wish to observe the production patterns of a stage crew at a live concert, you don't want to waste time observing the set-up of other concert elements such as catering or ticketing. Be sure the focus of your observation is closely linked to what you wish to uncover.

Overt observation vs. covert observation

If practising overt observation then it is usually a case where subjects are aware that they are being observed; for example a nurse may observe the coming and goings of an A&E department. In the case of events, you may wish to observe the movements and paths of participants at an exhibition. In so doing, you may learn more about what elements in the exhibition are appealing and attractive to the participants. By comparison, covert observation means that people are not aware that they are being observed. This approach to observation, and indeed data collection, is often a sticky point in terms of research ethics. In essence, it is deemed unethical (or in some cases illegal!) to undertake covert observational research. By the same token, if an area can be easily observed and there are no perceived issues with obtaining consent in for example public open spaces, for observing movement flows of people at a railway station within a mile of an event, then the notion of covert research would sometimes appear to be justified. It is a grey area though, so it is best to discuss your ideas with your supervisor in the first instance.

To conclude, observation can provide several different forms of data:

- Literal data – factual (can be numeric, e.g. the number of people at an event)
- Supporting data – e.g. statements by participants
- Interpretative data – incorporates assumptions made by the researcher, i.e. how they interpret what they observe
- Reflexive data – the researcher's own reaction to what they see or experience.

Interviews

As you will have realised, most acts of observation provide qualitative data, although occasionally quantitative data may also be obtained, for example, if the researcher observed and counted people in a queue. Next, we consider other methods that also predominantly deliver qualitative data (but like observation, can be set up in such a way that quantitative data can also be collected). We begin by asking questions to find out something we couldn't know from undertaking observation. This might be because we cannot access a research scene in which to do field work, or perhaps we want to know about something that has already happened or is going to happen, or maybe because we cannot see 'inside a person's head' and know what they are thinking. In these situations, we can ask people questions. First we consider when we want their answers to be uninfluenced by the responses of others, that is, a personal interview, which we discuss next. Or we can look at situations where we want people to think about what other people have said before they give their own responses, which are considered later.

Individuals

There are three forms of personal interview: *structured*, *semi-structured* and *unstructured*. The first is a quantitative method and the second two are qualitative. (These are sometimes referred to as standardised, semi-standardised and unstandardised.) Saunders et al. (2007) suggest that people may be more likely to agree to be interviewed than to complete a questionnaire, when the interview topic is seen to be interesting and relevant to them or provides them with an opportunity to reflect on events without needing to write anything down.

Structured interviews: surveys

This type of interview is often referred to as a survey (see Chapter 6) but needs to be distinguished from a survey in which the respondent completes the questionnaire themselves (self-completion). In a structured interview, the interviewer will read the questions to the interviewee and record their response either on paper or electronically (see Chapter 4). The interviewer is instructed to ask each question in the same tone of voice. This type of survey has advantages in that the interviewer does most of the work, and it is particularly suited either to respondents who may have difficulties in reading or writing; where the location is not suited to completing a questionnaire (for example on a clipboard at an event); or in a telephone interview. If face-to-face, an interviewer can also show the interviewee prompt cards which are not really suited to self-completion surveys. Whilst they follow a script an interviewer can skip irrelevant questions based on the responses they receive. The main disadvantage is that the questionnaire has to have fewer and simpler questions than a self-completion questionnaire. This type of interview provides quantitative data and hence a high degree of standardisation from which the results can be generalised to the population selected. It is often associated with market research (see Chapter 1). Designing the questions (see Chapter 9), undertaking the data collection and entry (Chapter 10) and analysing the data (Chapter 12) are the same for all surveys and so are discussed in those chapters.

Semi-structured interviews

Semi-structured interviews lie somewhere between structured and unstructured interviews. They are often used as they allow for some flexibility in questioning, but also some standardisation between participants.

The process of interviewing basically involves 'asymmetrical communication' whereby an interviewer facilitates a conversation with an interviewee with the goal of obtaining useful information for their research (Andrews et al. 2011). In the case of semi-structured interviews, the researcher can use open-ended questions, so the respondent has the opportunity to expand on their answer without restriction, and the researcher may further probe the issue if required, yet keep to some standardised focus of the research topic or aim.

Student vignette

Gina conducted research into the operational management challenges of small party planning businesses since the recession of 2008.

In addressing my research objectives, I knew that I wanted to concentrate on some particular perceived management challenges of this sector of the events business, and how these small party planning event enterprises went about overcoming these challenges. I designed an *initial interview structure* which I then piloted. Through this experience and thinking through my research approach again, I realised that my initial interview structure was not going to give me the depth of information that I was looking for. So I revised the interview structure to enable me to build the interview on solid open questions that would allow me to probe further with my participants in answering the questions. I ended up with an interview schedule that appears in the revised interview structure that follows:

Initial interview structure

- Do you recognise operations management as a management technique that you plan periodically (say at the beginning of each year) or that you recognise and design when an enquiry is made?

- Since the recession in 2008 have you recognised a change in the size of the events market?
- Have you recognised new entrants or closures within the market?
- Looking back since 2008 (5 years ago) do you recognise an increase or decrease in demand from customers?
- Have you recognised a change in the services that are demanded from you because of the recession?
- Do you feel that the recession has had an impact on the ease of gathering resources for an event? For example are suppliers emerging or closing? Is it easier or harder to find staff?
- Do you feel that by being a small business you face more operational challenges compared to a larger party planning company?
- Do you feel that having a small workforce has any effect on day to day productivity, does it enforce any challenges?
- As a small business do you feel you have the same access to resources that your larger competitors do?
- Do you have procedures in place to measure quality control of the events?
- Do you feel that by being a small events company you are at a disadvantage over your larger competitors to the variation of services which you are able to offer?
- As a small business do you do any formal planning for the future, if so how far into the future do you recognise?
- In your opinion do you believe that the future events market is changing? If so how?

Revised interview structure

- Understanding of operational management as a technique – when do you plan?
- Can you help me to understand the stages of your event operational management approach, e.g. market analysis, planning, implementation, and any performance evaluation?
- What type of change in types of services and customer demand has there been since the recession for you?
- What is the extent of your competition, i.e. how do you recognise this and how do you change to compete?
- Time constraints – what are they, lead time for events?
- As far as quality control is concerned, what measures if any do you put in place?
- What do you recognise as the main challenges that you face on a day to day basis? And how do you overcome these?
- What are the main challenges you face when working on a specific project? And how do you overcome these?
- As a small business do you recognise any formal planning for the future, how far into the future?
- In your opinion do you believe that the future event market is changing? How?
- How do you feel you would need to adapt your services to compete?
- What advantages do you feel you have?

You will see from the previous vignette that Gina thought through her research approach and realised that her initial interview structure was not going to give her the depth of information she was looking for. She then created a framework of questions which would guide the general enquiry of her research. This is the key benefit of semi-structured interviews, because although a framework or interview guide is set prior to the interview, you as the interviewer can also seek out further depth by probing the interviewee for more detail in their answers, and thus achieve more data to support your research objectives.

Unstructured interviews

As already acknowledged, interviews are typically carried out so as to capture research data that delves deeper into what people think, what they know, their attitudes and/or opinions on a certain subject or topic. In the context of unstructured interviews, it is maintained that the interviewee is typically encouraged to speak more freely on a subject, so that no stones are left unturned. A researcher is tasked with keeping a conversation going, but encouraging the participant to elaborate with open-ended questions such as: Can you tell me more about … ? What is important? Why? That is interesting; can you expand on it further? These are questions that can be used in any unstructured interview so as to solicit more in-depth content from participants. Typically, you want the participants to speak freely and openly in relation to your general line of inquiry.

It is then up to the researcher to guide the interview so that focus is still maintained, yet the openness of the information being shared is not compromised. For that reason, unstructured interviews can take more time to execute than would structured or semi-structured interviews as they follow more of a guide or script in their questioning.

With unstructured interviews, you usually have to allow for much more time for the participant to answer questions, go off track, come back around again (or not) and for the interviewee to bring the research query back around as the focus. It does, however, along the way allow for more enlightening, richer context to be divulged by participants to the researcher in relation to their potential input for data collection. For example, if a study was focusing on the experience of music festival attendees by way of structured or semi-structured interviews, the researcher might ask typical questions such as: How was the music? Food? Did you like the music? Which and why? What about other services? Were the activities appealing? Such questions allow for respondents to direct their answers to these particular questions. By comparison, by way of unstructured interviews (which by the way can very much mimic a conversation), a participant might reveal other aspects of the music festival that were enjoyable than would be the case if the interview were more structured. They may mention an impromptu game or a spontaneous group activity that allowed for them to enjoy the festival even more, such as having fun in a long queue for food or similar.

Of note is the fact that unstructured interviews can also be short or anecdotal in context, in that a researcher might seek informal and brief information from a resource that might be deemed a key source of information. This approach is not necessarily applied as the sole method of data collection, but it can be used alongside other sources of data collection such as surveys so as to further augment data in the findings. For example, music festival organisers might have a tally of total ticket sales shortly before an event, yet a gate manager as a key informant might be able to supply data with more accurate figures, for example that 92 per cent of ticket sales made actually attended the event.

Group interviews

Sometimes it can be useful to gain a better understanding of the dynamics of the event experience within a pair or group of visitors. Therefore, interviews can be carried out, where agreeable to the participants, with a group. In a study carried out at Disney theme parks, Bryman (2004) interviewed family groups. These interviews are similar to semi-structured interviews (see p. 114) in that an interview schedule is prepared, but it is expected that there may be some deviation from the planned questions depending on the responses. Also, the prompting may be different in that the interviewer can prompt not only the speaker but also the other interviewees to comment on what is said. These interviews therefore have many similarities to focus groups, which we discuss next. However, they tend to be much smaller – with a maximum of about five people.

Focus groups and panels

A focus group is a particular type of interview, where a group of people are interviewed together on a particular topic area. Sources differ on the ideal size of a focus group, but groups that contain twelve people or less are most suitable. To that end, a minimum size is also recommended, i.e. no less than six. Focus groups differ from other methods of data collection in that due to their nature they are focused in their intent and not necessarily representative of a population. They can be; however, if you want to conduct a focus group on the attendees of a latest edition product launch for users of a particular brand of smartphone, you wouldn't want or need to invite people who don't have one or are loyal to another type of phone. On the contrary however, it may be intended for a focus group to comprise a group of people unknown to each other and from a variety of different backgrounds to question them on their views or opinions, for example, of a nation's benefit (or not) from hosting a mega-event such as the Olympic Games.

Focus groups are typically used when soliciting qualitative types of data in research. The benefit of a focus group, which is very much a group interview, is that interaction between the participants can aid in bringing up issues and concerns that all have a view on, that might not ordinarily come up in individual interviews. Again to use the example from above, issues or problems with the functionality of some smartphone features may only be revealed in a focus group setting, whereas in individual interviews it may not be apparent or come up at all. This type of data collection method has its pluses and minuses. In terms of benefits to data collection, participants of focus groups are often at times able to expand on their views/perspectives when discussing a topic common to all in a session, thus they are able to share further depth of their experience.

Other advantages of focus groups over in-depth interviews arise from the social dynamics of the group. Ryan (1995) categorises them as:

- Synergism – a cumulative group effect produces a wider range of ideas than is possible from just interviewing individuals
- Snowballing – a single comment can elicit a whole range of additional confirmatory or modifying statements
- Security – the social ease generated by the situation reduces the sense of insecurity or defensiveness which some might feel, allowing such people to make their views known
- Spontaneity – more spontaneous, but possibly more unconventional views might result
- Stimulation – the members of the group can stimulate each other.

The logistics of organising a focus group are often overlooked. It can be time consuming and cumbersome, as you need to coordinate the commitments of a range of people to agree to a meeting time and place. Once done, however, the result is often worth it in terms of amount and depth of data collected.

Practical tip box

You should ask yourself the following questions in advance:

- Do you know of or have access to a room that would comfortably seat 12–14 people at the most, and permit moving around a little too (for cameras, etc.)? Typically your organisation may have facilities available for you to book in advance, such as a meeting room or study room for the purposes of bringing a group together. If your organisation doesn't present this as an option, local libraries often have community rooms for use that can be booked free of charge. It would be helpful to find out this information in your area. The important point is that it is in a public place (see Chapter 3 on health and safety).
- Is there a suitable time, when you can ensure that the type of people that you want to participate can all attend? This may be easy if your objectives can be met through a homogeneous group, that is, a very similar group, say mothers of young children. It may be much more difficult if they are a heterogeneous group, who may have for example, conflicting work schedules.
- Should you and will you record the session via video and/or audio? If so, can you obtain the consent of the participants to do that?
- Do you want to use any images or objects to stimulate discussion, for example a programme design?
- Could the focus group be undertaken electronically and therefore in a more environmentally friendly manner? Or might the synergy that you seek perhaps not develop so successfully with this method?

Some common pitfalls of focus groups remain. They have a high likelihood of participants going off course, or off track on a topic, and it is up to an experienced focus group facilitator (researcher) to ensure that the focus of the discussion gets back on course. The overall length of a focus group must also be taken into consideration. Usually, you can and should expect them to last at least an hour. Ordinarily, neither do you want it to run more than 90 minutes as participants can become restless or agitated. It is best for a focus group to have a facilitator generate a flow of well constructed questions (and to that end, no more than ten are usually required) and a second person to help manage the room, whether it is seating, comfort or even recording the session if that is what has been arranged, by video and/or audio.

To that end, the actual data collection of material that the focus group generates needs to be well planned in advance. For example, if you are going to record the session via video and/or audio, then consent is required and you will need the permission of participants to do that. If however, your preference is to capture notes (handwritten or typed) during the session, this can be an equally good approach to use. However, this type of data collection is quite intensive, so often you want another person dedicated specifically to taking notes. A facilitator continues to oversee the general flow of questions and reels in the discussion when necessary, but data collection is quite another task. Don't forget if you are video-recording the session ensure that the equipment you use is up to the task, i.e. test it first and be sure that it has enough capacity to record a longer session, for example 90 minutes or so. In focus groups, it is also wise to have a backup plan for your data collection methods of choice (recorded or handwritten) as it is often difficult to arrange a specific meeting time in the first instance that all participants agree to and can accommodate, so chances are if your technology fails, the opportunity to bring them all back a second time in a rescue attempt is highly unlikely. (See Chapter 4 for more details regarding using equipment such as video-conferencing or video link platforms such as Skype.)

Designing the questions to ask

In the next section, we discuss how to plan a key aspect of your data collection – the questions you will ask. Question design is a vital aspect of much research, and many research projects fail even before they begin to collect data simply as a result of a poorly designed research instrument. Question design can be challenging in both qualitative and quantitative research methodologies. Whilst the former tends to need a design that teases out some reasoning or feeling experienced by the participants, the latter is trying to get numerical data that can measure specific variables. This may be something quite simple such as the number of times that people attend an event, so that we can understand what segments of the population go to events or how people felt about the quality of the food served at an event. We will look at the design of surveys to obtain quantitative data in the next chapter.

Designing the questions to provide verbal data

Designing questions to provide verbal data in any form of interview, whether it is structured, semi-structured or unstructured, is something that takes care and thought, well before the interview takes place. Legard et al. (2003) offer some parameters by which the construction of interview questions can be formulated. On a basic level, it is useful to keep in mind the nature of the closed and open-ended question, e.g. Did you enjoy the festival? (leading to a yes or no answer, therefore closed) compared to an open question, which might be something like 'What did you enjoy about the festival?' This allows your participant to elaborate on their own individual experiences, and you can capture their answer verbatim.

A researcher is trying to uncover some of the buying decisions related to a field hockey weekend in Spain organised by Sport Touring Travel Company. The researcher's target group is fellow students so they already know that the financial aspect of deciding whether or not to attend the sports festival will play a big role in their decision to spend £200–300 to attend the event. The researcher also goes on a hunch that this group will be inclined to spend money on other so called 'luxury goods' alongside of, or instead of, a sports weekend away. The following series of questions shows examples of closed and open questions:

CLOSED   Have you heard about Sport Touring Travel Company? *Yes*.
CLOSED   Have you booked a sports holiday with us before? *No*.

OPEN   Can you tell us what you know about our company, if anything? *I know my mates have booked with you before, but I haven't personally. I think they went to Madrid or something. I remember they said it was a great time and I should go with them.*

OPEN   Why didn't you attend? *I didn't have the finances at the time. I would certainly like to go in the future though.*

OPEN   What would change your mind to attend in future? *My mates really. If they plan to book one again, I have already told them to count me in. That and this new job I have as a bartender. If some money is coming in and I can get the time off, I am there.*

CLOSED Are you willing to pay for a holiday away with them next time with our travel company? *Yes.*

OPEN   Thank you for your time. If you have any other comments to make, please do feel free to take the time now to do so. *Not much really, only that I am looking forward to my first trip with them. It means that I won't get a new mobile I was planning to get – but that can wait.*

As with the experience Gina had in redesigning her interview schedule (see her vignette earlier in this chapter), the above example also enables you to appreciate the nature of *open* and *closed* questions. Open questions can take many forms, but one good rule of thumb is to try and avoid leading questions. In such cases, the participant is more likely to frame an answer around a leading question instead of supplying a full picture. For example, festival organisers have phoned ahead to get an idea of whether or not more security is needed at the front gate where thousands of concert goers are about to come through the door. The festival director asks the front gate manager, 'We will open the theatre doors in an hour. Not many there yet, right?' To which the front gate manager replies 'No, not many.' There could be 200 and the front gate manager may think this is manageable, but the festival director knows that problems have cropped up in the past with concert-goer crowds at other venues which were much smaller, demanding entry and problems with confrontations and crowd management issues from those waiting. The festival director would have done better to ask, 'If we are opening the doors in an hour, can you tell me what the situation looks like outside the theatre right now?' He would get a more accurate description from the front gate manager, and could then best determine if more staff might be needed to handle crowd control.

It is also important to be aware of emotions whilst interviewing participants. This applies to structured, semi-structured and unstructured interviews. In relation to the latter, this is often the time when probing questions need to be applied as well. You have to be prepared for any answers and try to remain neutral without, again, asking leading questions. For example:

Q: Did you enjoy the role of stage manager?
A: *It wasn't offered to me in the end.*
Q: Why didn't you fill the role of stage manager?
A: *It was supposed to be given to me, but it was taken by the leading lady's husband instead. He didn't have the same experience as me, but what could I do in that situation? He was well connected.*
Q: That must have made you angry. Didn't you think that was unfair?

In these cases, you may wish to package your follow up interview question differently. For example, you could have asked *How did that make you feel?* instead of *That must have made you angry, didn't you think that was unfair?* in relation to being passed up for the stage manager role. In essence, the former ends up being an 'open' question, and the latter a 'closed' question that can only be answered with a 'yes' or 'no' when in fact you are looking for more information. You then get the participant to answer the question on their terms, without a bias to your question due to use of the words 'angry' and 'unfair'. Allow them to tell you the difference. In the above case, as it turned out, the participant was glad to remain an assistant because he made more contacts in the production house side of the tour than he would have in the 'management' role, thus setting him up for some solid work leads after that particular production.

Another factor to consider in asking questions is to avoid double-barrelled questions. You want to ask questions one at a time, and not:

Q: *Did your boss tell you in advance you were getting a promotion, and did you change your behaviour afterwards as a result?*
Q: *How ill were you before going to the show, and did you enjoy any of the performance as a result?*
Q: *How did you feel about waiting in a long queue before getting in, and was the wait worth it after the fact?*

Each of the above are examples of double-barrelled questions, and should be divided into two seperate questions and not asked together. It is important to ask questions clearly and be patient with the answers. You will also need to be aware that when interviewing your participants things will occasionally go off track. Legard et al. (2003: 165) offer some solutions to bring your research subject back to the fore without causing offence:

● If they are digressing and talking about other people, to bring the topic back to themselves ask, 'What about you?'
● Mention that time is moving on and that there are a few other topics that need to be addressed.
● If necessary, withdraw signs of encouragement and approval – remove eye contact, look down at a topic guide or use other ploys designed to indicate your less than rapt attention.
● Use body language to indicate that the researcher wants to interrupt (leaning forward, beginning to voice a question, raising a hand slightly).
● Rambling responses are sometimes an indication of tiredness and loss of concentration on the participant's part, and saying that only a little more of their time is required or that there is just one remaining issue for discussion will often reinvigorate them.

Remember, the research studies that you do are not asocial, ahistorical events:

You do not leave behind your anxieties, your hopes, your blindspots, your prejudices, your class, race or gender, your location in a global social structure, your age and historical positions, your emotions, your past and your sense of possible future when you set up an interview, and nor does your interviewee. Neither do you do so when you sit down to analyse the results.

(Wengraf 2001: 4)

Therefore you cannot ever state that research is unbiased. You are an intrinsic part of the process!!

Using images as data

As with other forms of data, primary or secondary data images may be suitable for a research study, depending as always on your aim and objectives. Photographs, videos, maps and other forms of images, whether paper based or electronic from websites, may be available for a research study. The use of photos, video and film as research tools has often been aligned in the past with studies that have been underpinned by visual sociology or visual anthropology. Indeed, the roots of this approach lie in works conducted by those engaged in cultural anthropology such as Bateson and Mead (1942), who studied the everyday life and routines of people in a Balinese mountain village. Therefore such visual media as a primary method of data collection has merit should you choose to use it for your research. You may, for example, wish to execute a 'photo elicitation interview' (Harper 2000) whereby your subjects are instructed to take photos of things that reflect a meaningful event experience for them. As a follow up, you would sit with your subject and have them explain the meaning behind their chosen photos. For example, they may take photos of a meaningful event experience they had while spending time in the Olympic Park during the Summer Games. From that point, they can explain to you, aided by the photographs, the reasoning behind their selected imagery. Their words combined with the photos as visual materials therefore aid in building content for your primary data.

Following on from Barthes (1996), four different approaches can be undertaken by the researcher and the subject researched:

1　The researcher can show photographs to persons under study and ask them questions about them (e.g. photos taken at a birthday party or family gathering).
2　The researcher can be the photographer and the research subjects be in a setting (e.g. going around an exhibition).
3　The researcher might ask a subject to show them photos of their choosing for discussion (e.g. participation at a music festival and related meanings).
4　A researcher might observe a subject taking photos and then inquire of the subject after the fact the reasoning behind the photograph, e.g. 'Why did you take a photo of the band playing but not the dance performance?'

Often, capturing information through photography or with a video camera forms a vital part of the field notes collected in the qualitative method of observation (see earlier in this chapter). But whether images are collected from existing sources or particularly when the researcher creates their own images, the ethical implications (see Chapter 3) are vitally important. On the one hand, the availability of modern mobile phones that can create images with a high pixel count provides opportunities for data collection without perhaps prior consideration. But on the other hand, the possibility of being too intrusive is equally likely. In most countries it is legally permitted to take a photograph or video of a crowd of people in a public place. However, special care should be taken if the images include children or vulnerable adults and permission should always be sought if feasible. Some places at some event locations may not be amenable to photography, particularly if national security is an issue. For example, at the London 2012 Olympics, attendees were not permitted to take photographs at the security checkpoints. If you want to undertake research in sensitive areas such as these, you must obtain full clearance in advance from the appropriate bodies.

Unlike still photographs, video recording offers an alternative way to collect visual data. Below, Knoblauch (2004: 126) lists several kinds of data which are used in video research:

- Scientific recording of natural social situations
- Scientific recording of experimental social situations
- Interviews
- Natural social situations recorded by the actors (surveillance, audio recording)
- Posed situations recorded by actors (video diaries)
- Situations recorded and edited by actors (wedding videos)
- Situations recorded by actors and edited by professionals (wedding videos, documentations).

As you can see from the list above, there are many different ways to approach visual research methods. Artefacts recorded in the form of photographs and film can also be used as the subject of analyses. Additionally, you may wish to capture or record a specific social situation, such as a wedding, via photo and/or film, and then analyse the footage after the fact. Also, you may give a subject(s) a camera with instructions to capture images with the camera as tool only and have them explain after the fact why they captured the visuals that they did, provided this underpins set research objectives. However, whatever the source of the data, all of the content must be screened and prepared (see Chapter 10) in an adequate way!

You can appreciate, then, how illuminating visual methods might be in the events field in terms of research. For example, would you be interested in capturing in photographs the elements of an event such as your favourite rock concert or a friend's twenty-first birthday party, so that you might learn a bit more of what it is about these events that makes them interesting and appealing to those who attend?

Scenario

Here are some questions and responses from a semi-structured interview with an organiser of a star gazing festival regarding some of the problems he faces. After each response, give a 'prompt question' or two that would help you gain a more in-depth understanding of his problems.

1. Which month of the year is the festival held?
   a. At the end of August or September, when we hope the sky will be clear.
2. Have you ever had to cancel the festival?
   a. No, we have always managed to go ahead somehow.
3. What is the most popular attraction for children?
   a. I think staying up late at night! No, seriously, we have several events during the day, especially for children.

(Continued)

Scenario (continued)

4   Are there particular problems with the night time events?
   a   Health and safety is obviously more complex and the electricity bill is much higher for those events. Also, we do have a problem in finding enough volunteers to cover the day and the night-time events, as they have to sleep at some point.
5   Is the festival sponsored or state funded?
   a   We have a mixture of both, but that in itself causes issues, particularly with last year's sponsors.

Summary

This chapter has highlighted:

● The differences between primary and secondary data and some of the issues that might arise with each
● The issues that arise in obtaining images as data
● Various forms of observation, including participant observation
● Different ways of asking questions – interviews and surveys – and to individuals and groups
● How to design the questions to provide verbal data.

Further reading

Journals

The first of these two articles provides information about a method and the second demonstrates a good application of a method.

Mackellar, J. (2013) 'Participant observation at events: Theory, practice, and potential'. *International Journal of Event and Festival Management*, 4: 56–65.
Stadler, R., Reid, S. and Fullagar, S. (2013) 'An ethnographic exploration of knowledge practices within the Queensland Music Festival'. *International Journal of Event and Festival Management*. Online. Available HTTP: www.emeraldinsight.com/journals. htm?articleid=17085034&show=abstract (accessed 7 April 2013).

Books

Adler, P.A. and Adler, P. (1998) 'Observation techniques' in N. Denzin and Y. S. Lincoln (eds) *Collecting and Interpreting Qualitative Materials*. London: Sage Publications. Gives useful details on observation.
Barrett, S. (2009) *Anthropology: A Student's Guide to Theory and Method*, 2nd edn. Toronto: Toronto University Press. This text has some good guidance into how to probe interviewees further to achieve your research objectives.

Bryman, A. and Bell, E. (2007) *Business Research Methods*, 2nd edn. Oxford: Oxford University Press. This text offers good insight into the differences between structured, semi-structured and unstructured interview techniques and approaches.

Denscombe, M. (2003) *The Good Research Guide* (2nd edn.) Maidenhead: Open University Press. Chapter 10 contains useful information on interviews.

Skinner, J. and Edwards, A. (2012) *Qualitative Research in Sport Management*. Burlington, MA: Elsevier. This text offers a good perspective into the process involved in conducting interviews.

Spradley, J. P. (1980) *Participant Observation*. New York: Hold, Rinehart, and Winston. Like Adler and Adler (1998) above, this similarly supplies useful details on observation.

Web links

Mahoe, R. (undated) 'Reflections on the dissertation process and the use of secondary data'. Online. Available HTTP: www.hawaii.edu/edper/pdf/Vol37Iss2/Reflections.pdf (accessed 10 August 2013), is based on the author's Ph.D. and provides some useful insights.

Video links

What to Observe in Participant Observation (26.16 minutes). Online. Available HTTP: www.youtube.com/watch?v=JADIR-J9Ht4 (accessed 10 August 2013). This particular video is part 2 of an ethnography series, yet offers some good insight and perspective into participant observation in general, and as a research method by itself outside of the ethnographic frame.

Chapter 9

Obtaining research material (2)

Chapter learning outcomes

In this chapter we:

- Provide an overview about quantitative methods and when they are used
- Briefly discuss thinking critically and an understanding of how to design a questionnaire
- Examine how to distinguish clearly between different types of measurement scales.

It's no surprise the UK festival circuit is struggling.

(British singer and rapper Example)

Example reckons the UK festival industry will continue to struggle in the wake of the recent cancellation of the 2012 Sonisphere Festival (*NME* 2012a). The rapper, who played a clutch of events in the UK in 2011, also said that a lot of festivals are going under because they are badly organised. He pointed out: 'A lot were promoted badly, had bad security, were in bad locations or the line-ups hadn't been programmed well, so they didn't make sense'. The rapper added: 'There was a boom a few years ago. Every second person wherever you went was starting a festival in the UK and anyone whose dad owned a farm. So obviously a lot of them are starting to go under.'

His comments came as Sonisphere Festival was axed. Queen were due to headline the Knebworth Park event on July 6–8 with vocals provided by Adam Lambert. Kiss and Faith No More were also due to play major shows at the metal and hard rock weekender.

Despite his bleak views on the festival circuit, Example said he still believes the bigger events will survive. 'There's still a demand for people to go to festivals even with the economy and the state that it's in.'

Introduction

So what role does research play in the success of such festivals? Could market research find out about the level of market demand for festivals in the UK? The answer is that, although market research does not provide the answer, it can perhaps help the organisers to make more informed decisions. This chapter will identify sources of socially mediated research material that is obtained by asking questions, such as through surveys, to obtain numerical data. It will also demonstrate that it is at this stage that the questions need to be correctly designed to ensure that the survey provides the type of answer required.

Perhaps one of the most daunting tasks as an undergraduate student is when, for the first time, you are required to produce a significant piece of independent work as a project or dissertation. Whilst the training you receive during your course will always help, the prospect of undertaking an independent piece of research for the first time is challenging and can be quite demanding. You may find that you have to select a topic or an approach towards a topic, set out your research aim and objectives and the type of research methodology you are going to use. Your decision on these matters will affect everything you do in your project or dissertation right from the word go!

As explained earlier in Chapter 2, your research *aim* and *objectives* are your starting point, then the objectives, if expressed properly, can inform you about the most appropriate research methodology you should use for your dissertation. For example, if you plan to identify people's perceptions about a music festival, such as Glastonbury (wellington boots and mud!!!) you may think of developing a survey instrument (questionnaire) and distributing it to collect information using a quantitative methods approach. However, you may also want to examine what the organisers have done to minimise damage to the land and improve facilities for visitors. Thus, you may need to undertake some in-depth interviews with the organisers (assuming you can get access!). This chapter will touch upon the first method mentioned above, the quantitative methods, with an emphasis on its application.

Quantitative methods

Quantitative research methods were initially developed for science subjects but are now well accepted and used within the social sciences and humanities. Quantitative methodologies are primarily concerned with numbers as the name suggests.

> ## Definition box
>
> *Quantitative research* is interested in information that can be assessed and used numerically and to examine the relationship between variables, and is often associated with hypothesis testing. It is usually more objective than qualitative research.

In many aspects of research in the social sciences quantitative methods are based on the collection of data from a sample of the population under investigation. The size of the *sample* (see Chapter 7) can be from quite a small number of respondents or it can extend into the thousands. Many textbooks associate quantitative methods with random sampling, however in reality there are other forms of sampling that are equally defensible. The appropriate size of the sample is dependent upon a variety of factors: the purpose of research, the level of confidence required, the size and nature of the population and the type of analyses you are likely to be undertaking. Achieving the desired sample size can be hampered by access, time, financial constraints, and, perhaps most of all, people's willingness to provide the information needed to complete the questionnaire. *Quantitative* research is more interested about the information that can be assessed and used numerically and to examine the relationship between the variables (for example, the relationship between age and the propensity to go clubbing weekly). Also it can be used for hypothesis testing, which is suited to more advanced types of research.

Almost all of us have, at some time, been asked to take part in a survey, or, if not, have seen many market research surveys that drop through the mailbox, received phone survey calls, or had our email in-boxes filled by requests to fill in an online survey. You often see people standing in high streets holding their clipboards, waiting for the right type of respondent or counting people past before they approach their next 'data victim'. There has been a surge of such surveys over the past few years and this means that many people simply ignore them, put them in their waste bin or, if kind enough, leave them in the recycling bin. What should be clear from this is that there are a variety of ways that researchers can collect their data. This includes not only the types of questions asked or the size of the sample, but also the design of online and physical questionnaires, their printing and even the delivery of them to people's houses (do mind the dogs though when sticking your fingers through letterboxes!).

Given the difficulties of collecting data through surveys, why do so many of us end up doing quantitative studies? The answer lies in the study's aim and the fact that events is a service related sector. Thus, there are many questions relating to the quality of events, the impact of events, people's perceptions towards a particular event, etc., that may need to be answered. For example, you may want to understand where visitors to the London Olympics came from, what their experience was, how long they stayed, how much they spent and on what did they make their expenditures. You may also want to examine their perceptions with respect to, say, pricing, quality, safety, access, etc. The fact that quantitative methods are meant to give us a general view about the population makes it a really useful method to use. However, it may lack the ability to address the underlying reasons for the answers obtained.

Quantitative data also gives you numerical data to analyse rather than the qualitative information you might gather from, say, an interview or a literature review. There are distinct advantages to obtaining and analysing quantitative data; mind you, those of you who didn't like mathematics at GCSE level or those of you who switch off when they see a decimal point, may think twice before deciding on your study's aim. This is because it will take more than a few multiplications or subtractions to answer your objectives. Indeed, you will be required to take these numbers, analyse them and write your story based on what the analyses tell you and, remember, take nothing for granted! You must bear in mind that understanding the numbers is essential but not sufficient on its own, and you will need to really apply the outcomes to the existing theories, concepts, current or previous hypotheses and be able to discuss them well beyond description. A good way of making more sense of what I have just outlined is to take a look at a few journal articles related to your discipline that have used quantitative research methods to see how they discuss the issues and how they apply their findings.

Questionnaire design

Some researchers have suggested that designing a survey instrument is not so much a science as it is an art. This suggests that there is no real theory behind the design process and that it is more down to the creativity of the researcher and their ability to find ways of constructing questions to provide the data needed to answer the research questions. However, there are some basic rules to questionnaire design and you will ignore them at your peril. You may now ask, where do we start? A good place to start is looking at the dissertation topic that you have chosen and then break this down into smaller elements that we call research objectives as these provide our research questions. When it comes to the design of individual questions it is really where the specific objectives are answered (Figure 9.1). In reality, no matter how many objectives you have, some of them will be met through reviewing the literature and some will be covered once you have conducted your primary research, in this case after you have run your survey (see Figure 9.1 and Example 9.1).

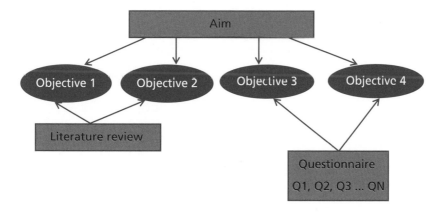

Figure 9.1 The design of questions

Example 9.1

Aim: To investigate travel risk perceptions and the effects of incidents on mega sport events.

- To examine the literature with respect to travel risk
- To determine the effects of major incidents on mega events
- To evaluate the work that has been done in determining risk perceptions
- To study the risk perceptions of travellers from different backgrounds to mega events
- To explore the effects of perceived risk on future travel.

One of the challenges of designing the correct questionnaire is how you break the objectives down into easily digestible questions that are clear, as short as possible and most importantly, providing data that is measureable. There is not a black and white answer to this problem and you may well find that two top researchers will design completely different types of questions even though they are both pursuing identical objective(s). As we said, designing a questionnaire can be more of an art than a science, but there are some clear cut rules that you need to follow relating to aspects such as the wording, sequencing and measurement scales (Malhorta and Birks 2006). These rules will enable you to collect the data objectively and measure it through statistical analysis using software such as Excel and SPSS.

Example 9.2

Mini case study

Johnny is a second-year student and he has been asked to design a questionnaire that is intended to find out how often undergraduates in each year group organise nights out each month. The university hopes to find out about students' clubbing habits to see if there is any relationship between going out and attendance at the early morning lectures. He designs a question asking them:
'How often do you organise nights out?'

1 Never
2 Rarely
3 Sometimes
4 Often
5 Always.

Johnny then needs to use his answers and inform his tutor about the average number of nights out. This information may be used to inform the university about their future decisions on lecture times, etc.

What do you think will be problematic in designing it as Johnny has done? How could you improve on it?

There seems to be no consensus among academics and researchers in terms of the sequencing of questions. However, using a rule of thumb can assist you in designing your questionnaire. There are several factors that need to be taken into account. Let's think of running a questionnaire asking people's satisfaction level about a recent sporting event. The aim is to find out the general level of satisfaction, i.e. the quality of the event, the quality of the swimming pool where the event took place, the atmosphere, levels of cleanliness, etc. However, the organiser is also looking to find out about the demographic characteristics of respondents and their spending patterns, so that they can relate these to their income, age, number of children, etc. Demographics are important for a variety of reasons, whether it is identifying target customers or giving the sample results greater contextual meaning and relating them to the wider population. One of the first issues is: with which questions do you start? Should you ask the demographic questions first to 'warm them up' or should you start asking them questions related to the quality of the event to engage them, and leave the demographic questions to the end?

Example 9.3

Q1 Can you tell us where you live? Please provide the first three letters of your postcode.
Q2 Do you have any children (aged 16 years and under)?
Yes/No
Q3 How satisfied are you with the overall quality of the event where 1 is least satisfied and 5 is most satisfied?
1/2/3/4/5

Where do you think you might experience the greatest hesitance in answering this snapshot of a questionnaire?

Individuals, or at least a fair percentage of them, tend to be self-conscious about their private life. Therefore, if you start off by asking them about their income band, age, place of residence, etc., it may affect their attitude towards the questionnaire and they may skip those questions or simply refuse to complete the questionnaire altogether. Indeed, some researchers suggest that you leave all of the demographic questions until the end of the questionnaire and start with the main theme to engage them with the central issue of the survey. In the example above, the questions relating to the quality of the event would be listed first.

To reduce the respondent's level of mistrust or hesitancy in filling in the questionnaire and to make sure that you get as honest answers as possible, an introductory paragraph at the start of your questionnaire is a necessary inclusion. Thus, an introduction to your questionnaire explaining the purpose of the questionnaire and guaranteeing (where appropriate) that the data collected will be treated confidentially and any results will not be attributed to the respondent in any publication is a good start (see Chapter 3).

The following example was written whilst conducting a survey. Let's have a look:

This survey is part of an unfunded research project that we are undertaking which examines the motivations and expectations of visitors to slum or township areas. The data collected through this survey is completely anonymous and no individual response will be identified in the results of the research. The survey is in two parts, Part A which should be completed prior to going on the tour and Part B which is a brief survey to capture your thoughts and feelings following the tour. The final section of the survey is to collect information that will allow the researchers to interpret the findings of the survey in a wider context. We are very grateful for your co-operation with this study.

Another issue you can see being addressed in the above is a brief explanation about the structure of the survey. This is a judgement call; sometimes you may need to give some additional information to help guide respondents through the questionnaire, or, say, a map of a region to put the questionnaire in context, but this is case related. Just think what other information respondents will need to be able to fill in your survey whilst you are not there to help. This is particularly important if it is a self-completion questionnaire.

Practical tip box

Variable boundaries or bands

With some questions it is better to get answers that fit into bands rather than precise answers. For instance questions relating to income may put people off if you are asking how much they earn, but they may be willing to tick a box that shows the band of income in which their income falls. The same is true with respect to age. I know from my personal experience that I always feel happier to tick a box relating to an age range rather than say how old I am – I am even happier if my age falls within an age band which is largely below my current age! However, there are important rules relating to the bands you use.

Example 9.4

What is your combined household income?

Less than £20,800
£20,800 and up to £25,000
£25,000 and up to £40,000
£40,000 and up to £45,000
£45,000 and up to £52,000
£52,000 and above.

Or instead: what is your combined household income?

Less than £20,800
£20,800 and up to £31,999
£32,000 and up to £41,999
£42,000 and up to £51,999
£52,000 and up to £61,999
£62,000 and up to £71,999
£72,000 and up to £81,999
£82,000 and above.

Which one do you think makes more sense? Why?

There are several factors that will determine what bands you should use for, say income or age. One of these factors will be the purpose of the study, if you are attempting to explore the behaviour of a specific age or income category. A second important factor may be the age or income bands that are used in secondary data. For example, if it is possible to get hold of census data and this is published in specific age bands, if you conduct your research using those same age bands it is more likely that you will be able to relate your results to the population as a whole by grossing up using age bands if you have a significant sample size. These bands also need to be consistent (where possible). For example, if we start categorising people in their twenties in the format of 20–29 then it might be expected that you would put people in their thirties in a similar format (30–39) and so on. Thus, the choice of age or income bands depends on several factors such as the research objectives, ease of completion (not having more categories than you need to have for your analyses) and the format of the published population data.

The next step in designing a questionnaire is about how to start the main theme. You can perhaps start with questions relating to the general theme to get the respondent engaged and thinking and then make the questions more detailed as it progresses. It is worth mentioning here that if the questionnaire is too long it might bore the individuals and this can have negative effects on your response rate. However, this does not mean a shorter questionnaire is necessarily better, because you need to be able to meet your research objective(s). It is a question of getting the balance right between data needs and length of questionnaire, and it depends on the particular case and your own professional judgement, timing and the number of responses you are hoping to achieve.

If you are interested in a particular category of respondent, for example only those people who have been to visit a particular type of car showroom, you can start your survey with a simple question asking:

Have you ever been to a BMW showroom?
Yes/No.

This can the be used as a filter, and if you are not interested in those who haven't been to a BMW showroom then they don't have to fill in any further questions, or if you want both groups for a comparative study, then you have immediately separated them.

The next issue to consider is how you design your questions, for example, if you are looking at the perceived quality of aspects of an event you might ask: Did you like the food in the canteen?

Yes
No
Did not consume.

What do you think you can get out of this question? Certainly it will provide you with the proportion of people who either liked or didn't like the food in the canteen and those who didn't consume it at all. But there are occasions with human related responses that are quite hard or almost impossible to understand fully without measuring people's attitudes, perceptions or beliefs, etc. in greater detail.

Therefore, instead of the above example we could use a *Likert scale* and ask them to reveal their response in terms of a scale of, say, 1–5 (see Figure 9.2).

The difference between the two approaches is that the previous one will only give you the proportion of people who say they like or disliked the food but it doesn't tell you how much they liked or disliked the food. The second approach provides the respondent with the ability to have some granularity in their answer to reflect their true feelings and provides you with the type of data that you could use to build up an index of satisfaction and compare different aspects. Let's look at the following example:

Example 9.5

Please state your level of agreement with the following statements.

	Agree strongly	Agree a little	Neither agree nor disagree	Disagree a little	Disagree strongly
I liked the food in the canteen.					
The choice of food in the vending machines was really good.					
The hygiene standard of the facility was good.					
I enjoyed the atmosphere of the event.					
The seating facilities were really good.					
The price of car parking at the event was reasonable.					
The timing of the event was good.					
I will come back to this event next year.					

How could you use the findings from this?

Please state level of your agreement with following statement:

I like the food in the canteen:

Agree strongly	Agree a little	Neither agree nor disagree	Disagree a little	Disagree strongly
1	2	3	4	5

Figure 9.2 Using a Likert scale

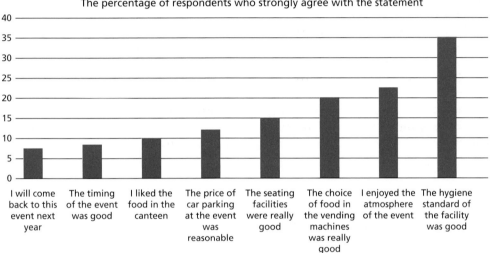

Graph 9.1 Example graph

Without going through complex types of tests, you can compare the findings of the above table to see which aspects of the event received more responses agreeing or strongly agreeing to the statements, and which disagreed or strongly disagreed. You can then put the percentage of each category in a spreadsheet and create a graph (see Graph 9.1) to show the results. This result does not show any more than descriptive statistics but, having said that, it is important to have a visual picture of what respondents thought of the quality of these aspects of the event before going on to look at further tests.

Question: What would you do if you wanted to find out why the respondents seem to be more satisfied with the hygiene than they are with, say, the food?

In social science using a Likert scale seems to be one of the most common ways of measuring a variety of responses to different questions. This, however, does not mean that it is the only way to tackle this problem. Multiple choice questionnaires, binary, ranking and ratios are all examples of other approaches that are widely used (see Malhorta and Birks 2006). But Likert scales are popular and many of the statistical packages that we use, such as SPSS, are able to perform tests such as non-parametric tests or factor analysis, etc., when using Likert scale data (see Chapter 12).

The way in which Likert scales are constructed has also been discussed at length in the literature. For instance, some researchers argue that we should use an odd number of scales such as that used in the previous example, whereas others argue in favour of an even number of scales. The main argument in favour of using the odd number is that if you use an even number you are forcing the respondent to provide either a positive or negative response and such an approach may end up as a lottery where the final result is down to pure chance. However, those that argue in favour of the even number of scales suggest that having a neutral scale in the middle can encourage respondents not to think too deeply and go for the middle (opt out) choice. Let's look at the example below:

Example 9.6

Please state whether you agree or disagree with the following statements.

	1 = strongly agree	2 = somewhat agree	3 = neither agree nor disagree	4 = somewhat disagree	5 = strongly disagree
I like going to the Glastonbury music festival knowing I may get wet and muddy.					

As explained above, some prefer not to have number 3 in the scale and therefore force the respondent to either agree or disagree, but many of the more complex modelling exercises also tend to be based around odd-numbered Likert scales.

Once you have made your decision to have either an odd or even number of scales the next issue is to decide upon how many Likert scales you should choose. For instance, should you go for 3, 5, 7 or 9 Likert scales? This depends on the purpose of the study, the target sample size and your ability to collapse the scales if needed during the analytical process. Of course, it is tempting to think that the more scales you have the better it will be because it gives the respondent the ability to be more precise in their choice of answer. But too many scales may confuse them, or you may end up with having some of the Likert scales not being selected sufficiently to be of use during the analyses and you then have to collapse your categories. Whilst it is perfectly possible to have 7 or 9 scales, the general practice, at least at undergraduate level where students tend to collect a few hundred responses, is to use a 5 Likert scale.

Measurement scales: an introduction

There are two main types of tests in quantitative methods which are related to the distribution of the data. *Parametric tests* which include tests such as the T test assume that the sample data come from a population with a normal (Gaussian) distribution, whereas *non-parametric tests* such as Mann Whitney U tests relate to data where there is no assumption about the distribution of the population from which the data are sampled. The non-parametric tests are quite common in the social sciences and are more relaxed about the assumptions relating to the population data, and this may throw in some element of scepticism as to the accuracy of such tests.

Let's go through this in slightly more detail to clarify it without being too statistical or complicated. In the previous section we have discussed the different ways of designing questions in a questionnaire and pointed also to the use of multiple choice questions, binary types of questions such as when we only have two possible answers (e.g. gender or multiple choice with two categories such as yes/no), ranking, ratios and Likert scales. Before you can determine whether or not you can use parametric or non-parametric techniques, you need to identify what types of variables you are dealing with. By variable in here it means if we have a question asking what is your gender, female or male are the variables. Another example is when we have a statement saying:

Answer 1 to 5 (where: 1 = strongly agree and 5 = strongly disagree):
I love chocolate cake ...

The variables determine the types of test we can use. Therefore, before designing your questionnaire, you need to be aware of the different types of variables so that you know what types of test you can use during your analyses. This is really important because sometimes you know what information you need to get out of your questionnaire to meet your objectives, but the way you design your questions may not give you the right variable(s) to run the required test, so you need to get your foundation right rather than rushing into the design of your questionnaire.

There are three main types of variables. The first one is *categorical/nominal* type of data; as the name indicates, they belong to categories and by categories we mean for example categories of male or female, pop or R&B, Glastonbury or Reading festivals. In other words, the response either belongs to one or another category.

So what? If we have these sorts of categories and we intend to use some statistical test, we might use SPSS. SPSS by nature does not like letters; it needs digits, because it takes digits in the formal sense and computes them. Indeed, SPSS does all of the calculations for you, and in return it expects you to feed the software with the appropriate data, in this case 'digits'.

OK, now let us go back to our categorical/nominal types of data that we had and try to prepare them from raw data to an appropriate set of data for SPSS. Imagine you have questions asking people:

1   What is your gender?
    (a) Female
    (b) Male
2   Which one of the following singers do you prefer (pick only one)?
    (a) Kylie Minogue
    (b) Bruno Mars
    (c) Lady Gaga
    (d) Eminem.

The aim here might be to find out if there is a relationship between gender and preferred singers for some event organisers. To look at the results of such a combination of questions a simple chi-square can help (see Field 2009 and Pallant 2010). The results will be based on each individual choosing male or female for their response to question 1 and selecting one of the singers from the choices a to d, in question 2. The important part to notice is you can either be a male or female and, as question 2 asks, you can only pick one of the singers. In such a situation when a variable belongs to one or another category, we say we have what is known as categorical data and although for SPSS, or another program, we can recode these answers to a digit, for example we give the value of 1 to females and 2 to males, these values are arbitrary and in reality they are still just females or males.

This means that we cannot measure the average. Say for example we have 300 females responding ($300 \times 1 = 300$) and 100 males ($100 \times 2 = 200$) we have a total 'score' of $300 + 200 = 500$, and with 400 total respondents this would yield an average of $500/400 = 1.25$, which is clearly nonsense in this context. However, we can look at the frequency and mode of responses, for instance. In this context, by frequency, we mean the number of times an answer occurs, and the mode is the most frequent response; if we have 300 responses, then the 300 is our frequency and if out of these 300 the majority were female (200) and the rest were male, we could say female is the mode, because it is the most frequent response. Or for example if in a Likert scale of 1–5, we have 100 who picked number 1, 200 picked number 2, 300 picked number 3, 500 picked number 4, and 400 picked number 5, then 200 will be frequency of Likert of 2, the mode will be number 4 because it is the most common response.

The next type of variable to consider is what is known as an *ordinal* variable which, as its name implies, indicates an ordering of the responses. Let me demonstrate: if we have age bands as our age variable, for example

1   Under 20 ($<$20)
2   20–29
3   30–39
4   40–49
5   50–59
6   60 and over.

If you are completing this questionnaire you may identify yourself as falling into the second band. Now if your parents are completing the questionnaire they may indicate that they are in the fourth or fifth band. Based on these results, you can identify which group is the youngest. In this example we still have categories of the different age bands but the difference with the previous type of variable is that you can not only distinguish between the responses but also put them in order and say who is older and who is younger, whereas with the categorical type of data such as gender you can know their category and there is no order to it. So does this mean you can take a step further and do tests other than chi-square? The answer is yes.

Furthermore, to link this discussion to the Likert scales introduced earlier, one could argue that we can also use Likert scales as ordinal types of data, although others might argue against this. The reason for this is that, unlike the age bands which are measurable in the strict sense, no one can be sure of the gap between each Likert scale, and that Likert scales are not continuous numbers, so it leaves us with the possibility of using them as ordinal variables most of the time. This also has other implications (which will be discussed in Chapter 12).

There is a third type of variable, called *continuous* variables. These are variables which have 'real' numbers with real values. For example, if you ask people 'How much did you spend on your night out last week?' it is likely, assuming they did go out, that they will respond with a value, for example £15.50, and that each respondent will give you a value that refers to their expenditure on the night out. These are variables that do not need any recoding; you can put them directly into your spreadsheet or SPSS. You can also measure the average spending of your survey sample simply by adding them up and then dividing that figure by the number of respondents. Indeed, a continuous variable can take any value, whereas in the previous cases they were limited – we either had to give arbitrary value to our variables so that the software would be able to handle them, or they were ordinal. This also applies to Likert scale responses which have very defined parameters, e.g. 1, 2, 3, 4 or 5.

Now let's think of the types of questions that are likely to appear in your questionnaire. You may ask questions about the satisfaction levels perceived, visitors' feelings, or attitudes towards an event using a Likert scale; you may give them multiple choice answers from which to select their answer; you might ask them their age, income, gender, etc.; all these types of questions will only let you have the first and second types of variable that we have already discussed, namely nominal/categorical and ordinal, in which case you are more likely to end up using non-parametric types of test.

On the other hand, if you ask your respondents how old they are (22 years 2 months and 2 days for example) or how tall they are (say, 5′ 6″), these are examples of questions that will give the prerequisites for the parametric type of test and yet you still need to test the shape of your data to see if you have normal distribution. You might ask, what about ratio types of variable? (see example 9.7). A ratio type of variable has all of the properties of an interval/continuous variable plus it has a fine definition of 0.0, and so when the variable equals 0.0 there is none of that variable. When you have ratio variables, just like when you have continuous/interval variables you can compute the mean, median, standard deviation or sum or differences; the only difference here with continuous type of data will be that you cannot compute ratio or coefficient of variable.

Example 9.7

Please divide 100 points among each of the following soft drinks according to your liking of each:

Cola ___
Lemonade ___
Orange juice ___
Tomato juice ___

This means respondents have to break 100 points down between the above four drinks to identify relative preferences.

Question: What are the limitations experienced by asking such questions?

Indeed, asking ratio questions will enable you to have more accurate measurements on the one hand, but it leaves the challenge for the respondents to do the sums! The numbers have to add up to 100 and in reality there is a chance of the respondent getting the numbers wrong when filling in the survey. Also, questions like this which transfer harder tasks on to the respondents are likely to reduce the response rates, so many researchers tend to stick with questions that ask the respondent to rank or order variables, give them a Likert scale from which to choose, or simply ask them to identify their favourite.

Event research in action

Each year a major Fair is held in the UK and is one of the world's leading country sport events. The Fair hosts not only sporting members, such as the hunting, shooting and fishing fraternity, it also showcases food, gardening, 4×4 vehicles, quad biking and clothing. The show regularly attracts around 150,000 visitors each year from all over the UK and from overseas. Handling such large numbers, particularly on a rotating venue basis, calls for excellent management data and to acquire this information the Fair have employed Bournemouth University's researchers to undertake various surveys.

There are three types of survey involved in these studies, the first being the visitor survey, the second a local business survey, and the third a participant survey.

The objectives of the visitor survey which takes place each year is to gather visitor information that will inform a variety of users including the event's organisers, sponsors and advertisers. The data collected includes demographic data such as origin, age, gender and socioeconomic grouping (SEG), together with more general contextual information such as holiday leisure habits, car usage, and postcode data to identify the type of area that people come from. The survey also seeks to establish the activities that visitors undertake during the Fair, membership information, length of time, distance travelled and visitor satisfaction. The visitor surveys have been undertaken using a conventional approach of a combination of face-to-face interviews together with distributed self-completion questionnaires. The target sample of questionnaires was 800 out of a distribution of 5,000, and 1,200 completed questionnaires are generally completed plus 200 face-to-face completed questionnaires. This approach was changed in 2011 to test the efficiency of using electronic data collection booths, which again has achieved 1,200 responses over the 4 days of the fair. In spite of the fact that the volume of responses has been maintained there are question marks relating to the range of respondents engaging with the electronic method, which seems to be favoured by the younger generation.

The purpose of the local business survey was to determine the economic impact of the Fair on the local economy at each of the different locations where it is held. An issue to be resolved when undertaking this element was to identify the appropriate geo-economic spatial area to be included. The selection of the area was informed by the travel to Fair time and the spatial distribution of the local population and businesses. Lists of suppliers were provided by event organisers which also helped the researchers trace the expenditure flows to determine the value and extent of economic impact.

The participant survey was again a combination of face-to-face and self-completion questionnaires. The aim of this element of the survey was to establish the proportion of money they received that was going into the local economy.

The expenditure data were used to feed an ad hoc multiplier model to estimate the direct and indirect economic impact of the Fair once a year at each of the locations where it was held. Thus, over a 4-year cycle the impacts were calculated for all four venues. The reason for undertaking this economic impact study was to provide positive information that could be used to balance any negative aspects that were identified by local authorities, such as road congestion. The value of the Fair was clearly demonstrated to all stakeholders using this technique.

An additional aspect of the visitor survey was to see if the Fair changed visitor's attitudes towards the membership organisation and towards their participation in country sports.

There were limitations to the study. There is always a balance to be achieved between the cost of undertaking such surveys and the accuracy of the final results. In an ideal world the researchers would undertake many more face-to-face interviews to overcome issues such as the self-selecting sample achieved by self-completion questionnaires. However, the sample size currently used is sufficient to be accurate and 99 per cent confident that the values obtained are plus or minus 3 per cent of the population.

The Fair organisers used the information from this study to organise their future events to enhance visitor satisfaction.

Student vignette

Gemma carried out a study of the relationship between the motivation and satisfaction of Chinese visitors to the Hong Kong Shopping Festival (see also Chapter 2).

Like all researchers, there were many issues I had to think about in designing my questionnaire. First, my respondents would be completing it online and so I would not be there to help answer any questions. It was vital therefore that all the questions were clear. My survey was more difficult than some, because I needed to translate it into Chinese, as my sample was mainland Chinese residents and I had to ensure that the words in both languages had the same meanings. Second, I did not want it to be too long, but I needed sufficient questions to meet all my objectives. It worked out at eleven questions over three pages, which seemed to work well when I piloted the survey. Third, I wanted a good response rate, so I made the introduction on the first page as welcoming as possible and I thanked respondents for their help at the end.

My introduction read as follows:

'I am a researcher from Bournemouth University, currently doing research about visitors' motivation and satisfaction in regard to the Hong Kong Shopping Festival. Could you please spend a few minutes filling in this survey form? All your answers will be treated confidentially and for my master's research dissertation. Thank you for your time.'

(Continued)

Student vignette (continued)

I began the questionnaire with a very easy question, to get respondents to start completing it. I simply asked how many times they had visited the Festival and gave three options for their response. I then asked them more about the events at the Festival they had visited before going on to the questions about their motivation and satisfaction with the Festival. Only at the end did I ask them the personal questions about their gender, age, occupation and income.

This chapter has touched upon the aim and objectives of a research project, the design of a questionnaire for quantitative techniques and the various types of data you may encounter together with the appropriate measurement scales with a focus on the application of these issues in relation to your own discipline. We saw that although the aim may be seen as the overarching target of your study, it can be broken down to smaller components which are called objectives, and we then discussed the fact that objectives can be met through both the literature review and primary research.

We then went on to discuss the do's and don'ts of questionnaire design and the fact that there is as much an art as there is a science behind such designs, whilst acknowledging that there are some basic rules which need to be taken on board when drafting the questionnaire in terms of clarity, sequencing and the purpose of your study and hence the types of data being collected.

The types of data you collect with your questionnaire can determine the types of test you can run and therefore the information that you can get out of your questionnaire. It was identified that there were two types of approaches to testing results, parametric and non-parametric, and what requirements each one needs to be able to give accurate results. The next chapter will go through these issues further and explain about the application of different tests which can be used at the undergraduate level for research projects related to event management studies.

Scenario

A student has started to design their questionnaire to identify the potential market for an inaugural Chinese New Year celebration in their city. Unfortunately, there are numerous mistakes, so redesign the following questions so that the responses will be of use. (Hint: try answering these questions yourself first!)

1 How old are you?
   a 16–21   b 21–30   c 30–40   d more than 40
2 Do you celebrate New Year?
   a Yes   b No   c Don't know
3 Are you Chinese?
   a Yes   b No   c Don't know
4 How likely are you to attend a Chinese New Year celebration?
   a Very unlikely   b Quite likely   c Very likely

5   Are you:
    a Male
6   How far would you want to travel?
    a Under 5   b 5–10   c 11–15   d 16 or more

Summary

This chapter has encouraged you:

- To be able to think critically about how to design a questionnaire to provide numerical data
- To distinguish clearly between different types of measurement scales.

Further reading

Journals

Forza, C. (2002) 'Survey research in operations management: A process-based perspective', *International Journal of Operations and Production Management*, 22: 152–194, provides guidelines for the design and execution of survey research.

Books

Malhotra, N. and Birks, D. F. (2006) *Marketing Research: An Applied Approach*, 3rd edn. Harlow: Prentice Hall. This book offers practical advice on quantitative methods.

Two books that are specific to using the SPSS software package for analysis are also very useful in designing your questionnaire:

Field, A. (2005) *Discovering Statistics Using SPSS*, 2nd edn. London: Sage Publications.
Pallant, J. (2010) *SPSS Survival Manual*, 4th edn. Maidenhead: Open University Press.

Web link

A glossary of statistical terms is available from: Easton, V. J. and McColl, J. H. (1997) Statistics Glossary. Online. Available HTTP: www.stats.gla.ac.uk/steps/glossary/hypothesis_testing.html#hypothtest (accessed 4 August 2013).

Video links

Questionnaire Design.mp4 (3.06 minutes). Online. Available HTTP: www.youtube.com/watch?v=WoRMJ2L4MgE (accessed 4 August 2013) is a market research source that provides a ten-point checklist for questionnaire design.

Whilst this clip helps you to design your questionnaire using Microsoft Word software: *Creating a Questionnaire in Word* (9.18 minutes). Online. Available HTTP: www.youtube.com/watch?v=W86mfwrP_ZA (accessed 4 August 2013).

PART III

Data collection and analysis

Chapter 10

Data collection and preparation for analysis

Chapter learning outcomes

In this chapter we:

- Guide you in preparing qualitative and quantitative data for analysis
- Discuss how to recode your quantitative data, label it and prepare it for analysis using SPSS
- Show how you can use Excel to enter your data.

John has successfully worked through all the earlier stages of his research project and has now collected a large pile of paper-based questionnaires at a basketball match, for his final year dissertation. He is really pleased to have received so many responses from the audience, but now he needs to prepare them for analysis. First, he allocated each survey a number, checking as he went through that they were all properly completed. He was a bit disappointed to discover that a few of the questionnaires only had the first couple of questions completed and the reminder left blank. These would be no use for analysis and so he put them in a separate pile. He was even more upset when he came across one questionnaire where the respondent had not only failed to complete many of the questions, but worse perhaps in John's view, had also written, in large letters all over it, some very disparaging comments about the home team, of which John was a lifelong fan!

Nonetheless, he found that he had 220 completed questionnaires that were usable and he was able to calculate his response rate (see Chapter 7). He had already been able to download the latest version of the statistical software package from his virtual learning environment and so he was ready to prepare the data for analysis.

Introduction

In Chapters 8 and 9 we have suggested ways through which you can collect three types of data: text, images and numbers. In this chapter we look at how these forms of data are prepared for analysis. However, first, we consider some of the practical aspects of collecting your data.

Undertaking the data collection

Hopefully, if you have worked through the earlier chapters in this book, you are ready to proceed with the data collection stage. However, there are still several practical considerations to consider if your data collection is to proceed successfully.

Practical tip box

1 Be sure in advance your kit works. Test your equipment well ahead of time in case you need something else. For example, a smartphone microphone may not be the best thing if interviewing people in crowds such as town centres or stadiums, so you might need a more sensitive microphone to fit that bill.
2 It's a good idea to have back up on site too (e.g. spare disposable batteries; a full battery charge, access to a power supply, back up hand-held digital recorder or similar). You can always support a recorded interview with hand written notes as well, but only if you take a notepad and pen with you.
3 Consider what your participants might need – for example, clipboards and pens for a paper based survey.
4 Think about safety or other protective clothing for yourself or other interviewers, such as a high visibility jacket or waterproofs.
5 Name badges or other identification, perhaps with your organisation's logo, can reassure participants that you are a genuine researcher.

6 Similarly, take bottles of water and sunscreen on hot days, if you will be collecting data for a long time.

7 Build in contingencies with the proviso that something might prevent your data collection. One of the biggest pitfalls is having interview participants drop out, for whatever reason (they may fall ill, have to cancel at short notice due to conflicting priorities or they may have second thoughts about meeting with you). In any case, don't assume that a commitment to be interviewed by you (verbally or otherwise) will actually happen until it does. It is best to line up some reserves in case your target participants fall through.

8 Consider the best time to approach someone if they are at a live event. For example, if you hope to find out their motivation for attending, it might be better at the start, but it is no good asking about their satisfaction at the beginning. Similarly, you cannot expect respondents to complete a questionnaire when an unmissable part of the event is taking place. When people are leaving they have usually already decided what they are going to do next and so will not want to stop to talk to you.

9 People waiting in queues often get bored, so this might be a good place to approach them; equally, having somewhere to sit can be advantageous.

10 Ensure that if you are stopping potential participants in a public place such as a shopping centre, you have obtained the property owner's permission beforehand.

11 Consider whether you are able to offer a small 'thank you' gift for assisting you, or perhaps entry into a free draw. Event sponsors may be generous in this respect if approached in advance.

12 If meeting in person with interviewees, take care getting to and from the interviews and allow plenty of time to find the right location for the meeting.

13 Similarly, allow time to set up the room for a focus group, whether in person or using e-conferencing.

14 At the beginning of interviews always check that you have informed consent.

15 At the end of interviews, similarly revisit the agreement of terms in relation to outputs – e.g. do you need them to proof-read any transcripts you construct after the fact? If so, make sure you comply with their request. Have you also promised that they can see a finished copy of your dissertation or research report? If so, be sure to deliver this as well. It is good practice, respectful and demonstrates your professionalism once you've finished. Who knows what contacts you'll make collecting data – it might lead to future job offers and the like!

16 Consider whether you have access to the research 'scene' as an insider or outsider. Being on the 'inside', for example as a volunteer, often allows access to the 'gatekeepers' and makes it more likely that they will be willing to help you.

17 Always pilot your data collection.

Piloting the data collection

A pilot study can take one of two forms. First, it may be a preliminary small scale feasibility study before a larger project is undertaken. Second, it might be to test a method, including a research instrument (such as a survey questionnaire or interview schedule) or the stimulus material for a focus group. It is the latter that we are interested in here.

To conduct a pilot study means to test your research method before actually undertaking your final version, and applies to both quantitative and qualitative approaches to research. The benefit of undertaking a pilot study is that you can overcome problems before you expend a lot of time and resources and before it is too late! Also, in quantitative research it can give an indication of the response rate, which can determine the sample size (see Chapter 7) or it may even highlight that you need to make changes to your method of data collection. For example, you could find that respondents are unwilling to complete a paper questionnaire, but would complete an electronic version, if it were online.

Event research in action

Fox and Edwards (2009) undertook a survey of residents to identify the market for small, medium and large horticultural shows in England. In the methodology section of the journal article, they mentioned, as is usual, that a pilot study was undertaken, but again as usual, none of the details as to changes that were made are given. But they did state that the number of households to survey was calculated by the response rate of the pilot study.

However, here we can give some of the details of the pilot study. The survey was piloted in two postcode areas, deliberately selected for their convenience and for being typical of the local housing stock. Questionnaires were delivered to thirty-five households in July 2002. At twenty households questionnaires were collected (57 per cent). All of the seven households at which the purpose of the questionnaire was explained verbally left a questionnaire out for collection. Four of the collected questionnaires had no questions answered, leaving 46 per cent at least partially completed. No questionnaires were subsequently received through the post after a 'reminder' letter.

The pilot study indicated that the itemised rating scale (of 'very important'; 'quite important'; 'quite unimportant' and 'very unimportant'); the definitions of attractions; the instructions and the skip patterns appeared to present no problems for respondents. Minor amendments, however, were required to the wording of a few of the questions. For example, the question asking about a respondent's membership of horticultural organisations had a 'none of the above' category added, so that during the data input it could be clear whether the respondent was not a member of an organisation or had simply not answered that question. Additionally an analysis of the respondents' pattern of answering the questions showed that the lowest number of responses was made to two of the open questions. These questions were therefore removed, as the main emphasis of the survey was on quantitative data and these questions were more appropriate to being asked in a face-to-face situation.

The delivery and collection was effective, particularly where a householder was present. The collection of 57 per cent of questionnaires indicates that the instruction letter had been read and the instructions understood. Although many residents placed the completed questionnaire in a plastic bag, as requested in the delivery letter, not all did, which could cause problems in wet weather. Additionally many residents placed a weight (such as a pebble or flower-pot) on the questionnaire on their doorstep, but two questionnaires were found to have blown away into their garden. Amending the instructions in the delivery letter was considered, but family and friends, consulted informally, felt that this could be interpreted as patronising, however carefully the instructions were worded. As an alternative, the instructions were given informally as a suggestion to house-holders who were at home. Despite the absence of responses to the 'reminder' letter, it was considered worthwhile repeating the process for the main delivery, the only additional cost being that of printing the letters.

The pilot indicated that each postcode block would take approximately 1 hour to deliver and collect the questionnaires (including transportation). The response rate to the pilot of completed questionnaires of 46 per cent, (that is a 54 per cent non-response) and a 'target' sample size of 400 suggested a minimum sample size of 400/0.46 = 870 for the principal survey.

As the journal article reports:

> the survey was delivered to the homes of 932 residents in November/December 2002. A total of 345 questionnaires were completely or partially completed (58 in response to the 'reminder' letter) giving a response rate of 37%.
>
> (Fox and Edwards 2009: 204)

This shows that a pilot survey is not an exact indication of what might happen in the main survey. On the one hand, Fox and Edwards had a lower response rate than the pilot indicated, but on the other hand, householders did respond to the 'reminder' letter, which they hadn't in the pilot, and this increased the response rate from 31 per cent to 37 per cent.

Pilot study procedures to improve the internal validity of a questionnaire:

- Administer the questionnaire to pilot subjects in exactly the same way as it will be administered in the main study
- Ask the subjects for feedback to identify ambiguities and difficult questions
- Record the time taken to complete the questionnaire and decide whether it is reasonable
- Discard all unnecessary, difficult or ambiguous questions
- Assess whether each question gives an adequate range of responses
- Establish that replies can be interpreted in terms of the information that is required
- Check that all questions are answered
- Re-word or re-scale any questions that are not answered as expected
- Shorten, revise and, if possible, pilot again.

(Peat et al. 2002: 123)

One important point to note is that you should not allow the results from your pilot study to 'contaminate' the final study. So do not combine data from both phases, where the questions may be slightly differently worded.

When using a qualitative method, going through the pilot stages also allows for you to practise your skills at asking questions, listening, and capturing detail, whether it is in field notes, audio or video-recorded. Jennings (2005) suggests some good guide-lines for interviewing:

- Listen more than talk
- Ask for elaboration
- Refrain from the use of leading questions
- Use open-ended questions
- Try not to interrupt, although judicious interruptions may save time budgets from being broken
- Give of yourself: it is an interaction
- Check your non-verbal interactions so that they do not bias interviewee reflections
- Ask interviewees to explain laughter, hesitations and emotions
- Trust your instincts – know when to ask hard questions or probe further
- Use guides carefully
- Feel comfortable about silences: they allow time for reflection
- Be genuine.

Student vignette

Events student Cassandra was conducting a study for her dissertation into how sports stadia go about marketing and promoting their facilities to host other event markets.

Question	Feedback	Change
How would you say most of your business originates? • Inbound enquiries • Outbound marketing activity	Expansion on meaning of inbound/ outbound marketing	'Inbound enquiries from potential customers (e.g. received through contact methods shown on your website)' 'Outbound marketing activity (e.g. you conducting trade shows or sales calls)'
Do you consider yourself to be marketing your stadium as an 'unusual' event venue?	Clarity of question can be improved.	'Do you believe you actively promote your stadium as an "unusual" event venue?'
Do you think that repeat visitation is an issue for you as an 'unusual event venue'?	Question is too leading.	'Do you benefit from repeat visitation by customers and companies?'
What marketing platforms do you use to market your stadium?	Value of information could be increased.	Please rate the importance of these different platforms in marketing your stadium as an events venue.

Above is a table of the changes I made to my interview schedule after practis-ing the interview. The first column captures my original questions that I piloted, i.e. test-ran on some willing volunteers. The second column captures the feedback I received from these pilot volunteers on how I should rephrase my questions so that my participants would understand my focus more clearly. The final column captures the changes I made which resulted in the final version of my interview schedule that I used with my sample group of interviewees.

As a result of going through the pilot process in making changes to a more usable format for her interview schedule, Cassandra was able to communicate with marketing managers of sports stadia in a clearer way, which meant that she was able to collect more relevant primary data from them to analyse her research findings.

In terms of the methodological approach, piloting the data collection also allows you to justify the approach you choose in a meaningful way. What that means is if you can provide evidence that you changed questions or say the focus of observation as a result of putting things through a dry run, i.e. pilot stage, it lends that much more credence and worth to your methodological position. In so doing, your results are more reliable and valid as a result. Therefore keep detailed notes of what you do and changes you make, ready to use when writing up the methodology section.

Data preparation

Text

Whenever possible, with qualitative methods of data collection by way of interviewing or group interviews (e.g. focus group scenarios) the session should be audio recorded at a minimum, so as to provide a backup form of data as well as an accurate record of what was said. Videotaping is also an option. Either of these methods, however, can be considered intrusive or uncomfortable for participants, so that you must first ascertain their consent. Equally, you may have to discuss the ethical considerations associated with recording data collection methods. This is where your supervisor can help you; do ask for advice in this case.

Nevertheless, whether data is collected by audio, video, handwritten or typed notes, it is usually transcribed in a systematic way in preparation for analysis. Your research supervisor should have and will have warned you of the tedious and time-consuming nature of transcribing text and data, as it can seem like an onerous and never ending task – but rest assured that when interesting results are found after the fact, the effort is worth it! So before you begin the task of concentrated and focused analyses, transcription of data (text or images) begins. Lay out the data in a way that is legible and convenient for you. Initially, you may want to consider transcribing data by time and day it was collected, or by subject it was collected from (e.g. interview respondent or focus group). In any case, find a system that works for you. You also need to decide how much to transcribe:

- All
- Only what is relevant to the research – with no transcription when a participant deviates widely from the subject
- Key sections with a summary of the remainder

- And whether to include every um or ah and the length of pauses (you must do this for conversation analysis – see Chapter 11).

You should be prepared to produce pages and pages of transcribed data, and you should also be aware that not all data captured will end up as being used in a systematic way in defining themes for your analyses. Transcription is very much a means to the analyses' end. For example, if you are interviewing a participant about their experience queuing for a high profile music event, you may expect and begin to transcribe data that includes how the participant travelled to the venue, whether or not they had any problems, e.g. a tube strike, or if indeed bad weather came into play at all. You may only be interested in what the queue was like, but other factors might crop up that shed more insight on the scene for you. When cross-referencing transcribed data with other participants, it is only then that you can often see relationships. On the other hand, interesting one-offs may also be of relevance to your research, for example did the participant win a contest so that they received VIP treatment and didn't have to queue in the first place? The point is, you often don't know the relevance of certain information in your transcribed data until it has all been written up in full from all your data collection efforts.

Practical tip box

To stop you feeling overwhelmed:

- Turn your data into a form that can be analysed (transcriptions)
- Add reference information (date of interview, person interviewed, etc.)
- Add identity label (e.g. interview number)
- Write the actual words, even if slang, or if they say the wong [sic] word. 'Sic' is used in parenthesis or square brackets and means 'Thus it was written' from the Latin *Sic erat scriptum*. It is exactly what is said or written, without being edited for any errors.
- Add any notes in brackets which may clarify the participant's meaning (e.g. facial or hand gestures)
- Develop a filing system!
- Keep your recordings – as evidence and good to listen to again

Consider

- One hour of interviewing with one person = about 1 day of typing if you are not an expert!
- More than one person in the interview takes much longer
- Focus groups take even longer

Images and other forms of data

The first important task in preparing images for data analysis is to ensure that there is a reliable means of identifying the images. They need to be labelled with a number, at the very least. Additional information should be included wherever possible, such as the person taking the image, the subject shown, the location, the date, etc.

Images are another form of data that can be transcribed. These can take many forms, but not unlike text, they need to be captured and accounted for in their entirety before the task of analysing image transcriptions begins. Images obviously take the form of photos, artwork, media, etc. One researcher used sketches from villagers to obtain sources of data as the people living there were illiterate, so the best way to express themselves in addition to speech was through their own drawings. This particular researcher used their drawings to expand on findings made from the research in a meaningful way, for example a villager expressed in a drawing how important their water source was by drawing their own version of a person collecting it at the well. The image itself is powerful and ends up being visual evidence in the research findings.

The point is, there can be many forms of images that you may need to capture for transcription, and not necessarily limited to the modern day domain. This form of image transcription would, by design, typically need more space than text transcription. In a physical form, you may want to consider laying out images in a common space such as a large empty wall or floor if space allows. The other alternative is electronic image transcription, which at a minimum acts as a good library of sources, but depending on the method of analysis, you may be confined to the size of the monitor in your image transcription efforts. If, for example, you captured your own personal photos of crowd flow at a music festival over a period of a day or two, you would need to take shots periodically, at least hourly, to get a good representation of this for your analysis. It is then up to the researcher to decide if viewing in one common physical form (e.g. posting images on a large empty wall) or viewing them electronically is of benefit for the information you seek. If in doubt, you should consult your research supervisor on a good approach.

Numbers

Once you have collected your data, the first step is to prepare them in a format that facilitates the analysis of your data. When undertaking quantitative studies the intention is to 'quantify' the data and therefore this means that the data that you have collected need to be transferred into a format so that you can analyse them. This involves a process known as coding. (Note this is a similar but different operation to qualitative coding, which we describe in Chapter 11.)

Definition box

Coding is a process by which raw data is transformed into a standard form which can be processed and analysed by a computer.

In this part of the chapter, we show you how you can prepare your data for SPSS, which is a software package that is widely used to analyse research data (see Chapter 4). SPSS can only do this for you once you have transformed words or letters into digits. This is a process known as coding.

Imagine you have asked respondents:

Do you buy heavy metal songs?

And the responses can be one of the following:

- Definitely would not buy
- Definitely would buy
- I am not sure.

Now if you plan to enter this information into SPSS, you need to code these labels such as:

Definitely would not buy = 1
Definitely would buy = 2
I am not sure = 3.

This transformation is known as coding. Let's now look at how you enter this information into SPSS using 'variable view'. You can switch between 'data view' and 'variable view' by using the yellow and blue boxes at the bottom of the screen. Figure 10.1 shows an empty image of 'variable view' in SPSS.

As you can see there is a series of columns with which you need to make yourself familiar once you plan to enter the information into SPSS.

The first column is 'name'. In this column you can put in the question number or code it in any way you wish, but remember this only allows you to type a certain number of letters or digits. For instance, you could just enter the question number such as Q1 for question 1.

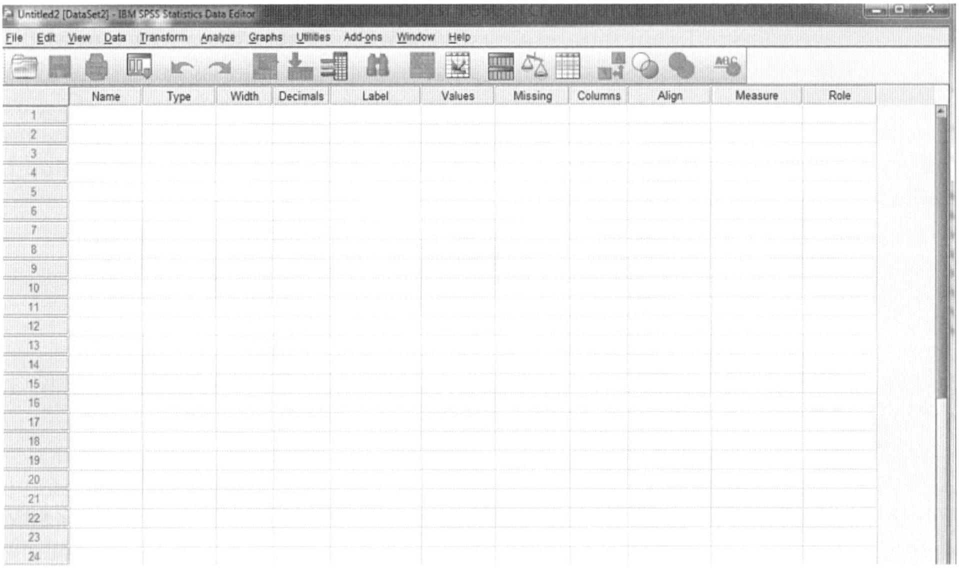

Figure 10.1 A snapshot of an empty SPSS variable view

As soon as you enter Q1 in the name column you will see a range of different inputs in the other columns (see Figure 10.2).

The second column in Figure 10.1 is titled 'type'. Type relates to the type of variable you are entering. In most cases we are dealing with digits (numeric data) but you must make sure that you clarify this so that SPSS can understand. If you click on 'numeric' in the second column you will see a blue square on the right-hand side, and if you click on that you will see that a new window opens up (see Figure 10.3). In this new window you can choose what type of variable; in our example our variable is numeric and so you don't need to change anything.

The next column, 'width', allows you to select the number of characters to be entered in each cell. In SPSS, for example, up to eight digits or ten letters (if it is a 'string' variable) can be selected. You do this by assigning the right number to this cell, remember that it is about the number of characters, and therefore even decimal points count as one.

In the next column, 'decimal', you tell SPSS how many decimal points you need in terms of the data. For example, your data might be in a form that has, say, two decimal points or zero decimal points. In our example earlier on we had no decimal points in our coding; our answer to the questions could have been 1 or 2 or 3 and therefore you can tell SPSS that you don't need any decimal points simply by clicking on number 2 in

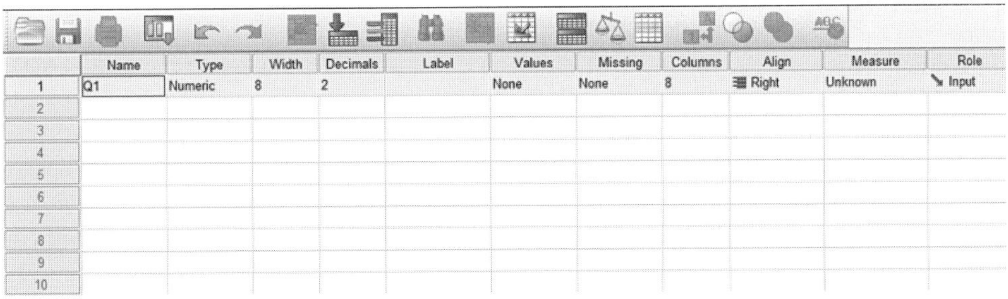

Figure 10.2 Labelling the columns

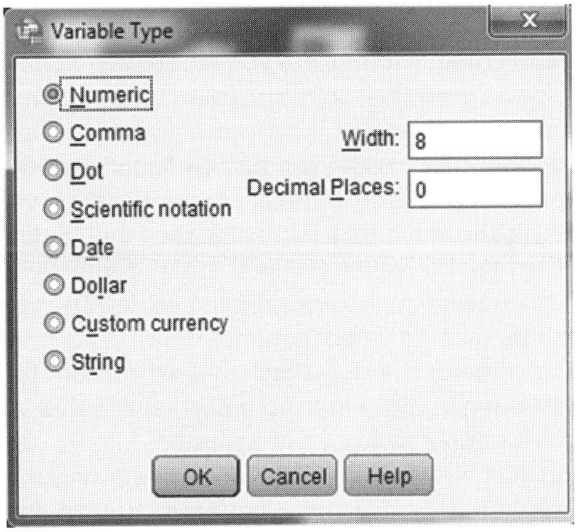

Figure 10.3 Variable type

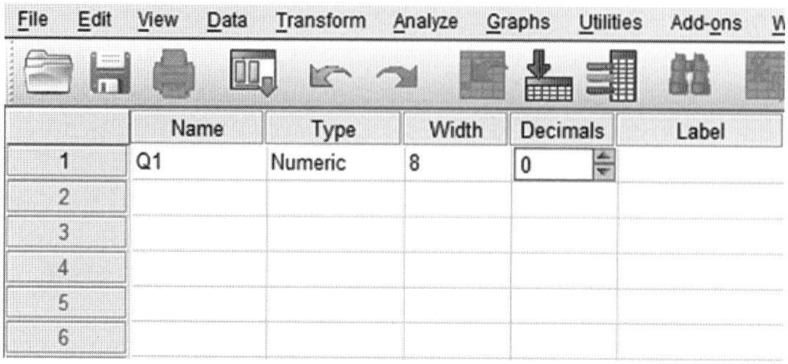

Figure 10.4 Decimal box

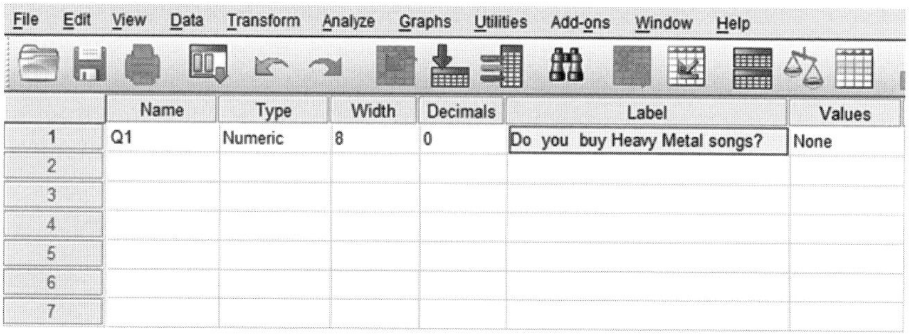

Figure 10.5 The label column

the decimal box and then scrolling up or down to select the appropriate number (see Figure 10.4).

The next column is 'label', which is helpful, and you can enter the entire question here if you wish (see Figure 10.5).

This means that once you start analysing Q1, the output will display the question for you in the results page, which makes analysis much easier for you. We will show you this later on in this chapter.

'Values' is an important column: it is where you tell SPSS what each digit stands for. For instance, in the example above you tell SPSS that every time you see '1' in this row of data it means 'definitely would not buy'. Let's take a look at Figure 10.6 and see how this works.

We do the same routine: click on the cell named 'label' and then click on the small square blue box on the right-hand side of the cell. A new window will open up. Then enter the label for our value. To the value of 1 you enter the label 'definitely would not buy', then press 'add' and then for the value of 2 you enter 'definitely would buy' and press 'add' until all three of them have their corresponding values. Then press OK (Figure 10.6).

The next column is the 'missing value' column, which is for those respondents who failed to answer one or some of the questions. In here you can tell SPSS that for every cell which is missing a value you are entering a particular value which is not a digit in any of the answers: most people tend to use a number like 99 or 999, but really it can be any number as long as it is not counted for any answer (Figure 10.7).

'Columns' and 'align columns' are more cosmetic adjustments, which show how wide your columns are and where the characters can be aligned, left, right or in the middle. Basically they relate to the presentation of your data in the data entry page.

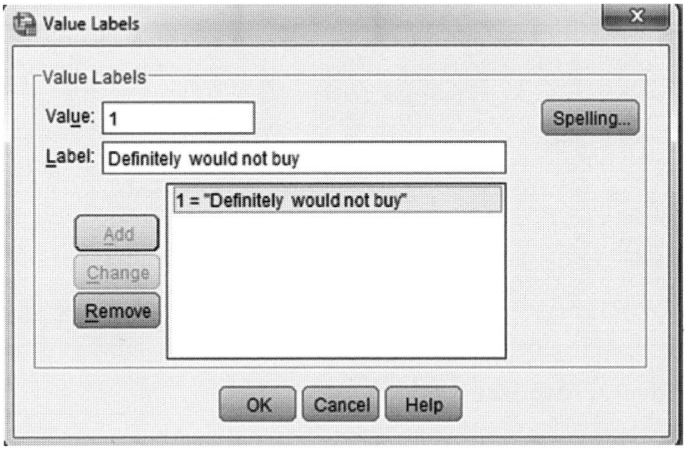

Figure 10.6 Value labels

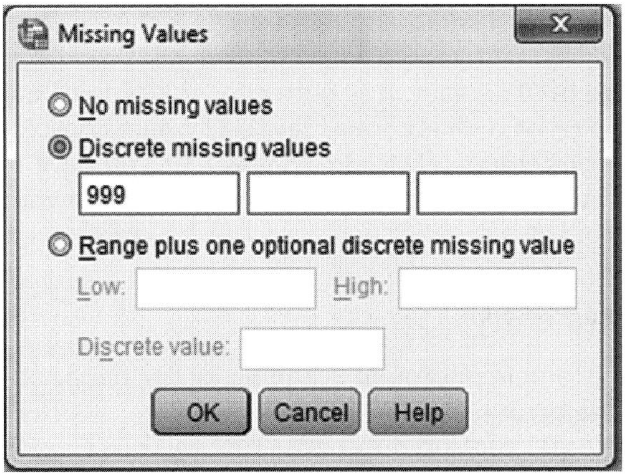

Figure 10.7 Missing values

The column called 'measure' addresses the measurement scales that were discussed in Chapter 9. Once you have identified what types of variable you have (nominal, ordinal or continuous) you can change the label in this column.

Question: which of the following aspects are the important factor for choosing a football match? Choose as many answers as appropriate.

1 Proximity
2 Ticket price
3 Teams that are playing
4 Weather
5 Transport types.

The challenge now is how to enter this information into SPSS, because respondents can choose as many answers as they wish, even though there is only one question.

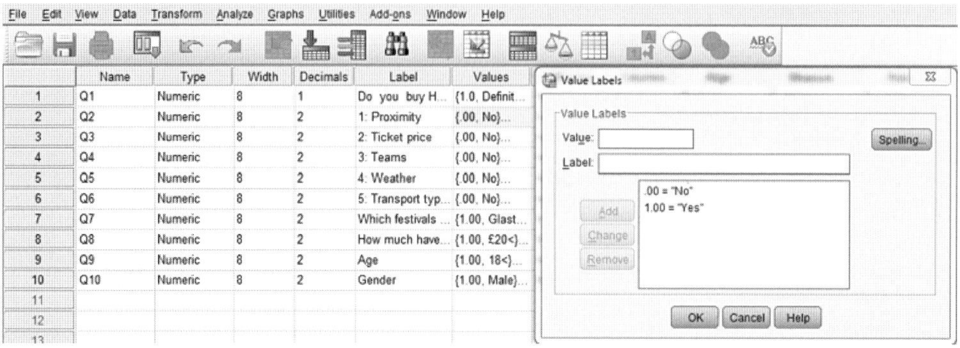

Figure 10.8 Several response options

Therefore you need to break this question down into as many options as you have given the respondents, in this case to five questions (see Figure 10.8).

As Figure 10.8 shows, we first broke this question down in to five questions (the same number as the possible answers they can choose) and then labelled the values. If the respondent said yes we entered value of '1' and if the respondent said no we entered value of '0'. Ideally, it is better for this type of question to give your respondents the choice of a Likert scale, say 1–5, where they can choose 1, 2, 3, 4 or 5 to reflect their preferences. This also means that you have more useful data to analyse, although it still means that you have to break down your question into five questions.

Checking the data entry

Whether the data is entered through scanning or by hand, checks should always be undertaken on the accuracy of the data entry. Simple tasks include listing the columns in size order (using the sort function). This will quickly show whether coding that, for example, should be from 1 to 6, includes an 11 or 22. This is a simple error – where the key has been pressed twice – but one that frequently happens. The original questionnaire should always be checked to find the correct code and the amendment made to the data set. This is one of the reasons why it is important to number each questionnaire as it is returned, unless it is pre-printed with a number.

Using Excel software

Although it is generally preferable to undertake analysis with specialist software (such as SPSS) some analysis can be undertaken in Excel. There are some issues with this, outlined below:

- Data Analysis ToolPak is an 'add-on' for Excel and may not be available, for example if you are using a university computer it may not be possible to get it installed.
- There are some potential problems with analyses involving missing data.
- There is a lack of flexibility.
- There is a high risk of human error both in terms of misidentifying outputs and when defining functions/formulae.

If you have the Data Analysis ToolPak available, use of this is recommended. It is relatively self-explanatory and therefore instructions for use are not included here. The ToolPak allows a variety of analysis, including simple frequencies, descriptive statistics, correlations, two-sample t-test, paired t-test, crosstabulation and chi-squared test of independence.

If the ToolPak isn't available then some manual creation of frequency tables can be undertaken.

Frequency

Table 10.1 below shows a sample of a survey of the number of items of fruit eaten at a festival and the respondents' favourite item of fruit.

Table 10.2 below shows the frequency and valid percentage for the number of items of fruit eaten.

Table 10.3 below shows how Table 10.2 below can be constructed using a formula. The = sign denotes that the formula is commencing the COUNTIF function as the formula that is being used, that is, Excel calculates whether the conditions that follow are satisfied. In the brackets the first element is the range (B3:B12: this denotes where the

Table 10.1 Sample of a survey for entry into Excel

Respondent	Number	Fruit
1	4	Apple
2	3	Orange
3	4	Grapes
4	2	Apple
5	1	Apple
6	4	Mango
7	1	Apple
8	4	Orange
9	2	Apple
10	5	Orange

Table 10.2 The frequency and valid percentage

Number	Frequency	Valid %
1	2	20
2	2	20
3	1	10
4	4	40
5	1	10
Total	10	100

Table 10.3 Using formula

Number	Frequency	Valid %
1	=COUNTIF(B3:B12,1)	=(F5/F$10)*100
2	=COUNTIF(B3:B12,2)	=(F6/F$10)*100
3	=COUNTIF(B3:B12,3)	=(F7/F$10)*100
4	=COUNTIF(B3:B12,4)	=(F8/F$10)*100
5	=COUNTIF(B3:B12,5)	=(F9/F$10)*100
Total	=SUM(F5:F9)	=SUM(G5:G9)

formula will look for the criteria. The second element is the criteria, 1): this is what the formula is looking for.

So in this case Excel will look in cells B3–B12 to see how many times the number 1 appears. This is repeated in the cells below with the criteria changing each time from 1 to 2 to 3 and so on. The 'Valid %' is calculated by taking the number of responses to each criterion, dividing it by the total number of responses and multiplying that result by 100.

Table 10.4 below shows the frequency and valid percentage for the respondents' favourite item of fruit.

Table 10.5 shows how the table above can be constructed using a formula. This is similar to the first table but instead of looking for a number, the criterion is text, as denoted by the speech marks. Extreme caution is urged when using this technique, as any variation in spelling, etc., will result in the response not being counted.

Average (mean)

An average (mean) can be calculated for the number of items of fruit eaten during the festival. This is written '=AVERAGE(B3:B12)'. The = sign denotes that the formula is commencing, AVERAGE is the function to be executed, and is followed by the range (the cells in which the formula will look), in this case (B3:B12).

Average (median)

An average (median) can be calculated for the number of items of fruit eaten during the festival. This is written '=MEDIAN(B3:B12)'. The = sign denotes that the formula is

Table 10.4 The frequency and valid percentage for the respondents' favourite item of fruit

Fruit	Frequency	Valid %
Apple	5	50
Orange	3	30
Grapes	1	10
Mango	1	10
Total	10	100

Table 10.5 Using formula with text

Fruit	Frequency	Valid %
Apple	=COUNTIF(C3:C12, 'Apple')	=(J5/J$9)*100
Orange	=COUNTIF(C3:C12, 'Orange')	=(J6/J$9)*100
Grapes	=COUNTIF(C3:C12, 'Grapes')	=(J7/J$9)*100
Mango	=COUNTIF(C3:C12, 'Mango')	=(J8/J$9)*100
Total	=SUM(J5:J8)	=SUM(K5:K8)

commencing, MEDIAN is the function to be executed and is followed by the range (the cells in which the formula will look), in this case (B3:B12).

Average (mode)

An average (mode) can be calculated for the number of items of fruit eaten during the festival. This is written '=MODE(B3:B12)'. The = sign denotes that the formula is commencing, MODE is the function to be executed and is followed by the range (the cells in which the formula will look), in this case (B3:B12).

Numerous other types of analysis can be undertaken using the same basic principle and the 'insert function' option gives assistance with this.

Scenario

Look back at the questions in the scenario in Chapter 9. Using SPSS, or another statistical software package that you are familiar with, create the appropriate headings.

Summary

This chapter has highlighted:

- Some advice on data collection, including piloting the method
- How data should be labelled for identification purposes
- The checks that should be undertaken having entered the data into SPSS
- How Excel can be used for basic statistical analysis.

Further reading

Journals

Meho, L. I. (2006) 'E-Mail interviewing in qualitative research: A methodological discussion'. *Journal of the American Society for Information Science and Technology*, 57: 1284–1295. This discusses the benefits and challenges of using emails to undertake in-depth interviews.

Books

Pallant, J. (2010) *SPSS Survival Manual*, 4th edn. Maidenhead: Open University Press. This discusses the screening and cleaning of quantitative data in chapter 5.

Web links

Tools4Dev (2013) 'How to pretest and pilot a survey questionnaire'. Online. Available HTTP: www.tools4dev.org/resources/how-to-pretest-and-pilot-a-survey-questionnaire/ (accessed 12 August 2013). This is a simple guide to piloting a survey.

Bristol Online Surveys (2007) 'How do I pilot a survey?' Online. Available HTTP: www.survey.bris.ac.uk/support/faq/surveys/how-do-i-pilot-a-survey (accessed 12 August 2013). This offers detailed advice if you are using that software for an e-questionnaire.

Video links

Practical Issues of Social Research: Part 1 of 3 on Practical Issues and Ethics (22.03 minutes). Available HTTP: www.youtube.com/watch?v=rKgm1TiQFh0 (accessed 12 August 2013). This discusses amongst other aspects the practicalities of gaining access to participants.

Entering Data in SPSS (9.20 minutes). Online. Available HTTP: www.youtube.com/watch?v=QQykoF1ZMXY&feature=related (accessed 10 August 2013).

Focus Group Facilitation (6.53 minutes). Online. Available HTTP: www.youtube.com/watch?v=rt5W7tXvljo (accessed 10 August 2013). This describes the role of the facilitator at a focus group.

Chapter 11

Analysing text and images

Chapter learning outcomes

In this chapter we:

- Discuss the tools (both computer-based and traditional) that can be used to analyse qualitative data.
- Describe various forms of qualitative analysis.
- Discuss the tools that can be used to analyse images, videos, etc.
- Consider the producer and the viewer as well as the image.

Christine is organising a fashion show for a leading humanitarian charity. They have been fortunate in obtaining the support and involvement of several leading fashion designers and a celebrity chef. However, the chef has made his involvement conditional on Christine using the occasion to undertake research into the market for his new range of canapés, which he is keen to promote. The charity representative, however, is adamant that the guests must not be directly involved in the data collection in any way, as he thinks that their evening might be 'spoilt by researchers'.

Christine resolves their dilemma by suggesting that they photograph each plate of canapés whilst it is in the preparation room before it is served and then again when the waiting staff have circulated around. This, she explains to the chef, will enable them to accurately count which canapés are the most popular, by the ones that are selected by the guests. The charity representative is delighted by this idea, as it will be totally unobtrusive to the guests, and the chef is happy because it will give him accurate data to inform his next range. However, he doesn't just want quantitative data but also qualitative data that will help explain why one canapé has been chosen and not another and whether the guests actually enjoyed what they had selected. Christine suggests therefore that some of the waiting staff could be her events management students who are experienced at working at this type of high profile event. They will discreetly observe the reactions to the canapés and report back each time as they return to the preparation room, so that notes can be taken. They will even, she offers, check the flower arrangements at the end of the show for any discarded canapés. Both the chef and the charity representative look horrified that their guests might do such a thing, but Christine has been involved in enough events to know exactly what some attendees do. Because of Christine's mixed methods research, the chef becomes a leading supporter of the event and contributes generously, first to the event outgoings, second, the charity and third, Christine is relieved to hear, to the costs of the research study.

Introduction

In the social sciences, qualitative data inquiry often engages in studying in more depth the behaviour, thoughts, emotions and feelings of people in everyday life scenarios. As Bernard and Ryan (2010: 5) have stated, 'when we reduce people's thoughts, behaviors, emotions, artefacts, and environments to sounds, words, or pictures, the result is qualitative data'.

What this chapter sets out to do is to differentiate the ways in which qualitative data can be analysed. The chapter begins by considering the written word, whether from secondary data sources (see Chapter 8) or the transcripts from interviews or focus groups whose preparation was discussed in Chapter 10, or field notes from observation. It then explores the range of visual data that can be obtained when collecting primary data for research. Visual materials can be used as a primary source of data (e.g. a study of photo albums) or can also be used to support other data collection methods (e.g. using a videotape of an interview to capture gestures and expressions as part of the primary data). The discussion in this section focuses on visual data types such as photos and film, but also acknowledges the subject(s) as creators of visual data, for example where a researcher asks subjects to capture photos of a context that is important to them – such as taking photos at a food festival – before subjecting the content of the photos to data analysis.

Analysing text

To begin with, based on your aim and objectives, research questions, the literature and practical issues (including personal preferences), you need to decide:

- The degree of subjectivity (see Chapter 2)
- The research design (see Chapter 5)
- The data source(s) (see Chapter 8)
- The level of transcription (see Chapter 10)
- An analytic tool(s)
- And the form(s) of coding.

We describe these last two in this chapter, but first, as we discussed in Chapter 10, you need to be organised, to prevent you feeling overwhelmed. So make sure you have:

- Turned your data into a form that can be analysed (transcriptions)
- Added reference information (date of interview, person interviewed, etc.)
- Added an identity label (e.g. interview number)
- Sorted your literature
- Developed a filing system!

Having done that, students and practitioners often have problems in starting an analysis, but it is actually a very simple process, although one that requires thought. We wouldn't like to suggest it is child's play, but it is a process that you have followed, perhaps unwittingly, since you were a child. Figure 11.1 shows a mess of toy bricks, farm animals, etc. This is like your data – many different bits from different participants that all together, initially don't seem to make much sense.

But, when you start sorting and re-reading or listening to the data, you'll realise that there are some parts that have something in common relating to your aim and objectives – the bricks, animals and people in Figure 11.2.

Then, the more you look at the 'data' you may start to see more similarities or patterns – see Figures 11.3 and 11.4. You probably sorted your own toys in this way.

Figure 11.1 So much information – aaagh!

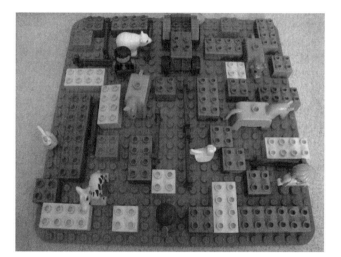

Figure 11.2 The sorted 'data'

Figure 11.3 Patterns emerge in the 'data'

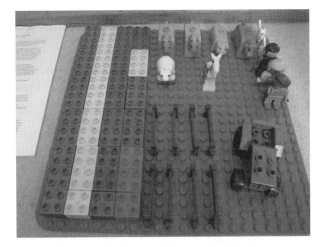

Figure 11.4 The reworked 'data'

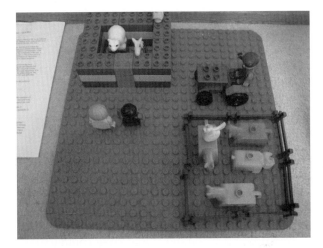

Figure 11.5 The finished 'analysis'

We have shown two examples, because you will often have to 'play' with the data to make it work for you. The outputs won't just jump straight out at you – it takes some thought and reworking.

However, this is just the beginning of qualitative analysis; somehow, you have to take the data and make it 'tell a story'. The story of course, needs to relate to your aim and objectives and research questions. In Figure 11.5, we have done that – the exact same 'data' now tells a story of a farmyard with domesticated animals secured by a fence. There is also walled enclosure for the wild animals. From this simple example, we hope that you are able to grasp in outline what qualitative analysis seeks to achieve.

The process of qualitative analysis is therefore very cyclical in nature. You have to be prepared to not only collect the data, but digest it and search for patterns and why they are there. From that point, you can begin to code and categorise your data. A code in qualitative research is different to the quantitative coding we discussed in the previous chapter, but is similar in that it helps with the analysis.

Definition box

'a *code* in qualitative enquiry is most often a word or short phrase that symbolically assigns a summative, salient, essence-capturing, and/or evocative attribute for a portion of language-based or visual data' (Saldaña 2009: 3).

You begin the process by creating codes and a *coding framework*:

At one end of the continuum, we can have prespecified codes or more general coding frameworks. At the other end, we can start coding with no prespecified codes, and let the data suggest initial codes ... Nor ... does it need to be an either-or decision. Thus, even when guided by an initial coding scheme, we can be alert to other labels and categories suggested by the data.

(Punch 2005: 200)

So, you can create or identify codes as you:

- Write your literature review
- Draft the interview schedule
- Write up your field notes
- Transcribe the interviews
- Prepare for the next interview
- Or finally sit down 'to do the analysis'.

Now, have a look at the pictures of chocolate and sweets in Figure 11.6.

Already, we have applied labels to these pictures by distinguishing between chocolates and sweets. We might be interested in confectionary that could be eaten at events for different target markets. So we could code the sweets as suitable for children and the chocolates for adults. For a more formal event, the chocolates in the centre of the figure might be most suitable: what code could you give to them?

Here are some different forms of coding:

- Attribute coding – basic descriptive information, e.g. setting (ticket office); participant characteristics (female, manager); data format (focus group)
- Holistic coding – basic theme or issue
- Provisional coding (from objectives, literature review, data collection)
- 'Great quote for writing up' coding. This one is useful when you come to write up your research (see Chapter 13). Some participants are very articulate and can express themselves well; others may stumble around looking for the appropriate words to express themselves. They may both be saying the same thing, but it is obviously better to use the quote from the first example as your evidence than the second.

Saldaña, (2009) lists other forms of coding, which may give you some ideas when you are carrying out your own analysis:

- Descriptive coding – identifies the topic not the content, usually a noun
- Process coding – 'doing words' (gerunds) – activities or actions

Figure 11.6 Coding chocolate and sweets

- Emotion coding – the emotions recalled or experienced (possibly inferred by the researcher)
- Values coding – reflect the participant's values, attitudes or beliefs
- Versus coding – binary conflicts
- Evaluation coding – assign judgements about the merit or worth of something/someone
- InVivo coding – a word or short phrase in the participant's language that has resonance
- Magnitude coding – indicates frequency, direction, intensity, etc.

Try to think of when these types of codes could be applied to the images of the chocolates and sweets.

All sections of text can be given more than one code, so using our example in Figure 11.6, the confectionary in the centre of the image could be coded in numerous ways such as 'chocolate'; 'unwrapped', 'delicious' or 'expensive'. However, another participant could describe the chocolate not as 'delicious' but as 'disgusting', so adding a fifth code, and so on.

Analytic tools

How do you break down the data and record the codes? We have identified a number of tools to assist in the analysis stage. Which one you use depends on how you like to work. Some people are happier working at a computer, whilst others like to be surrounded by pieces of paper. Be aware though that these tools are like a washing machine, in that they help you to do the job better and more effectively, but you will still need to work and do the thinking. In the same way that you have to sort your clothes, put them in the washing machine and decide on the wash programme. If you put a bright coloured article in with white shirts (and we've all done that at some time) the shirts will come out coloured; similarly, code ineffectively and your analysis will be flawed.

Here are some tools that we and our students have found to be effective, which you can try.

1 CAQDAS (Computer Assisted Qualitative Data Analysis Software)

In Chapter 4, we discussed the use of specialist software to analyse qualitative data such as NVivo, ATLASti or MAXQDA, and if your organisation has a license to use one of these software programmes, they are very effective, but can be time consuming to learn.

2 Coding using columns/tables in Word (Figure 11.7)

In Figure 11.7 we have coded a section of transcript using columns in a table. The right hand column shows the different code labels that are appropriate to each section. For example, 'a nice little park' is an attraction to visit, whilst 'we go there quite often' can be coded as the frequency of visiting. This tool has the advantage of showing the code labels and it is easy to give a section of text more than one code at a time. It might also suit you, if you have a problem distinguishing between colours.

D: And do you ever visit gardens at home?	
VI98: Well I live near Sherwood Forest.	
D: Oh do you, Nottingham?	
VI98: There's a nice little park, so we go there quite often and have a walk, very nice.	Attraction Frequency Experience
D: Do you ever go to the sorts of gardens that people pay to visit?	
VI98: Well you have to pay to go in there.	Paying
D: Oh you have to pay for that one?	
VI98: Three pounds a car unless you've got one of these, you know, that you can get in, pay for the year. Get in without paying each time, I think it's a bit cheaper to do it that way.	Paying

Figure 11.7 Coding using columns/tables in Word

3 Colour highlighting in Word (Figure 11.8)

This time we used the same section of transcript but used the highlighting tool in the Microsoft Word package to identify the phrases, with each having a different colour. This method requires you to keep a key to identify the code label for each colour. One colour is designated for the frequency of visiting, in this case that they visit 'quite often'. A different shade of the colour could be used on another transcript if a different interviewee visits 'rarely'. Alternatively, you can use different fonts, underlining, bold, italics or combinations of text effects to differentiate between codes.

Some students like to combine these two methods and highlight the codes in the right hand column of a table, using different colours or text effects.

D: And do you ever visit gardens at home?

VI98: Well I live near Sherwood Forest.

D: Oh do you, Nottingham?

VI98: There's a nice little park, so we go there quite often and have a walk, very nice.

D: Do you ever go to the sorts of gardens that people pay to visit?

VI98: Well you have to pay to go in there.

D: Oh you have to pay for that one?

VI98: Three pounds a car unless you've got one of these, you know, that you can get in, pay for the year. Get in without paying each time, I think it's a bit cheaper to do it that way.

Figure 11.8 Colour highlighting in Word

4 Coloured highlighter pens on paper (Figure 11.9)

This example is similar to the one above, but instead of using technology, the printed scripts can be highlighted using colour pens. This is good if you like to work on paper rather than a screen, but you can run out of pens of different colours. Again like example 3, you will need to make a key to show which code relates to each colour.

D: And do you ever visit gardens at home?

VI98: Well I live near Sherwood Forest.

D: Oh do you, Nottingham?

VI98: There's a nice little park, so we go there quite often and have a walk, very nice.

D: Do you ever go to the sorts of gardens that people pay to visit?

VI98: Well you have to pay to go in there.

D: Oh you have to pay for that one?

VI98: Three pounds a car unless you've got one of these, you know, that you can get in, pay for the year. Get in without paying each time, I think it's a bit cheaper to do it that way.

Figure 11.9 Coloured highlighter pens on paper

5 Cutting up paper into sections

With this method, the transcripts each need to be printed several times and then cut up into pieces, with one piece for each code. All the pieces that relate to a particular code are then stapled on to another sheet of paper. You need to write a label at the top of the sheet of paper, so that you know which code, the pieces of transcript refer to. This method is not environmentally friendly, but useful, because you gather together all the sections relating to one code from the various transcripts. This is a step that with some of the other tools needs to be carried out afterwards.

6 Cut and paste sections using Word

This method is the same as the one above, but is undertaken electronically rather than using pieces of paper. Using the computer is helpful, because you can later use the 'find' function, if needed. However, it is harder with both of these tools to find the section of text in a transcript, because there are no colours to stand out.

7 Using comment boxes in Word (Figure 11.10)

Our final suggested tool is using the comments function in Word. The code can be written in the comment box, together with any additional thoughts or notes. Multiple coding of the same sections of text is more feasible with this method.

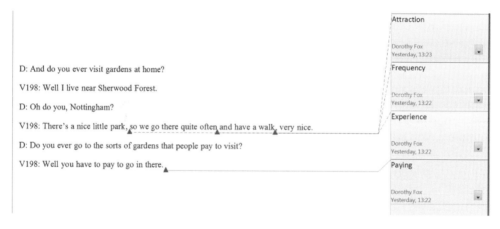

Figure 11.10 Using comment boxes in Word

Coding framework

Having established the codes and identified the relevant sections of the transcripts, you then need a way of seeing how the codes inter-relate; you do this by creating a coding framework or code book. If you have used one of the methods involving colours, you can also use it as your key by colouring the code book, highlighting the codes in the appropriate colours or text effects.

In developing a code book, it can sometimes be difficult to see the patterns or rela-tionships between the codes. So you could try creating a mind map, or a tree, or a list in the same format as folders and files in older versions of Windows Explorer. Remember that as with the children's toys discussed earlier, there is not just one way to relate the data and it may take several attempts to create a logical framework that meets the needs of your aim and objectives.

As you progress, you can organise your data into:

- Categories
- Higher order themes
- General dimensions

A computer generated codebook in NVivo and a manual code book are shown in Figures 11.11 and 11.12. On the left of a codebook are the general dimensions, moving to higher order themes and categories or specific codes toward the right hand side. In our example earlier, *frequency* becomes a category, with *never, rarely* and *often* being the codes.

Similarly to quantitative analysis, data can be recoded, but unlike that, in qualitative research, you need to revisit your coding as you collect data and be prepared to re-code and re-categorise the data. Themes and concepts will then rise to the surface in a more purposeful manner. According to Miles and Huberman (1994: 49):

Analysis during data collection lets the fieldworker cycle back and forth between thinking about the existing data and generating strategies for collecting new – often better data.

Coding can therefore be useful:

- Through recoding – more accurate words or phrases may come to mind or have been identified.
- You may have missed codes!
- You may see pattern codes which are 'explanatory or inferential codes … that identify an emergent theme, configuration, or explanation … They are a sort of meta-code' (Miles and Huberman 1994: 69).

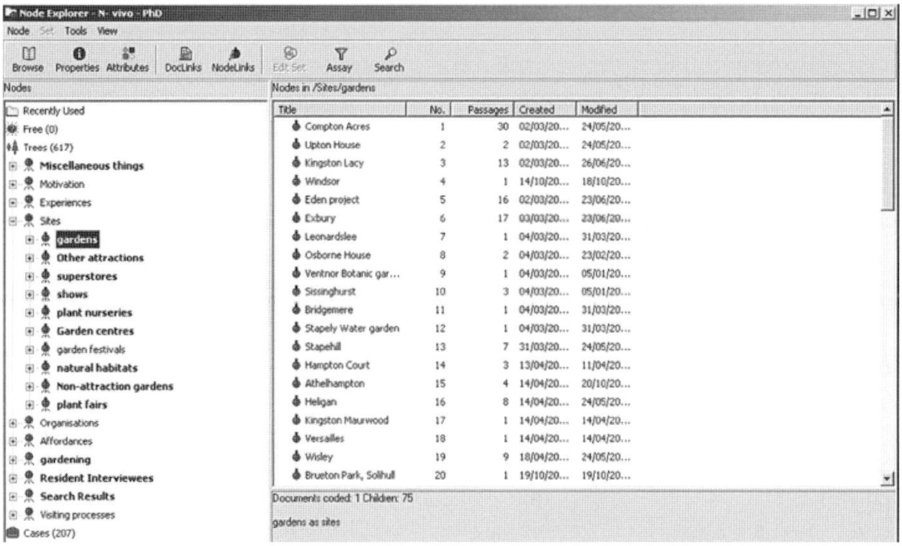

Figure 11.11 Coding framework in NVivo

Attractions	Gardens	Domestic
		Open to the public
	Parks	Private
		Public
	Shows	Small, local
		Medium, regional
		Large, national
Frequency	Never	
	Rarely	
	Often	

Figure 11.12 Manual code book

As we discussed in Chapter 7, a question often asked by students is, do I have enough data? But as we said before, one approach is to continue interviewing until you are learning nothing new – this is called saturation. Often, though, you may run out of participants, time and/or money.

Practical tip box

Some texts refer to immersion in the data – however, when you are new to qualitative analysis, this may feel more like 'drowning' than 'immersion'. If this happens, try:

- Re-listening to the recordings or read the transcripts again
- Reflection – think about it when you are relaxed (out walking, listening to music)
- Read some of the literature again
- Give up, do something else, start again next day
- But most importantly, don't press delete or throw anything away!

In terms of analyses, a good qualitative output should possess the following characteristics:

- It should address your purpose and goal, giving an answer to your 'researchable question'.

- It should offer analysis, not just description.
- It should offer at least a new theory or explanation.
- It should offer something more than the participants in your research could have reported.
- And it should account for your data. This has to be an adequate account, so you will be able to claim that it 'makes sense' of what's going on in the data.

(Richards 2009: 198)

It can be useful to write memos – these are simply notes. Glaser defines a memo as 'the theorizing write-up of ideas about codes and their relationships as they strike the analyst while coding' (Glaser 1978: 83). Codes are the prompts or triggers for analytic memos and so the memos are created as a tool of the analysis. They can also be used to influence subsequent interviews. The contents of the memos can include the researcher's reflections on the related literature, any difficulties they have faced in understanding the interviewee's meaning, and any patterns which are emerging, as well as any contradictions. They are also a good place to record your thoughts on the code contents as you think of them. This can occur either sporadically (as referred to by Glaser 1978) or systematically, when you apply yourself to really considering the meaning line by line.

So at this stage, make notes (or memos) about your findings and what they might mean, while your ideas are fresh in your mind. These will be invaluable when you come to writing up the findings, which we discuss in Chapter 13.

Student vignette

Gina undertook research with small party planning businesses (see Chapter 8).

My research objectives were:

A *To investigate how 'operational management' is viewed as a management technique in small party planning businesses*
B *To investigate the operational challenges experienced within small party planning businesses forced upon them by the competition, the external environment and customers*
C *To investigate the operational challenges occurring internally within small party planning businesses*
D *To investigate if key success factors are identified and if strategies for the future are implemented in small party planning businesses.*

I wanted to align these objectives with my primary data, namely the interview transcripts, an example of which is shown in Table 11.1 that follows. I used a simple form of the analytic tool of highlighting sections of text in various colours to represent different codes and categories. For example, I assigned two shades in my coding framework (Table 11.2) to text found in the transcript relating to the categories of the constraints to operational challenges in the party planning business, and the measures the interviewee said they took to overcome these constraints.

Table 11.1 Gina's coded transcript

G: I've got some objectives and the questions sort of relate to each of the objectives.

IC: Right.

G: The first one ... my first objective is to investigate how operational management is viewed as a management technique. So ... is operational management a technique that you understand or that you plan, or something ...

IC: No, No. umm I think it's just something that you...umm I think you have to be quite good at strategic planning.

G: Uh ha.

IC: You have to be quite good at being methodical about logistics. So you have to, when you get a brief from a client you have to really go through it, step by step, all the notes that you have taken from the meeting with the client and then plan from your diary. So say you've got six weeks to plan and collate everything for an event, ummm that's how I would do it. I have to time everything in steps, you have to allow for things to be delivered that you've ordered, especially if you've ordered stuff from America.

G: Okay, cool. So my second objective is to investigate the operational challenges experienced within small party planning businesses forced upon by the external environment, the competition and the customers.

IC: Uh ha.

G: Do you think that the recession has had an impact on the change of services that are demanded from you?

IC: Hmmm... well in that there is not the amount of enquiries that there used to be and certainly in corporate events they now will not accept your first price, you price everything up and give it to them, and they always try to get it lower.

G: So pricing has become a lot more competitive?

IC: Yes, yes that's right. Whereas before 2008 you would do a fair price and nine times out of ten they would be happy with it so ummm and I suppose it's just budgets. I mean corporate budgets, private individuals aren't affected so much I think for say weddings, 40th, 50th celebrations it's more the corporate stuff whereas before the recession they would go mad and money would be no object. No it's not like that anymore.

G: Do you try to target more private clients then?

IC: No, even though corporate clients are having tighter budgets they are still spending more than private clients when they do book.

G: So how do you manage to keep up with the competitive prices, does it just come down to sourcing at competitive costs?

IC: Yes exactly ... If I can get the supplies at competitive costs then I can price competitively.

G: Do you think the size of the market has changed ... have a lot of companies closed down or opened up?

IC: Yes I think, because I do a lot of work in London I think the best case scenario is to be like me. i.e. small, just me, and then I hire people to help me if I need them.

G: Okay cool. Human resources, do you ever need to gather staff for parties? Is this easy?

IC: Well yes I do. I do ask I mean here in Weymouth there is quite a lot of freelance event designers and stylists, so like me used to work in London and have now moved down here so yeah, that's all quite easy. I mean obviously can't do everything myself so sometimes it's a bit much.

(Continued)

Table 11.1 Continued

G: The next objective is to investigate the operational constraints incurred internally within the company. Ummm what would you recognise as the main challenges that you face on a day to day basis and how would you overcome them?

IC: Umm, it is I suppose it's all about getting things done in the right order. I mean this goes back to taking the brief and working out how you're going to do it to ensure that you are running to schedule and can get everything done in the time frame. I mean when you are working by yourself, or even if you're working with someone, it is just up to you to get on and do it so I can't see that there really is any constraints. I mean apart from workload, say you've got loads of work on and you've got four different projects going on at the same time, then you've got to be really careful about what you're doing and organising your time so that you fit everything in.

Table 11.2 Gina's coding framework

Objective's and codes	Colour key to categories	
Research objective A		
Extent of awareness		
Understanding of operational management as a technique		
Relevance of structure		
Understanding of event operations management		
Research objective B	Constraint	Overcome constraint
Size of market		
Demand in the market		
Availability in the market		
Extent of competition		
Demand of products/services		
Availability of human resources		
Legal constraints		
Recession		
Cost constraint		
Time constraint		
Quality control		
Research objective C	Constraint	Overcome constraint
Time constraints		
Human resource constraints		
Manage customer contact/relations		
Managerial skills		
Resources and capabilities		
Research objective D		
Key success factors		
Differentiation from competition		
Operational business planning structure		

You can see from the interview transcript the natural progress of the interview discussion, i.e. Gina's conversation with her interview participant, in its fluid and naturally occurring flow. As Gina adopted a semi-structured approach to her interview schedule she was able to probe and steer the questions so she obtained the depth of perspective needed from her interviewee in addressing her research objectives.

Types of analysis

We have suggested above a generic form of analysis of qualitative data because as Sarantakos (2005) states, qualitative analyses

> transform and interpret qualitative data in a rigorous and scholarly manner. ... Beyond this there is simply no consensus as to how qualitative analysis should proceed, or what makes an acceptable analysis.
>
> (Sarantakos 2005: 344)

However, some more standardised and specialised forms of analysis have emerged in the literature and we discuss some of these next. If you are interested in these or other forms, such as narrative analysis or critical incident analysis, consult sources (such as Bryman 2008 and Seale 2004) to gain an understanding of their foundation and approach. If you are unsure which to use, consult your dissertation supervisor in the first instance.

Thematic analysis

This form of analysis attempts to identify 'patterns and processes, commonalities and differences' (Miles and Huberman 1994: 9) and is therefore used quite frequently. You will be looking out for themes and interconnections that occur in the data (Denscombe 2003). It therefore requires several iterations; namely reading and coding, rereading and recoding several times. This form of analysis is often associated with grounded theory (see Chapter 5), but can be used in other forms of qualitative research.

Content analysis

Content analysis usually applies to a certain context or case. A content analysis most often involves a researcher who is looking for common themes/occurrences in the content of documents and other supporting sources such as blogs, television/video footage, media, etc. The analyses of the content will depend on the set objectives of the enquiry, but it can be things associated with determining the recurring presence of certain meanings, words or relationships within the data captured from sources such as the above. Such 'meanings' can go further so that it is framed within a historical or political influence, the researcher themselves, or issues related to, for example, environment, social class or financial status.

An example of this was conducted by undertaking a study related to the perception of the availability of Olympic ticket sales for purchase by the general public in the lead-up to the start of the 2012 Olympic Games in London. Having conducted a content analysis of the media reports on their promotion, along with websites and official sources, as well as travel companies, the content analysis concluded that the perception of available tickets was quite low among the public, even if it was the view of the organisers that the process had been transparent, fair and equitable.

Other sources that can be used in a content analysis include public records, diaries, letters, advertising and photographs. Obviously the internet provides endless opportunities to access content, but the important thing with content analysis is being able to authenticate the accuracy of certain accounts and reports. A fuller content analysis benefits from sourcing from a number of different places. It is common, no matter the set research objectives, for content analyses to apply codes to certain variables/themes so as to break down the data further. For example, a content analysis of the promotion frequency of charity fun runs in a region may uncover a relationship between registration demand and promotional efforts of those promoting them. From this description, you can see that content analysis often, but not always, results in quantified findings.

Discourse analysis

Discourse analysis is presented and packaged in different ways in the literature, yet often it depends on the contextual and/or theoretical influence of a study. Contextual may mean how it exists within a certain entity or environment, for example, a legal, medical or environmental realm. As for the theoretical, it may mean making sense of social practices including priorities in relation to aspects such as the influence of gender, power or poverty. In essence, however, discourse analysis seeks to make sense of patterns of communication, the information shared within a certain study, as opposed to a semantic analysis of the text within a data set. This means that you need to maintain a certain 'distance' from the text, as the text formations are the object of the study as opposed to direct inferences of the 'words'. To that end, the variability of the content is understood to be present, as opposed to a purely objectivist approach to the data. Bernard and Ryan (2010: 221) are of the mind that discourse analyses consists of three factors:

1 The grammar beyond the sentence
2 The language in use
3 The rhetoric of power.

Accordingly for Flick (2006), the emphasis in discourse analysis is the emphasis on the construction of versions of certain events, be it in reports or presentations, as part of the data collected. It is the study of analysing the construction of whole conversations or narratives as part of this. One of the more common influences for a critical approach to discourse analysis is that of Michel Foucault (1980). Using a critical discourse analysis approach that adopts the Foucauldian school of thought would include the presence of power as one of the main themes of the analysis.

Conversation analysis

Conversation analysis is the study of speech interchange between people. It is also about the sequence of who speaks first, second and so on – as well as broken sentences, interruptions, or overlapping conversation. Depending on the nature and detail required (e.g. adjacent pairs – once an utterance like 'Hello, how are you?' is made, a response from the second is expected – a pair), conversation analysis can also engage in the features of speech including intonation, vowels, gestures and body language, as well as fillers such as 'ahhh', 'erm', and 'ummmm'. In essence, the structure of the unfolding conversation and how the interaction unfolds is the focus of the study. This includes the analysis of 'turn taking' whereby the sequence is also classified into analysis/coding. In essence, conversational analysis is undertaken under the premise that conversation allows for social order to take shape – so we might study how action is obtained, sustained or side-stepped through the analysis of conversation in sequence.

An example of a conversational analysis applied to a specific setting would be the study of conversation occurring in a community 'safety awareness' event. Depending first on a set agenda, conversational analysis might make some conclusions about the sequence of the conversation that takes place at a meeting. If there is a space for an 'open forum', a researcher might begin to make some conclusions as to how order is maintained in this setting, and how and where priority is placed in addressing issues, and where and how action is decidedly taken, and by whom. For example, a resident may make suggestions that others take turns monitoring the church graveyard as a result of recent vandalism. If a decision is made, what 'conversations' and transitions on the subject took place to get there?

Analysing images

In this technological age, it is fair to say that photographs, video and film are increasingly becoming a ready-made source of primary or complementary data for research, as we discussed in Chapter 8. Equally, such visual evidence may be used as a tool in undertaking research, such as using an old photo album to prompt memories of a former family holiday. This section concentrates on how these media (photos, video and film) can be analysed, whether on their own or in combination with another data source.

Event research in action

Sharples et al. (2003) undertook a study in which cameras were distributed amongst children to collect visual materials as part of the data collection. Their sample was 180 children in three different age groups (7, 11 and 15) who were given cameras to take photos of whatever they wanted over a weekend. More than 4,000 photos were generated, and the researchers analysed them using the following criteria:

● What is the content of each photo?
● Are people or objects shown posed?
● Who are the people in the photos?
● Are there any particular themes in the photographs of certain age groups?

Upon analysis of the photographs, the following trends were revealed. Seven-year-olds tended to take photos of toys and other possessions, as well as their family and the home. The 11-year-olds tended to take photos of an outdoor nature and of animals, including pets. Last, the 15-year-olds tended to take mostly photos of their friends, often of an informal nature.

> Such a visual analysis enabled the researchers to gain an understanding of those things that are meaningful and have priority in these particular age groups of children. By comparison, by interviewing the children individually, they may not have been able to verbalise those things that are important and of interest to them in quite as much depth. This is a classic example where multiple forms of data collection augment the effort in achieving the research objectives, as the added visuals chosen and selected by the children give a broader perspective to consult as part of presenting the findings for this research.

Images

The unique thing about photographs as a source of data and therefore analysis (as with film and video to some extent as well) is that they are symbolic representations of subjects in the world, i.e. they may mean different things to different people. But that doesn't make them any less important than words – in fact, they may be more important in terms of expression. This may sound daunting but need not be any more so than, say, when you compare it to doing a statistical analysis of variables in SPSS. On the contrary, it is an alternative and unique form of data collection that also is subject to alternative data analysis approaches.

Video analysis

An analysis of video can be approached solely by what is recorded, but equally what is not, or what is edited out, i.e. what meanings lie behind the choice of material viewed/ reviewed? There are, equally, problems with the approach. Film/video content can be very complex in that a lot of information and context is captured; there are technological challenges; there is the relationship between the video and text produced from it, i.e. is it representative; and finally legal and ethical implications of recording – who is permitted to record and how is permission justified? However, when compared to audio recording, video recording allows for non-verbal elements of a situation to be captured and analysed, which can provide richer data source.

Pink (2001, 2004) has written widely on the use of visual data collection as a complement to other forms of data collection, such as interviews. If you think about the video recorded interview, a researcher has the ability to consider not only the verbal content, but visual images, gestures and body movements too. Speech is often emphasised by body gestures, enabling the researcher to get a clearer indication of the true meaning of a context. Thus, in analysing the data, the researcher could be left combining the verbal context (e.g. speech) with visual cues found from body gestures in the participants in video footage. For example, if you videotaped an interview with two different people, such as a criminal in a pending court case, or a sports star in an international event, can you envision how different their body language might be as a result of studying their 'words' alongside their body language? The criminal might fidget in their seat, and be sombre in their communication. By comparison, a sports star may stand up tall and smile a lot, showing their confidence in a very direct way. If you strip away a visual image of these interviews to an audiotape-only recording, you can appreciate how some of the context can be overlooked, yet with visual tools the data collected can be enhanced in its description and interpretation.

A research inquiry that involves analysis of visual materials will likely focus on descriptions of the images and reality that photos or film capture. From this approach, visual data ends up being transitioned to text. To that end, the same type of analysis often applied to text data is then applied to visual data. Genuine analytical approaches that apply solely to the analysis of images remain to be developed (Flick 2009). Visual methods are often subject to other methodological approaches to analysis, for example: semiotics, ethnography, content analysis or ethnomethodology. Don't let the sound of these approaches scare you; if you think you would like to explore visual methods it can be a rewarding learning experience in conducting research, so do discuss with your supervisor.

Scenario

You are interested in the clothes that students wear to events – you'd particularly like to know whether practicality in their choices outweighs fashion. At your request, many of your fellow students have sent you photographs of events they have attended over the long break, in which they are the subjects. How will you proceed?

1 What form of analysis could you use?
2 How will you code the images?
3 What will be the basis of your assigning an item of clothing as practical or fashionable?
4 What other aspects of the event, may be relevant, e.g. indoors/outdoors?

Summary

This chapter has discussed:

- Coding and memo writing
- Various analytic tools that you can use to code qualitative data
- Several different forms of qualitative analysis
- The means of analysing images, both stills and video
- The role of the producer and the viewer.

Further reading

Journals

The Journal of Visual Culture contains a range of articles, although not specific to events management.
Derrett, R. (2003) 'Making sense of how festivals demonstrate a community sense of place', *Event Management*, 8: 49–58, uses visual observations of community festival participants to draw conclusions on attendees' sense of belonging as a result of going to the festival.

Books

The following books all discuss analysing text as data:

Bernard, H. R. and Ryan, G. W. (2010) *Analyzing Qualitative Data: Systematic Approaches*. London: Sage Publications.
Miles, M. B. and Huberman, A. M. (1994) *Qualitative Data Analysis*, 2nd edn. London: Sage Publications.
Richards, L. (2009) *Handling Qualitative Data*, 2nd edn. London: Sage Publications.
Saldaña, J. (2009) *The Coding Manual for Qualitative Researchers*. London: Sage Publications.

Whilst these cover analysing images:

Banks, M. (2008) *Using Visual Data in Qualitative Research*. London: Sage Publications.
Flick, U. (2009) *An Introduction to Qualitative Research*, 4th edn. London: Sage Publications, pp. 239–253.
Silverman, D. (2006) *Interpreting Qualitative Data*, 3rd edn. London: Sage Publications, pp. 241–267.

Chapters 1 and 2 of Rose's book below are particularly good at capturing the context and scope of visual research methods. Chapter 1 captures the range of visual methodologies and Chapter 2 captures the compositional interpretation that can be applied to visual materials.

Rose, G. (2001) *Visual Methodologies: An Introduction to the Interpretation of Visual Materials*. London: Sage Publications.

Web links

Banks, M. (1995) *Visual Methods in Social Research*. Guildford: University of Surrey. Online. Available HTTP: http://sru.soc.surrey.ac.uk/SRU11/SRU11.html (accessed 14 August 2013), discusses visual records produced by the researcher and those being studied.

Videolinks

Visual Research Methodologies: Dr Rasoul Mowatt Part 1 (10.0 minutes). Online. Available HTTP: www.youtube.com/watch?v=phuh-0ibJh8. This video gives a good overview of visual research methodologies. It is part 1 of a 6-part series, so if you enjoy it, carry on!

Analysing numbers

Album sales are down for the seventh year in a row (*NME* 2012b). At the same time UK fans spent £1.45 billion on gigs in 2009 – up 4 per cent from 2008 despite the ongoing recession, according to the songwriters' body PRS For Music (Youngs 2010). Williams (2010) in her blog questions whether 'Music Festivals [are] offline versions of online Communities'; she goes on to say 'if Social Media is bringing like-minded people together online, music festivals are bringing bodies together offline', suggesting that 'at a time when the record companies claim music is in dire straits it seems live music is more popular than ever'.

For the music festival organiser, however, the challenge remains that of ensuring the quality, timing, access, satisfaction, etc., are all appropriate. This brings us to our discussion on 'can surveys help?' Although surveys might not give an accurate answer, they should be able to guide the decision maker to make an informed decision. This leads us on to consider how to measure variables, how to identify the relationships, how to compare frequencies, and for instance how to identify the relationship between visitor types and event and their satisfaction levels, spending, etc.

Introduction

Chapter 9 explored the different types of variable that you may want to use and briefly explained the implications of each type. This chapter will take that exploration further, examining the types of data, and then move on to explain about the main statistical tests you may need to use, before finally working through some of these tests in greater detail. This chapter has been written purely for the non-statistician, with the focus being placed on the implications of each test rather than the mathematical formulation or proofs underpinning each of the tests.

Identifying the right test which will allow you to answer your research questions can be a challenge. As a researcher you need to understand what types of test are required for you to gain a better understanding of how your data helps to answer your research question. But before even you start thinking about the type of test you are going to use, you need to know your data. In the following section we discuss exploring the data, and then move on to identify different types of data and the different associated tests.

Exploring data

Imagine you are organising an event for a group. For you to be able to prepare the event and make sure that it is appropriate to your aims, you need know for whom the event is being staged, how many participants you could expect (approximately), for what sort of duration the event will run and whether there are any other aspects that would determine the size and location of the event, etc. To answer these questions you need to collect information (data) and before you start applying research methods to these data you need to understand what you have collected. For instance, how many respondents have you had? What are the demographics of the respondents? And so on.

In Chapter 9 we briefly mentioned the demographic questions, in terms of where such questions should be placed (sequencing) in the questionnaire. Almost every questionnaire will need some form of descriptive or demographic background questions.

Descriptive data

Can you think why it is worth showing the profile of the data you have collected in your data analysis? The profile of the data will allow you to put the data into context; it helps to explain the sample size, whether it is people (as is often the case in events management), or places, or companies. There are ways of deriving the appropriate sample size based on this background information. This is because it is likely that there are differences between people from different (for instance, socio-economic) back-grounds, or differences between age groups or gender. Therefore it is useful to have this information so that the researcher can explore whether there are differences in the responses explained by demographic differences.

Now let us to take a look at a sample of data and see what this means, beginning with Figure 12.1, in which we have selected two variables, age and gender.

Table 12.1 shows that 395 people responded and that they can be broken down into different age bands (note that the age bands must not overlap), by gender and by the

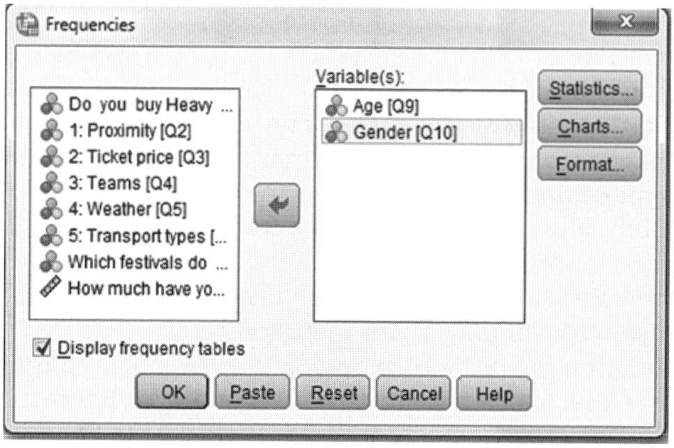

Figure 12.1 Sample of frequencies

Table 12.1 Descriptive differences of respondents

Age in band	Frequency	Percentage
18<	1	0.3
18–29	65	16.45
30–39	80	20.2
40–49	99	25.0
50–59	84	21.26
60–65	56	14.1
65+	8	2.0
Missing	1	0.3
Gender		
Male	195	50.4
Female	199	49.4
Missing	1	0.3

distribution of responses; these are shown in the frequency column and also in terms of the percentage of the total attributable to each category or grouping. There is also a 'missing' row, which shows the number of respondents who did not fill in the box(es). The percentage column provides a better picture in terms of the distribution of respondents by age and gender. One of the most important things when you collect data is ensuring that the proportion of respondents falling into each of the categories is a good reflection of the overall population, otherwise you may have biased results. For example, if you had received 49.4 per cent of your total responses from female respondents and 50.4 per cent from male respondents.

The descriptive tests/frequency tests give you a series of options from which you can choose and in SPSS, for example, you will find that there is a series of boxes from which you can select the tests you wish to run. You need to be aware that just because there is a series of boxes there, you cannot tick all the boxes, as some of them may not be relevant to the type of data you have collected. Consider a quick question. For the example shown in Table 12.1, do you think you can tick the box which selects the descriptive statistic 'mean' when you are considering the gender variable?

The answer is obviously no, you cannot because gender is a categorical type of variable and therefore you can only choose to look at the frequency and it makes no sense at all to measure the average of males and females. In order to explain your data with respect to gender it is really the frequency of responses, the percentage of frequency, and mode, although even mode itself is meaningless because mode simply presents us with the most frequent response, and with respect to the male versus female responses you will be able to tell which one is the most frequent simply by looking at the frequency percentage.

Some researchers might calculate the standard deviation when working with ordinal variables. Do you think this an appropriate tool to use?

Our preferred answer is that nobody would try to calculate the standard deviation for data based on a Likert scale as that would involve several invalid arithmetic operations on a non-numeric scale. So how do they do it? Would they? They would use median as the central tendency and the upper and lower quartiles as an indication of dispersion. Of course, you can calculate means and SDs for such variables (and many people do, especially in the social sciences). The question as to what these numbers actually mean is an interesting one; but it is not a question that seems to engage many who use these values on Likert scales.

Putting ticks into boxes to select the descriptive statistics associated with your data set seems to be a very easy task, but it is important to select the right options from those available to demonstrate that you understand the nature of your data and that your understanding of the types of variables you have collected extends into the areas appropriate for your level of research.

Event research in action

Edwards et al. (2011) undertook a study entitled 'Beyond tourism benefits' in association with Business Events Sydney to measure the social legacies of business events. They carried out an online survey of 1,090 attendees to five international

(Continued)

Event research in action (continued)

congresses held in Sydney, Australia, between 2009 and 2011. The congress attendees comprised delegates, sponsors, exhibitors and members of the organising committee. A key finding of the study was that:

Congress attendees are not a homogenous [sic] group. Significant differences were identified between: males and females; younger age groups and older age groups; delegates with less than 5 years' experience in the field and those with greater experience; academics and practitioners; and international and domestic delegates.

(Edwards et al. 2011: vii)

Before reporting their results it was vital to show who had completed the online survey if their findings, and the recommendations they made on the basis of them, were to be of value. They began the findings and discussion section of their report with a subsection headed 'Respondent characteristics'. First they reported the gender of the respondents – 63 per cent were male and 37 per cent were female. However, there was considerable variation within the five congresses and so they also included a table showing the gender by congress. Then they reported the age distribution, which overall showed a greater proportion of older delegates. Thereafter they gave the split between domestic and international delegates, the place of residence of attendees by region and the length of time respondents had worked in their main occupation. Further detailed breakdowns of the respondents' characteristics were given in the appendices.

In the following sections of this chapter we will go through some of the tests that tend to be popularly used in your discipline. The focus is on the application of these tests, as much as this is possible, rather than an explanation of the way in which these tests are calculated or their proofs. For those of you who are more interested in the latter, there is an indicative list of references at the end of this chapter that should help. The difficulty is to understand the principles associated with some of the tests and to become more familiar with the use of SPSS. Once you know where things are within the SPSS software, understand about terms such as 'sig.' or 'p' values and know what each test can do for you, then you are on the road to understanding these aspects of research methods.

Crosstabulation: Pearson chi-square

Categorical variables are those variables that are not *ordinal* or *continuous* (interval). Such variables are those where the response belongs to either one category or another. For instance, with the demographics of a person, they can be either male or female. The value for this type of variable is arbitrary, which means that the value being given to them, such as a value of 1 for females or 2 for males, etc., is simply a device we use to be able to identify which responses are from a respondent from a specific gender. Now we are clear about the characteristics of categorical variables, the following example will look at the application of crosstabulation.

You might have always thought, instinctively or through observation, that males tend to like heavy metal music more than females, but is it possible to actually see if there is any relationship between choice of music and gender? The simple answer to this question is yes, you should be able to get an answer of sorts, for instance, by running a crosstabulation and looking at a test statistic known as chi-square.

To make this investigation a bit more formal you can set a hypothesis. If your prediction is that there is a relationship between gender and the types of music respondents like, this will be your explanatory hypothesis. Assuming there is not a relationship

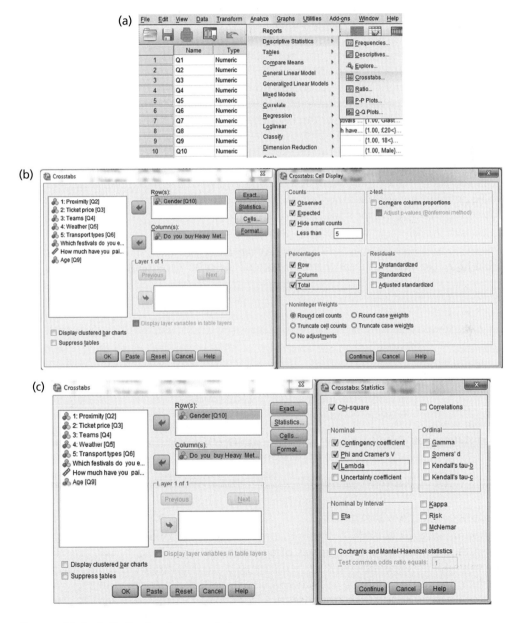

Figure 12.2 Cell display in crosstabs

between gender and the choice of music therefore becomes your null hypothesis. What the chi-square test will do for you is to compare the frequencies you observe in certain categories, assuming that the variables are independent and that there is no relationship between the variables. However, if the significance value for the chi-square statistic is less than 0.05 then it suggests that the variables (music choice and gender) are somehow related.

Figure 12.2 shows the dialogue box from SPSS so that you can see which options you need to select when faced with the crosstabs statistics. One important point that you should take into consideration is the fact that you have a contingency table of 2×2. In this example, then, you need to ask for expected counts because, for the chi-square to be precise, your expected count should be more than 5; for some larger tables up to 20 per cent of the expected frequency showing less than 5 may be quite acceptable. This is because chi-square tests are 'approximate' tests and so for approximate tests you need to understand the conditions under which the approximation is good enough to use. Now you might ask, what do you do if you have more of your expected count less than 5? For a contingency table of 2×2 you can, instead of looking at the value of the chi-square, take the value of the Fisher test into account (see Table 12.3).

The crosstabs table (Table 12.2) shows the number of respondents that fall into the male and female categories. It can be seen that 122 said they 'definitely would not buy (heavy metal songs)' and 132 said that they 'definitely would buy [heavy metal songs]'. It can also be seen that there were 125 females and 74 of them said that they definitely would not buy heavy metal songs, which is 60.7 per cent of the total female respondents. Out of the 129 male respondents, 48 of them said they would not buy, which is just

Table 12.2 'Do you buy heavy metal songs?' gender crosstabulation

Do you buy heavy metal songs?		Gender		
		Female	Male	Total
Definitely would not buy	Count	74	48	122
	Expected count	60.0	62.0	122.0
	% within Do you buy heavy metal songs?	60.7%	39.3%	100.0%
	% within gender	59.2%	37.2%	48.0%
	% of total	29.1%	18.9%	48.0%
Definitely would buy	Count	51	81	132
	Expected count	65.0	67.0	132.0
	% within Do you buy heavy metal songs?	38.6%	61.4%	100.0%
	% within gender	40.8%	62.8%	52.0%
	% of total	20.1%	31.9%	52.0%
Total	Count	125	129	254
	Expected count	125.0	129.0	254.0
	% within Do you buy heavy metal songs?	49.2%	50.8%	100.0%
	% within gender	100.0%	100.0%	100.0%
	% of total	49.2%	50.8%	100.0%

39.3 per cent of the total. You might at this point think this result shows that men are much more in favour of heavy metal songs than their female counterparts, but this finding so far is not sufficient to indicate such a conclusion, and you need to look at the Pearson chi-square statistics (shown in Table 12.3).

The *Pearson chi-square* statistic examines to see if there is an association between two categorical variables. In our example, these variables are gender and whether or not they decide to buy heavy metal songs. Table 12.3 shows the result of the chi-square test as part of the crosstabs output generated by SPSS, and it shows the value of the chi-square statistic and its significance value. The Pearson chi-square tests to see if the two variables are independent. But if the asymptotic significance value (asymp. sig.) is smaller than 0.05 then this means we can reject our null hypothesis that the variables are independent and instead consider them to be in some way related. As Table 12.3 shows, our chi-square statistic, with value of 14.765, is significant at 001 < 0.05 indicating that there is a relationship between gender and choice of heavy metal songs where male respondents seem to have a greater propensity to be associated with buying heavy metal songs than their female counterparts.

As Table 12.3 shows, 0 cells (0 per cent) have an expected count less than 5, which means that the chi-square value can be reported. However, if the results had shown that some of the cells have an expected frequency of less than 5, then the value of the Fisher's Exact Test could instead be reported. As mentioned earlier, the chi-square test is only an approximation and it works well with larger samples. Yates' continuity correction is designed to make the chi-square approximation better, but it is regarded as being 'too conservative' by some (Feinstein 2001), and Field (2005) suggests that this test can be ignored. The challenge is with the smaller sample sizes (and it is difficult to say how small is small, but if you have less than ten in each cell of your table this is likely to be considered small) the chi-square statistic is not accurate, with or without Yates' correction, and Fisher's Exact Test seems to be the best resolution; and yet some other authors have suggested that the Fisher's test gives the exact answer to the wrong question (see Feinstein 2001). Overall, to reject the null hypothesis (variables are independent) the value of the Fisher's Exact Test should be less than 0.05, just like the significance value in chi-square, and you can report it similar to chi-square.

Table 12.3 Chi-square test

Chi-square tests

	Value	df	Asymp. sig. (2-sided)	Exact sig. (2-sided)	Exact sig. (1-sided)
Pearson chi-square	12.299[a]	1	.000		
Continuity correction[b]	11.434	1	.001		
Likelihood ratio	12.399	1	.000		
Fisher's Exact Test				.001	.000
Linear-by-linear association	12.251	1	.000		
N of valid cases	254				

Note:
[a]0 cells (.0%) have expected count less than 5. The minimum expected count is 60.04.
[b]Computed only for a 2×2 table.

Table 12.4 Crosstabulation

	1	2	3	4	5
I buy heavy metal songs	*Strongly disagree*	*Disagree*	*Not agree or disagree*	*Agree*	*Strongly agree*
Female					
Male					

Table 12.5 Collapsed Likert scale

	1	2	3
I buy heavy metal songs	*Disagree*	*Neither agree nor disagree*	*Agree*
Female			
Male			

Question: why can you not confirm an hypothesis?

Logically, there is no statistical test which can confirm an hypothesis; you can only argue that the test statistic is so improbable for the null hypothesis to be true, that it would be reasonable to reject it (the null hypothesis) in favour of the alternative you set before doing the test.

For those occasions when you have a larger contingency table than 2×2, it is said that up to 20 per cent of the cells can have an expected frequency (expected count) of less than 5. Some researchers also suggest that another resolution to this problem is to collapse the data to reduce the possible range of responses. For example, if you have a Likert scale of 1–5 asking respondents to indicate how strongly they agree or disagree with a statement regarding the purchase of heavy metal songs, where 1 is that they strongly disagree with the statement (i.e. they don't buy heavy metal songs) and 5 is where they strongly agree with the statement (see Table 12.4).

So that once you have collected your data and run the crosstabulation routine and realise from the output that you have more than 20 per cent of your expected count less than 5, you can collapse the Likert scale of 1 and 2 to into a single category (call it 1) and leave 3 as a single category but call it 2, and then again collapse 4 and 5 into a single category (call it 3). This way you might be able to get rid of the issue of too many cells with an expected count of less than 5 (see Table 12.5).

However, for the larger contingency tables, where you have ordinal variables, which is true in most instances, there are more advanced tests that you can undertake instead of crosstabulation.

Student vignette

Susi was interested in wedding planning services for her final year dissertation.

I attended two wedding exhibitions in the south of England with the organisers' permission to undertake a survey. The questionnaire focused on the planning stages of the wedding and all other related events pre- and post-wedding ceremony. The aim of the questions was to find out which aspects of wedding celebrations brides choose to include, what they spend on them and how much help they receive planning them. By the end of 3 days 123 questionnaires had been handed out to 'brides-to-be', but only 101 were returned to me. One of the questions in the survey was 'What is the overall budget for your celebrations?' I then wanted to establish whether there was a relationship between the overall budget and whether this was the respondent's first marriage. I used the chi-square test, and the table giving the Pearson chi-square value looked like this:

Chi-square tests	Value	df	Asymp. sig. (2-sided)
Pearson chi-square	10.511[a]	7	.161
Likelihood ratio	12.582	7	.083
Linear-by-linear association	5.396	1	.020
N of valid cases	101		

Note: [a]10 cells (62.5%) have expected count less than 5. The minimum expected count is .12.

Unfortunately, because I only had 101 completed questionnaires and eight categories for the amount of the budget, ten of the cells had a count less than 5 (62.5 per cent). The analysis therefore did not meet the assumptions of the test and I couldn't claim any statistical significance. As it was, the p-value was 0.161 and was therefore greater than 0.05, so there was no statistical significance at the 95 per cent confidence level anyway. I thought it was interesting, though, that 20 per cent of the first weddings cost more than £20,000, whereas none of the second or subsequent marriages cost this much.

The following section provides you with an example of a test that can be used to replace the chi-square test for ordinal variables. But before we go to that we need to run through some of the fundamental concepts that allow you to choose the most appropriate tests.

Normal vs. non-normal distribution

Definition box

A *normal distribution* is a pattern for the distribution of a set of data which is symmetrical. That is there is a similar number of low values as high values, with most values being in the middle. It is referred to as a bell shaped curve because it is concentrated in the centre and decreases on either side.

The distribution of your data has got a lot to do with the type of test that you will be using for your analysis. However, some people ignore this fact and go on to produce results that are likely to be incorrect (Field 2005). The distribution of your data can either be normal (see Graph 12.1) or non-normal (see Graphs 12.2 and 12.3).

Practical tip box

How do you know if the data you have collected is distributed normally or not? Once you have collected your data and have entered them on to your software, such as SPSS, you can plot a graph and see how many times each score is repeated. By score we mean, for example, if you have age in different bands, how many times you get responses from people who fall into each age group. To do this you simply go to analysis in SPSS, choose frequency and use histogram (Figure 12.3) that will give you the shape of the frequency distribution curve.

The frequency distribution curve may not be represented by a normal distribution curve as shown in Graph 12.1, but may be similar to that shown in Graphs 12.2 or 12.3.

This also enables you to immediately see the mode, which is represented by the tallest bar in the graph. You can then look at your data to find out how close your data are to a normal distribution. If you put a ruler, or draw a vertical line through the centre of the distribution (see Graph 12.4) you will immediately be able to see if you have a symmetric shape (which means that both sides of the central line are identical, like a mirror image of each other). If your data do have such a distribution (normal) you can use *parametric tests*. In reality parametric tests require data from a large sample and from a population which meets other assumptions (see Field 2005).

Graph 12.2 shows almost a normal distribution, although one can argue this is not a normal distribution given that the left and right side of the centre don't look exactly the

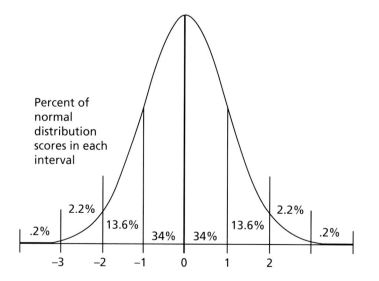

Graph 12.1 A normal distribution

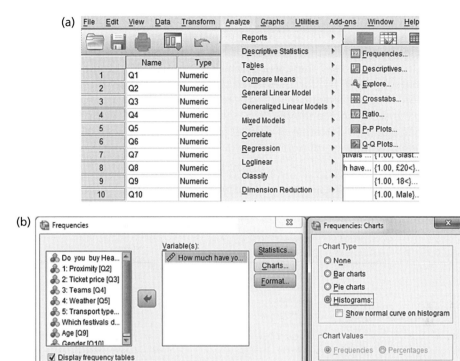

Figure 12.3 Plotting a histogram

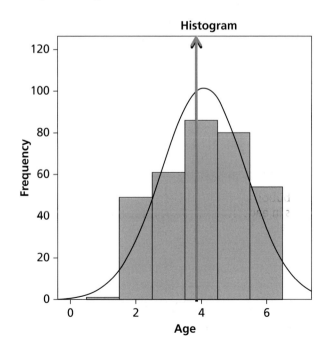

Graph 12.2 Age distribution

same. Although in contrast one could argue that the majority of scores (frequency) lie around the centre of distribution and as we get further away from the centre (mode) the bars get smaller. In other words as we get further away from the centre age the scores become less frequent. Indeed there is a common bias towards histograms and it does seem to be very subjective, but for cases when one cannot be certain on the distribution, Kolmogorov-Smirnov and Shapiro-Wilk tests can help. Field (2005) argues that they actually compare the scores in the sample to a normally distributed set of scores with the same mean and standard deviation. If the test is non-significant (p > 0.05) it tells us that the distribution of sample is not significantly different from a normal distribution.

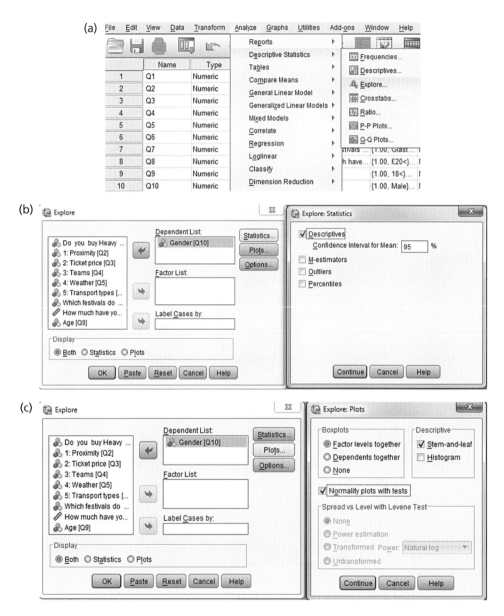

Figure 12.4 Dialogue boxes for the explore command

SPSS will create a table showing the descriptive statistics first, followed by the information shown in Table 12.6. The K test (see Table 12.6) is the important one.

Table 12.6 contains the test statistic, the degrees of freedom which should be equal to the sample size, in our case 394, and the significance value of this. As mentioned above, a significance value (p-value) smaller than 0.05 shows a deviation from normality and therefore, in this case it indicates that the distribution of age is not normal. For further details see Field (2005).

Question: What if you use a Likert scale? Can you look at the distribution and use parametric tests if, by any chance, you have a normal distribution?

The simplistic, purist answer is something like: NO! But it is much more subtle than this, and there are many things to consider. So, a better provisional answer is: not if you have an acceptable non-parametric test.

Types of test

Now that we know that the types of test you can use will very much depend on the distribution of your data, we can look at some of the tests that you can use to measure these variables, or to make comparisons between the different groups, to test your hypotheses.

Imagine you have a group of male and a group of female respondents and you want to find out if there is a difference in terms of the level of enjoyment that they derived from participating in the Glastonbury Festival. You design a statement which states 'I enjoyed Glastonbury', where 1 indicates that the respondent strongly disagrees with the statement and 5 indicates that the respondent strongly agrees. The intervening scores indicate varying degrees of agreement or disagreement. The easiest way to tackle this will be to look at the percentage (frequencies) of responses and see which group seems to be more in agreement or more in disagreement with the statement to determine which group enjoyed the Festival more, males or females (see Table 12.7).

Table 12.6 Test for normality

	Kolmogorov-Smirnova[a]			Shapiro-Wilk		
	Statistic	df	Sig.	Statistic	df	Sig.
Gender	.344	394	.000	.636	394	.000

Note: [a]Lilliefors significance correction.

Table 12.7 Frequency percentage for each scale

	1	2	3	4	5
I enjoyed Glastonbury	Strongly disagree	Disagree	Neither agree nor disagree	Agree	Strongly agree
Female	17.08	51.25	26.13	4.02	1.50
Male	36.2	47.15	15.02	0.51	1.03

But using the percentage of frequency does not seem to be statistically sufficient because it does not tell us whether this difference is statistically significant or has simply happened by chance.

So the next question will be, what sort of test can you use to measure the differences between the two groups and how can we find out if any differences are statistically significant? Both the T-test and the Mann Whitney U can be employed, as they are both applicable when you have two independent groups; in this case your groups are males and females. The next question is, which of these tests should you use? Strictly speaking you need to look at the distribution of your data. To use the T-test you at least need to have a normal distribution; if not then Mann Whitney U is the appropriate test to use.

To look at this within your software (SPSS) you need to go to 'analysis', and then choose 'frequency', and then select 'chart' and click on the option for 'histogram with normal curve'. The result is shown in Graph 12.3.

If you look at the distribution of the data each side of the central line, it is obvious that the distribution of frequencies is not symmetric. In other words, the left and right sides are not mirror images of each other and therefore you can assume that you do not have a normal distribution. This means that it is better to run non-parametric tests and therefore the Mann Whitney U test is appropriate. You can also assume that given you were dealing with responses to a Likert scale, the chances of having a normal distribution were quite remote.

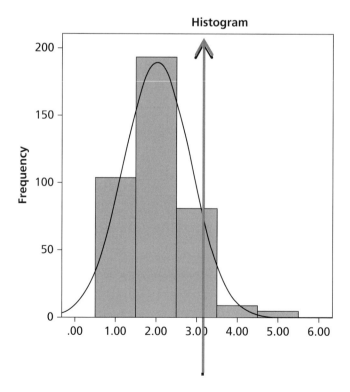

Graph 12.3 Non-symmetrical distribution

To run the Mann Whitney U Test you need to go to 'analysis' and then to 'non-parametric test' and select the 'two-independent-sample tests' (see Figure 12.5).

Experiment hypothesis: there is a relationship between gender and the level of enjoyment.

Null hypothesis: there is no relationship between gender and the level of enjoyment.

Table 12.8 shows the results of running the Mann Whitney U test on these data, and it can be seen that the mean rank of females is higher than the mean rank of males, indicating that females seem to derive more enjoyment from going to the Glastonbury Festival than their male counterparts (see Table 12.8). The higher mean rank means

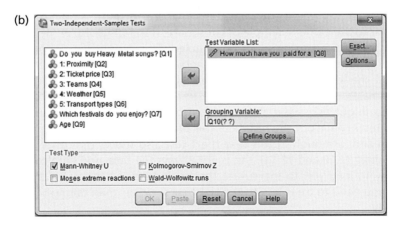

Figure 12.5 Two independent samples, Mann Whitney U

Table 12.8 Mean ranks

	Gender	N	Mean rank	Sum of ranks
I enjoyed Glastonbury	Female	199	221.59	44097.00
	Male	193	170.63	32931.00
	Total	392		

Table12.9 Test statistics[a]

	I enjoyed Glastonbury
Mann Whitney U	14210.000
Wilcoxon W	32931.000
Z	−4.820
Asymp. sig. (2-tailed)	.000

Note: [a]Grouping variable: 6. Gender?

Table 12.10 Group statistics

	Gender	N	Mean	Std deviation	Std error mean
I enjoyed	Female	199	2.2161	.82789	.05869
Glastonbury	Male	193	1.8290	.77513	.05579

greater satisfaction because of the way that the Likert scale was constructed with higher scores being associated with higher enjoyment (see Table 12.8).

Thus, the next question to ask is whether or not this difference is statistically significant, and this can be observed in Table 12.9. Table 12.9 shows the results of the non-parametric tests where the important element in there is asymp. sig. (2-tailed). This is similar to the earlier example of chi-square, if the value sig. or 'p-value' is smaller than 0.05, the null hypothesis can be rejected. This suggests we should favour the alternative hypothesis because the results indicate that there is a difference between gender and the level of enjoyment, as females seem to have enjoyed Glastonbury more than males.

Now you might ask, what if we had employed the T-test instead of the Mann Whitney U test? I have put the results of the T-test here for you as well just to show the comparison and, although in this case the T-test also shows that difference is significant (see Tables 12.10 and 12.11), this is not always the case, and employing the wrong test is likely to lead you to inaccurate results. Indeed, once you have identified the symptom, you need to treat it with the right cure, rather than taking the risk of doing it doubtfully.

Indeed the T-test as it is shown in Table 12.11 calculates the SD, whereas the variables we are dealing with are ordinal and therefore the results are quite meaningless.

Table 12.11 Independent samples test

		Levene's test for equality of variances		T-test for equality of means						95% confidence interval of the difference	
		F	Sig.	t	df	Sig. (2-tailed)	Mean difference	Std error difference		Lower	Upper
I enjoyed Glastonbury	Equal variances assumed	.484	.487	4.775	390	.000	.38706	.08106		.22770	.54643
	Equal variances not assumed			4.780	389.520	.000	.38706	.08098		.22786	.54627

Other conditions

The next point to consider is the fact that you do not always have just two independent groups, and might have more than this. Can you think of any examples? For example, you might have people of differing age groups attending the Glastonbury Festival and therefore you may be interested to see if the age group plays a significant role in determining the level of enjoyment of participants. In this sort of situation you can use either ANOVA or Kruskal Wallis; these two tests also use the same assumptions as the T-test and Mann Whitney U, where the former is a parametric test and so the data need to be distributed normally and the latter is non-parametric test and therefore is more relaxed in terms of the assumption regarding the distribution of your data. The procedure is similar to that undertaken in the previous example; you will first need to look at the distribution of the data and, if it is normally distributed, you will choose ANOVA over Kruskal Wallis. For details of how to run this test, see Field (2005).

> Brian is trying to find out if he can predict people's satisfaction levels by looking at the way their team has performed in a sporting event and their attitudes towards the particular sports venue. The reason for this is that the event organiser wants to know if it is only the physical attributes of the event that affect people's attitudes towards that venue or whether there are other factors important in determining successful events. So how could Brian measure if the level of satisfaction can determine attitudes?

This example goes one step further and is trying to set a hypothesis which states that two kinds of quantities vary together in some predictable way. If more satisfaction results in a more positive attitude towards the venue, then it can be said that there is a positive correlation between the two variables, and if more satisfaction results in a more negative attitude then it can be concluded there is a negative relationship between the two. In either case we are looking at correlation as a means to measuring the relationship. The principle here is no different to that used during the other tests. You need to first look at the distribution of your data. If it is normal distribution then the Pearson correlation can be employed and if the distribution of the data is non-normal, which is likely to be the case when handling ordinal variables, then the Spearman correlation is the important statistic. Correlation looks at two things. First it looks at the strength of the relationship, and if so then it tries to determine whether or not the relationship is significant (p-value smaller than 0.05). Table 12.12 summarises these tests.

In the social sciences many of the variables (but not all) are ordinal variables and this will lead you to undertaking non-parametric tests. It is similar if you have interval data which can also lead you to using non-parametric tests, if your sample size is small (which means you will not have enough data to give you the characteristic bell shape to your frequency histogram). With categorical types of data you are only able to use tests that can compare aspects such as frequencies (e.g. chi-square).

This chapter has only managed to touch the surface of these issues, but is intended to make you aware of these aspects so that you can take them into account without going into the formulae and mathematics that underpin them.

Table 12.12 A selection of some of the tests

Normal distribution	Non-normal distribution	Application
T-test	Mann Whitney U	Look at the two groups to see if there are differences between them
ANOVA	Kruskal Wallis	Look at more than two groups to see if there are differences between them
Pearson correlation	Spearman and Kendall's Tau	Try to predict a change in one variable from changes in other variables
Crosstabulation chi-square	Not applicable	Compares the frequency

Scenario

Organisers of a major new international surfing competition have commissioned a survey of participants in existing competitions in Australia, South Africa, the USA and the UK. However, they are concerned when they read the results that the sample of surfers who completed a questionnaire may not be representative of surfers in these countries, and that the results may not be generalisable to surfers in other countries around the world.

● What descriptive statistics should they want to see to reassure them?
● Which statistical tests would they expect to have seen performed on the data?
● Why these tests?

Summary

This chapter has highlighted:

● Which statistical tests to use and when it is appropriate to use them.
● You should know that, by exploring your data to determine whether or not the distribution of it is normal or non-normal, you can choose a test that takes this distribution into account.
● You should be able to understand or acquire a feel about your data once you have designed the questionnaire (research instrument) you'll use to collect it.

Further reading

Journals

Cheng, E. and Jarvis, N. (2010) 'Residents' perception of the social-cultural impacts of the 2008 Formula 1 Singtel Singapore Grand Prix'. *Event Management*, 14: 91–106. This article reports the results of a residents' survey to elicit responses to host residents' perceptions of social-cultural impacts of the F1. This is a good example of how chi-square analysis was used to explore relationships between different types of respondents and their perceived social-cultural impacts.

Books

The following books can help you with quantitative analysis:

Field, A. (2005) *Discovering Statistics Using SPSS*, 2nd edn. London: Sage Publications.
Malhotra, N. and Birks, D. F. (2006) *Marketing Research: An Applied Approach*, 3rd edn. Harlow: Prentice Hall.
Pallant, J. (2010) *SPSS Survival Manual*, 4th edn. Maidenhead: Open University Press.

Web links

A comprehensive guide to data analysis using SPSS can be found at: Gaur, A. S. and Gaur, S. S. (2009) *Statistical Methods for Practice and Research*, 2nd edn. London: Sage Publications. Online. Available HTTP: www.scribd.com/doc/30873720/Guide-to-Data-Analysis-Using-SPSS#page=133 (accessed 4 August 2013).

GraphPad Software (2013) 'Ordinal, interval and ratio variables'.Online. Available HTTP: www.graphpad.com/guides/prism/6/statistics/index.htm?the_different_kinds_of_variable.htm (accessed 10 August 2013), sets out in their section on ordinal, interval and ratio variables what you can display in your results page, with respect to each type of variable you have collected.

Video links

More information on chi-square analysis is available from: *Chi-square Analysis on SPSS* (4.15 minutes). Online Available HTTP: www.youtube.com/watch?v=Ahs8jS5mJKk (accessed 4 August 2013).

SPSS for Beginners 2: Frequency Counts and Descriptive Statistics (10.19 minutes). Online. Available HTTP: www.youtube.com/watch?v=4CWeHF3Mn00 (accessed 4 August 2013), guides you on the basics of analysis using SPSS.

Data set for lecturers (see Chapter 12 SPSS file)

Chapter 13

'Ending at the beginning'

Chapter learning outcomes

In this chapter we:

- Suggest approaches to assist you in evaluating your research effectively
- Discuss how to organise the material from your study
- Provide guidance on creating the macro- and microstructure of the research output
- Give advice on writing up research.

Kate had finished evaluating her findings and was about to begin writing up her dissertation, when she received an email from her tutor asking whether she would like to present her research at a national undergraduate conference. She was immediately pleased as she realised that her tutor must have been impressed with what she had done so far. She hoped that this was a good sign that the outcome that she sought from her dissertation, that is, a high mark, was definitely achievable. She read the conference guidelines carefully and saw that she had a choice of submitting a poster or presenting for 20 minutes. She decided that giving a presentation would be more nerve-racking but would look good on her CV and give her something to talk about when she had an interview for a graduate job. Writing an abstract was fairly easy – she based it on her research proposal and briefly added the findings and conclusion. She sent it off, together with the completed form asking her faculty to pay the conference costs, and crossed her fingers.

Kate had forgotten all about the conference as she concentrated on her lectures and assignments and was therefore surprised when there was an email in her in-box from the conference organisers informing her that her abstract had been accepted. She forwarded it to her tutor and made an appointment to thank her for recommending that she apply and to discuss the presentation. Her tutor suggested at the meeting that she aim for a maximum of eighteen PowerPoint slides, which with an opening and closing slide would be about one a minute for the 15 minutes she would have to present. The remaining 5 minutes, her tutor reminded her, was for questions from the audience.

As Kate began preparing the slides she realised that this was a very good way of summarising her research and seeing the most important points that she'd want to make. This was really helpful as she wrote the final chapter of her dissertation. She was glad that she had taken some photographs as she had collected her data, as these enhanced the look of the presentation. Her tutor made a few comments when Kate showed her the presentation and by the time she had acted on the suggestions, Kate was confident that she had a good presentation. Then all she had to worry about was what to wear!

Introduction

This chapter ends where this book began in Chapter 1; that is with the output of the research. This could be, for example, a report, dissertation or presentation. We begin by considering how to organise the content, suggest ways to help make decisions about the main sections and then provide some advice on writing up. First, however, you need to consider how effective you have been in undertaking your research and whether a reader can place trust in your findings; that is, you need to evaluate the study.

Reliability, validity and trustworthiness

Imagine that a researcher has collected a sample of 200 questionnaires to discover the perceptions of local people regarding the congestion resulting from football matches played every Saturday in their neighbourhood. The results suggest that local people in general are fairly happy with the way traffic is managed. The findings of this research are supposed to inform policy makers so that they can take them into account for their future planning. However, the committee that received the researcher's report are not convinced by the results and they ask for exactly the same questionnaire survey to be undertaken again to verify the results from the earlier study. This time the results present quite a different picture, suggesting that local people are not at all happy with the congestion levels and traffic management, prior to and after football matches.

Reliability in research

This is a typical scenario where the reliability of the research is questionable. Reliability refers to the fact that results of these two rounds of survey should have been consistent. In other words, the results from the first survey should have been duplicated by the results from the second survey.

As discussed in Chapter 7 regarding sampling, reliability can present more of a challenge when the sampling undertaken is non-random, which means that it is likely that the sample is not representative of the population. This, however, doesn't mean random sampling guarantees reliability, nor does it mean that non-random sampling will provide non-reliable data. However, in general one would expect random sampling to provide reliable results if it has been collected correctly. More importantly, in such cases, the tests of significance would also make sense. However, as demonstrated in Chapter 7, if the data is collected non-randomly then rejecting hypotheses based on significant differences is somewhat meaningless. Remember, that tests of significance try to ensure that the results cannot simply be down to chance. When the sampling method is, for example, convenience sampling, it is more likely that results could indeed have happened as a result of chance or accident.

There are, of course, other issues that may affect the reliability of research outcomes, such as when one uses parametric tests on non-parametric data sets.

Validity

In addition to reliability, it is important that statistical outcomes of research also have a high degree of validity if they are to be trusted. Validity refers to whether or not the research measures what it is intended to measure. It can be argued that checking the validity of research is easier when undertaking quantitative research than when undertaking qualitative research. However, any type of research needs to be designed in such a way that it is both reliable and valid and if not, then this can be considered to be the difference between good research and bad research (ActiveCampaign 2009). A researcher should be concerned with *external validity*, which refers to whether or not you can make generalisations from your research outcomes (see Chapter 7 on sampling). One also needs to be concerned about *internal validity*, which refers to the consistency with which the study was conducted. For studies that try to measure any causal relationship, then, it may be important for the researcher to be able to explain other influences found in the causal relationships.

There are three main types of validity in research. *Face validity* is probably the least scientific term when measuring the validity of a piece of research (Fink 1995). It questions whether or not the research measures what it says it is measuring, whether the research has any face value. For example, does a question being asked make the right sense to the respondents? This issue can be quite subjective, for while a question may make sense to one person it may have a different meaning for another.

Another type of validity is referred to as *construct validity*, which is generally whether or not a scale does in fact correlate or measure the theoretical relationships being hypothesised. For example a researcher may want to find out how stressed students are just before their exams. The researcher might look at indicators such as sleeping hours or lack of appetite and then measure whether these are related to stress levels. But you may counter this by saying that the number of sleeping hours has nothing to do with students being under stress but is more related to social patterns. Construct validity needs to be evaluated on the basis of the correlation between the variables being measured with the theoretical relationships being tested.

Finally, *content validity* is based on the extent to which a measurement reflects the specific intended domain of content (Carmines and Zeller 1991). For example, if a researcher tries to find out how satisfied customers are with a particular event, they might ask about the quality of the venue and based on the answers they receive, conclude that visitors are very happy with the event. However, one might argue that you could have instead asked about the price, the quality of food, the accessibility of the car park and then, with a better set of indicators, explain what is significant in determining the overall satisfaction levels. This again could be a subjective measure because we might all have slightly different views about which variables determine overall satisfaction levels.

Overall, reliability refers to the accuracy of the measuring tools or procedures; validity is concerned with the study's success in precisely measuring what the researchers set out to measure.

Trustworthiness

There is some divergence in relation to the validity and reliability of the output from some forms of data, and sometimes their related analysis. To that end, generally speaking as we discussed above, quantitative data is aligned with positivistic outcomes i.e. data uncovered is 'true and valid' whereas qualitative data does not necessarily fit so easily in that framework. In essence, other terms of reference can and should be applied to data findings that are able to justify their 'worthiness'. Denzin and Lincoln (2000: 21) point out that the more common positivist criteria of 'validity, reliability, and objectivity' is giving way to terms such as 'credibility, transferability, dependability, and conformability' in qualitative accounts of research. In undertaking qualitative forms of data collection, a researcher should be able to offer in-depth examination, interpretation and analysis in addressing the research objectives. Indeed, if qualitative data is subject to being interpreted by different approaches (see e.g. Chapters 5 and 12) and not necessarily in pursuit of 'truths', then 'by creating different truth-criteria ... such as conformability, trustworthiness and transparency' (Tribe 2006: 369), a researcher is able to demonstrate that rigorous analysis has been applied to the data.

Richards (2009: 198) suggests that a good qualitative output should:

- Address your purpose and goal, giving an answer to your 'researchable question'
- Offer analysis, not just description
- Offer at least a new theory or explanation
- Offer something more than the participants in your research could have reported
- And it should account for your data. This has to be an adequate account, so you will be able to claim that it 'makes sense' of what's going on in the data.

How can you demonstrate that your research is reliable, valid or trustworthy? First, by using credible and correctly referenced reliable, valid and trustworthy sources in your literature review. Then you need to give an honest and detailed account of your methodology, so that the reader can judge for themselves. If the method hasn't gone as planned, and hopefully that won't be the case as you would have piloted it (see Chapter 10), then you have to consider how much impact the error has had. It may have an indirect effect on one small part, so for example, if you discover that a question has been badly worded, you could simply not report the results, provided of course that you are still meeting your aim and objectives. Larger issues need to be clearly pointed out as limitations in the methodology, so that the reader can decide how much reliance they can place on your findings and any recommendations that you might make.

Having evaluated your research, it is now appropriate to begin presenting your findings.

The macrostructure

The macrostructure is the overall scheme of organisation of the research output. What-ever output you need to produce, begin by reading any guidance that has been pro-vided and find a good example to guide you. This can be on a totally different topic, as it is the structure that you want to look at rather than the detailed content at this stage. Next, think about the way you work best; some people like to plan with lists, others see better spatially. If you are a list person, begin by listing the topics, chapters or sections. If you prefer to see matters spatially, you can create a mind map, using either software or pen and paper. Some people use 'post it' notes stuck to the floor or wall. Whichever format you use, make sure that you move the themes around or up or down until you have a structure that you are happy with. A good structure will flow well, like a story; it will have a beginning, middle and end. If you have already pre-pared a *research proposal*, much of the structure will be the same.

A standard format is often:

- Introduction
- Literature review
- Methodology
- Results
- Conclusions and recommendations.

The microstructure

When preparing a report or dissertation, a very useful tool in Microsoft Word 2010 is the 'navigation pane' (formerly 'document map' in Word 2007). You create headings in your document using the appropriate heading styles (for example, 'heading 1' and then subti-tles using 'heading 2' and so on). The heading view shows a group of nested tabs of each of your headings. Figure 13.1 provides an example using student Claire's dissertation on the importance of global event companies understanding divergent cultures.

This allows you to:

- See your headings clearly and check the order
- Ensure that you have not used the same heading twice!
- Move up and down a large document quickly (left-click on the tab in the navigation pane and it jumps the cursor to that position in the document, which saves a lot of scrolling up and down).

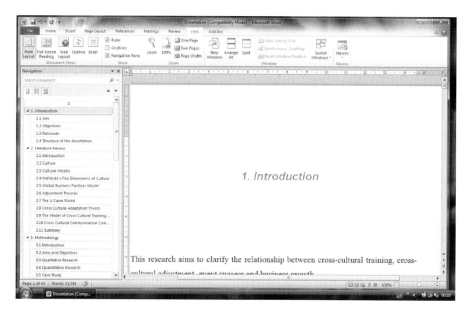

Figure 13.1 Using navigation pane to review section headings

The five stages of research writing

Hannon (2000) suggests that there are five stages of research writing:

- Prewriting
- Drafting
- Revising
- Editing
- Sharing.

Prewriting

You have undertaken much of the prewriting whilst you were making notes on your literature search and carrying out the analysis, for example. Therefore this stage should already be finished.

Drafting

Practical tip box

- Use a chapter format and numbered headings and sub-headings.
- Begin each chapter with an introduction and finish with a summary or conclusion.
- Write in the third person. So do not say 'I sent out questionnaires', or 'the author/researcher sent out questionnaires', but instead 'questionnaires were sent out'.

Only refer to 'the researcher' if it is something particular to you, for example, 'The researcher had been employed at the Company during her placement year and therefore knew ... ' The only exception to using the third person is if you are undertaking some forms of qualitative study, such as an *autoethnography*, when using the first person may be appropriate. To be on the safe side, always specifically agree this with your tutor first, if undertaking a dissertation.

- Use the present tense, except for the methodology chapter which is written in the past tense.
- Students should avoid sounding like an authority on the subject; they are not experts, so avoid saying for example 'in my opinion' or 'in the researcher's opinion'. Similarly, stating what you think or believe is not appropriate.
- Use the correct form of English, whether UK, US or Australian, as appropriate to where the output is being submitted.
- When using an abbreviation, write the term in full on the first occasion that you use it and indicate the abbreviation in brackets. Thereafter use the abbreviation and add it to your list of abbreviations. For example: 'the United States of America (USA) ... ' This is shown in the UK English form of writing. In the United States it is spelt 'U.S.A.' using fullstops or periods. In Chapter 6 we reminded you that if you are showing that there are three or more authors and hence using 'et al.' ('and others'), this has a full stop or period at the end as it is an abbreviation.
- Avoid abbreviating words such as 'can't' and 'won't', so write 'cannot' and 'will not' in full.

How you write your first draft may depend on your approach to time management when working. Some people are polychronic, that is can undertake more than one task at a time. So they may begin a draft whilst they are collecting their data, for example. Other people are monochronic and like to work on one thing at a time (Wilson 2010). Whichever you are, we suggest that you start writing as early as possible. If you leave writing up your research until you have more time, this is often a sign of procrastination and you may run out of time altogether! Also, like any skill, good academic writing requires practice, which does take time. However, the disadvantage of writing earlier rather than later is that your work may require more additions or amendments, which can be annoying.

In Chapter 6 we considered critical evaluation, and linked to this, and another area that many students struggle with, is crafting an argument. An argument is the main idea of your research that should flow throughout your research writing. It is often called a 'claim' or a 'thesis statement'. A good place to begin is 'What is the point of this research?' leaving aside the output or the outcome. So the point of this book is to guide you in the process of undertaking research in the context of events management. Our argument could be that many events students find this a difficult topic to study and that to date there are no other context-specific books that can guide them. We could demonstrate our understanding of this argument by presenting a counter-argument – in our case that would be that there are many general research methods books in publication that a student could use. By discussing this aspect we are demonstrating that we have thought this through and that the reader can therefore dismiss this argument too. The important thing to remember is that your argument must be consistent throughout your writing – don't 'change sides' as you progress from the abstract to the conclusion.

Language

- Always only use words that you understand. If you do not know what the word or sentence means, use a dictionary or ask someone. Consider these two sentences:
  - 'It is our job to continually leverage others' performance-based methods of empowerment.'
  - 'The subject is contextualised into a precapitalist theory that includes truth as a paradox. But the main theme of Dietrich's analysis of dialectic precultural theory is not patriarchialism per se, but postpatriarchialism.'
  Do you understand exactly what is being referred to? Fisher (2007: 341) gives these two very useful examples of how not to write. He refers to these styles of writing as 'Bizno-bollocks' and 'Professorial pompousness'. In fact both of these sentences were computer generated and are meaningless.
- Use language appropriate to the philosophical approach that you have employed, for example, *post-positivist* or *interpretivist* (see Chapter 2). In a *quantitative*, *deductive* study, refer, for example, to *hypotheses/research questions*, respondents, results, *reliability* and *validity*. Whereas in a *qualitative*, *inductive* study, the appropriate terms are *research questions*, participants, findings and *trustworthiness* (see Chapter 7).
- Use non-discriminatory language, although it is sometimes referred to disparagingly as 'political correctness'. So don't use expressions that may be perceived as insulting to a group of people because they are discriminated against or disadvantaged. So avoid sexism and terms such as policeman and waiter, instead use police officer and waiting staff.
- In doing this, don't replace 'he' with 'he/she', but use 'they'. Similarly, not 'his' with 'his/hers' but use 'theirs'.
- Write formally and in an academic style and don't use slang, like 'mojo'. A sign that your sentence structure is too informal is if you use shorter sentences which sound more like a conversation. We have deliberately written this book in an informal style, so that it is more accessible to novice researchers, so please don't copy our style!
- Avoid vagueness, such as 'many researchers suggest ... ' Be specific and state who the researchers are.
- Avoid emotional language, including both positive and negative emotions, so subjects are not 'amazing' or 'dreadful'.
- If you use terms or phrases in a second language, other than the one you are writing in, do not assume that the reader will understand and so provide a translation.

All of these recommendations do not apply of course, if you are either quoting a reference directly or a participant's words in qualitative research.

Using tables, boxes, figures, images and maps

Information can also be provided in formats other than prose, such as tables, boxes (that is, a table with only one column and one or more rows), images and maps. Maps, for example, are a good means of demonstrating the geographic scope of your research (see Chapter 3), but check your institution's requirements as some do not allow the use of boxes, images or maps. Ensure that each format is given a title (caption) and that the font size of any writing is legible in the finished format. Provide the reference for the source as usual, if you have not created it yourself. If you have adapted a table or figure from another source, you should show this as '*Source*: Adapted from Smith and Doe', with the year of publication and page number in the standard format required. It is easier for the reader if you refer to the insertion before it is shown for the first time (for example, 'see Table 1 below'), so that you can explain why they should look at it and how it relates to your study. Thereafter any subsequent mentions of it are shown as '(see Table 1 above)' and it is useful for the reader to give the page number as well. Many of us find reading page after page of text laborious, so judicious use of other formats for presenting information can help break up the text as well as providing the information in a more succinct or clear format.

Revising

Don't expect to get the finished document right first time. You are likely to need to write and rewrite several drafts before it reads well. Ensure that each draft is numbered, for example, v1, v2, v3, and always keep earlier versions in case you need to refer back to them. Remember too, to keep a backup copy of the current version, either on a main server or for students, if this is not possible, email it to yourself from your home email account to your university email address.

As you read a draft, check not only the grammar and spelling but also that there is some variation in the lengths of sentences. If all sentences are short or conversely all are long, the reader finds it a more difficult read. Also, read aloud or vary the format in which you read the draft from a screen to a paper copy. When you have written something and read it back, your mind sees what it expects to see, rather than what is actually there. Reading aloud also demonstrates when your sentences are too long or lack punctuation, because you will run out of breath! If your sentences fail the 'breath test', divide them into two parts or even three. Similarly check that your paragraphs are not too long – they should discuss just one principal point. Finally, check that you have not written 'a laundry list of previous studies, with sentences or paragraphs beginning with the words, "Smith found ... ", "Jones concluded ... ", "Anderson stated ... ", and so on' (Rudestam and Newton 1992: 46).

As you revise your drafts bear in mind that the standard of writing that you are aiming for is so that an educated person, but not an expert in events management, can understand your research.

Practical tip box

Using the 'find' function in Microsoft Word can help you in several ways:

- Type 'n't' into 'find' and it will quickly show you where you have written 'can't', 'won't', etc. by mistake, which you should not use. Do not, however, use the 'replace all' function as it will change quotes, for example, that should not be revised.

(Continued)

> ## Practical tip box (continued)
>
> - If you may have omitted the full stop (period) after 'et al.' in your references, you can go quickly through checking them.
> - Also, you may be aware that you often make the same mistake such as typing 'their' instead of 'there' or vice versa, and again the 'find' function can be useful.
> - To check that you have the correct references in the list at the end, open the chapter and type '19' in 'find' and it will highlight all the references from the twentieth century, so that you can check that they are included. Tick or highlight those that are. Do the same typing in '20' for the twenty-first-century references. You can now see which references you don't need to include in the list because they are not in the text, and those which you have missed out.

Editing

At this stage, it can be very useful to obtain feedback from a colleague or your tutor, but don't ask too many people as they may give you conflicting advice. As you plan the final stages of your research allow sufficient time for a colleague or tutor to read your drafts and for you to make amendments. Students should check too, in their guidance or regulations how often tutors are permitted to read the same chapter. Many institutions allow work to be read on one occasion only. If this is the case, ensure that sufficient time has been allowed to be able to send a later rather than an earlier draft. Remember that a tutor is likely to have many other students' work to read, as well as their other academic duties.

Similarly, if English is not your first language, you should consider the time needed for a proof reader to help you.

Word count

Whilst professional reports are unlikely to have limitations as to the maximum number of words, this will be the case for a journal article and almost definitely for a dissertation. For each, check the submission guidelines as to what precisely is to be included in the word count. For example, often the abstract, tables, references and appendices are excluded.

Table 13.1 shows a typical breakdown of a dissertation word count. However this is only a guide. Again, check the institution's guidance, but if none is given, the percentage marks allocated to each section provide an approximate itemisation. Be aware, however, that these percentages are only approximations, depending on the methodology you have adopted. The literature review is likely to be briefer, if an *inductive* approach has been used and longer, if the approach is *deductive*. If the data is *qualitative* the findings chapter will have a greater word count than if there is *quantitative* data because of the increased number of words in the direct quotes from the participants. Wilson (2010) also points out that if only *secondary data* is used, the methodology chapter may have fewer words.

Table 13.1 Approximate word counts in a dissertation

Chapter	% of overall word count
Introduction	15
Literature review	25
Methodology	25
Results and analysis	25
Conclusion and recommendations	10

Be aware that not all of the data collected has to be used, if you are considerably exceeding a maximum word count. However, you should consider the ethical position of taking up people's time in collecting data that is then not put to good use.

For a dissertation, read carefully any marking criteria that have been supplied to ensure that everything that is required is included. Marks cannot be given for something that is essential but not in the dissertation, however good other sections may be. Similarly for a professional report, ensure that nothing is omitted.

Formatting

Finally check that the instructions regarding font size and double spacing, for example, have been fully complied with. Read the details of the number of copies that are required and the format, whether paper-based or in an electronic format, and ensure that directives regarding binding and submission are understood.

Student vignette

Aimee had worked for O2 during her industry placement. Her final year dissertation was titled 'An exploratory study into O2's events using brand molecule theory'.

Whilst I was working in the O2 Events Team, a mobile network provider in the UK, I read *The Brand Innovation Manifesto: How to Build Brands, Redefine Markets and Defy Conventions*' (Grant 2006). Inspired by this I decided to focus my dissertation project on O2, as I had gained an interest in the company and the events and partnerships that they were involved with. With a large portfolio of events and sponsorships, the company's continued efforts in the sport and music industry was seen by Fletcher (2005), an industry specialist from *Event Magazine* to be pushing 'the company further ahead in the event marketing arena, previously dominated by rival network Orange'. O2 spent on average around £40 million a year on promotional activity, which was considerably less than the £65 million that Orange dedicates each year (Mintel International Group Ltd 2007). With smaller expenditure on promotional activity I wondered how it was that O2 had a larger market share. I was interested in developing a better understanding

(Continued)

Student vignette (continued)

of the culture associated with O2's events and whether employees believed it had something to do with the company's success.

I conducted seven semi-structured interviews with employees from O2's Events and Sponsorship Team. These were recorded and transcribed to assist with analysis. The research showed that the cultural ideas associated with O2's events were much more than the organisation's brand values. This created difficulties in constructing a brand molecule diagram as the cultural ideas associated with O2's events were much interconnected due to integrated campaigns. I soon realised that a three-dimensional diagram would provide a more realistic representation of how the ideas interconnected.

I met my tutor often throughout the process of carrying out the research and we had some interesting discussions at the meetings. Brand molecule theory wasn't one of the areas in which she taught or undertook research; however, after I lent her my copy of Grant's book to read, she became very interested in my topic. As I was drawing to the end of the process, she asked if she could present my research at the Global Events Congress (Figure 13.2). I was working in New York at the time of the conference, so couldn't attend, but it was really great to see my research reach an audience of academics and industry practitioners from around the world.

Brand molecule theory: An exploratory study of a telecommunication company's events

Aimee Goodwin and Dr Dorothy Fox

Global Events Congress IV: Events and Festivals Research:
State of the Art
The Rose Bowl, Leeds
14th – 16th of July 2010

dfox@bournemouth.ac.uk

Figure 13.2 The opening slide from the conference presentation

Sharing

Upon completion, you have to submit your study for assessment or dissemination to interested parties as a formal output based on the reasons for undertaking the research. It is also good to invite participants who have contributed to your study if doing qualitative research, to read your work, or to send it to employers or other organisations that have supported you in the study as acknowledgement and thanks for their backing.

In the next section, the specific requirements of a dissertation are discussed, but many of the suggestions are also appropriate to other prose-based formats such as a journal article or professional report. Specific differences with these are highlighted at the end. Thereafter, the creation of a presentation is considered.

The individual sections of a dissertation

These are usually very similar to the list below, but do check your organisation's guidelines. The discussion of the results or findings is shown in brackets in Chapters 4 and 5, because they often fit better with the findings in a qualitative piece of research and with the conclusions and recommendations in quantitative research. However, there is no fixed rule, just select which chapter suits your study better.

- Title page
- Acknowledgements
- Abstract
- List of abbreviations
- List of tables
- List of figures
- List of images
- Contents page
- Chapter 1: Introduction
- Chapter 2: Literature review
- Chapter 3: Research methodology
- Chapter 4: Results/findings/(discussion)
- Chapter 5: (discussion) Conclusions and recommendations
- References
- Appendices.

However, we suggest you write the dissertation starting with the chapter you feel most comfortable with. This is often not the introduction chapter, but the literature review; and then progress as follows:

1 Literature review (initial draft if qualitative)
2 Methodology
3 Results/findings/discussion
4 Conclusions
5 Introduction
6 Abstract
7 Title
8 Lists (contents, abbreviations, tables, figures, images, maps, references, appendices) and acknowledgements.

The literature review

This was discussed in detail in Chapter 6, to which you should refer.

The methodology chapter

- Whenever possible write this as soon as possible after collecting the data and undertaking the analysis, so that the precise detail is still fresh in your memory.
- Use the past tense when you state what has been done.
- Give an honest account of the research process.
- Explain and justify (using the literature) each aspect of what you did.
- Give full details so that someone could replicate each part of your research, including both data collection and analytical methods.
- So, for example, if translating questions or data, state the stages, for example, 'The questions were designed in English and then translated into Chinese, by the first author, a native Chinese speaker. A back translation (Werner and Campbell 1973) was used to ensure the clarity of translation. A pilot test was conducted among twenty university students (ten in China and ten in Britain) to clarify the wording; some statements were reworded to improve understanding of the question' (Xu and Fox 2012).
- Identify the limitations – be specific, not just time and money.
- Include ethics, and health and safety.
- Describe what went wrong or was ineffective, including any changes after piloting.
- Critically evaluate the methods.

Results/findings/discussion

You need not only to report your results or findings, but also to provide evidence of them, interpret your findings and show the similarities or differences between your study and those of other researchers.

Presenting your results – quantitative data

Begin with descriptive statistics of the respondents before progressing to the later results. Present the results in a coherent order, which will probably not be the same order as the questions were asked in a survey. As Chapter 10 showed, the order of the questions in the survey instrument was designed to encourage the participant to respond, which is likely to be different to what is required when writing up.

Decisions need to be made how to best present the data, whether in prose or visually in a chart or table. If in a tabular or graphic form, the minimum number of figures or tables that make sense of the data and can present it in a coherent way should be used. Consider carefully whether a table or a figure would be best, as you should only use one or the other in each instance. Frequencies, for example, are often best displayed in a pie chart, whereas if you are presenting means and standard deviations, these would be best in a table.

Presenting your results – qualitative data

Consider carefully what the 'evidence' is in a qualitative study. It is most likely to be reports of observations or quotations from interviews or documents. Depending on the form of analysis (see Chapter 12), usually a variety of viewpoints of the participants are presented with an emphasis of what is typical.

Qualitative data is rarely presented in figures or tables with the exceptions of descriptions of participants and the findings of content analyses. Instead quotations should be integrated into the text. Here are some examples of evidential quotations from Crowther (2010):

> James remarked that, 'events remain a cottage industry ... '

When she first arrived in her current role, she remembered that, 'there were no structures anywhere ... '

> Claire, who is the event manager for recruitment and outreach events supported this and emphasised the prevalence of the brand values, stating that, 'I think everyone in my team's conscious of them ... '

The selection of quotations should be carefully made to ensure that they are neither too short nor too long. It is also not always necessary to use the participant's exact words; instead they can be paraphrased. So for example, again from Crowther (2010):

> A frustration for Stephen, Director of Communications, is that events occur across the institution and the central, and localised, marketing and PR teams are often oblivious to their existence.

In qualitative research you also need to take greater care when reporting your findings to consider your ethical position (look back at Chapter 3) and also the trustworthiness of the research (see above).

The conclusions to your research

Drawing conclusions from their research is often problematic for students (and also sometimes academics and industry practitioners) but can also be the most rewarding as you finally have the opportunity to express what you think rather than what those who have undertaken research in the past have thought. 'An imaginative conclusion will move on from the careful description and analysis of your earlier chapters to a stimulating but critical view of the overall implications of your research' (Silverman 2010: 356).

- Don't just write a summary of your results/findings, but link back to the aims and objectives.
- If you convert your objective into each of your headings, you will ensure that you have discussed each one.
- Use evidence from your results/findings chapter to draw conclusions.
- Bring in literature from your review (add to the literature chapter if something new comes out in the findings, but don't introduce new material into this chapter).
- Save any value judgements for this section – but ensure you are clear about the criteria for making these judgements and the basis for them.
- Suggest what the implications for practice are; that is, recommendations for event managers and policy makers and any implications that have arisen from your methodology, for example.
- Identify future research that would be of value – but avoid simply suggesting that the research be repeated using a larger sample.

A useful way of getting started is to create a table with three columns. In the first column, write the research questions/hypotheses with each in one row. In the second column enter the specific findings/results in relation to each row of column one. Finally, in the third column make a judgement based on the specific findings/results, that is, a conclusion.

Introduction

The introduction chapter should tell exactly what the research is about and provide a clear rationale for undertaking the study. Wilson (2010) suggests that you include a statement of any problem and who will benefit from the research. As you write up the introduction chapter, ensure that you have completely *met* your aim and objectives. It may be that they may need rewriting at this stage to guarantee that this is the case. When you first drafted them, you would have had much less knowledge than you do near the end. If you are undertaking *quantitative research*, refer briefly to the theory or model that is being adopted and the variables to be tested, including their relationship with each other, begin with *independent variable(s)*, then the *dependent variable(s)*. In *qualitative research*, define the key concept(s) that are of interest.

You may want to include some contextual literature here rather than in the literature review, as sometimes the theoretical literature is better in a chapter on its own. Finish with a 'map' of the subsequent chapters setting out what each contains (use the present tense for this, not the future tense). It is tempting to write up your project as a 'whodunnit' with the reveal at the end, but this is not the way research should be presented. The reader needs to know from the outset where you are going and how you are going to get there. If you are having problems getting started, have another look at the journal articles you have read and see how they have written the introduction to their studies. Don't, of course, plagiarise, but they may give you inspiration to begin writing.

Abstract

> ## Definition box
>
> An *abstract* is a summary of an article, book or research project report. It gives the reader a quick but accurate insight into the research.

The abstract should succinctly cover:

- Your research problem
- Why that problem is important and worth studying
- Your data and methods
- Your main findings
- Their implications in the light of other research (Silverman 2010: 314).

You should by now have become used to reading the abstracts of journal articles and deciding very quickly whether it is relevant and worth obtaining and reading more. This is what the reader of your abstract will also be doing, so make sure you inspire them. Abstracts vary in length, so check your institution's requirements.

Title

This is the first aspect of your research that will be read, so ensure it guides the reader accurately.

- Convert your working question title into the final title
- Can be one part or two parts
- Check key words are included
- Make sure it refers to exactly what you have done, but is not too wordy.

You will also need to create a title page, including other information based on the requirements of your organisation, such as your full name, study programme, etc.

Lists and acknowledgements

Most institutions give you the opportunity to acknowledge the help and support you have received in undertaking the research. This could be individuals, such as family, colleagues, your tutor, supervisor and research participants, and groups such as funding bodies.

The lists

The 'lists' play an important role for the reader and so it is vital that they are correct. Have a look at the lists at the beginning and end of this book for guidance on their format. At this stage it is a good tactic to combine any separate files into one Microsoft Word document as you can then use several useful features in the 'references' tab of Word 2010. These create your lists instantly and automatically make adjustments to them if you make amendments to the text.

Contents page(s). Ensure that your pages are numbered as required and that headings have been formatted appropriately, using the 'navigation pane' (see above) to check them. You can then use the 'table of contents' tab to create it automatically. Avoid numbering sections to too many decimals. For example:

1.1   Chapter 1 begins with an introduction to the chapter
1.1.1   Sub-heading
1.1.1   Sub-heading.

Further sub-headings are usually better underlined, rather than numbering 1.1.2.1 and so on.

List of abbreviations. These are given in alphabetical order – see above for guidance on punctuation.

List of tables. This should be in order that they appear in the final draft. Use the 'table of contents' tab to create it instantly or list manually. Check that each table has a different title as they should not show the same information. If you have used the same title for two tables, this is an indication that your headings are imprecise.

List of figures. This can be created and checked in the same way as the list of tables.

List of images. This is an optional list if you have included any photographs or other pictures.

List of maps. If there are just one or two maps, they are usually better included in the list of images (unless your institution has specific requirements). So this is again an optional list if you have included a number of maps.

List of references. This should be included at the end of your dissertation as a Bibliography (or in some institutions, as References). See Chapter 6 for details of referencing. A useful tip at this stage, to ensure that no references are omitted in the list, is to use the 'find' tab and type in first '19' and then '20'. This shows all the references published in the twentieth century and then the twenty-first century. You may want to omit some chapters in the checking, particularly if you have undertaken quantitative research as this method will highlight numerous '19's and '20's in the tables of results.

Appendices. The appendices should include any additional information that is of secondary importance to the reader. Usually the appendices are not included in the word count, but this is not an excuse to use them as a 'dumping ground' for information purely to meet the word limit requirements. Example contents include:

- A list of meetings between students and tutor (as before, check your institution's requirements)
- Interview schedule or survey instrument
- One coded interview transcript as an example of the coding tool adopted (see Chapter 12)
- Any boxes or tables of information that extend over a single page.

Other outputs

Oral presentation

You may have to share your work as part of the assessment procedure of your institution, by attending a viva voce *oral* examination. This is the opportunity to defend your research, justify what you have done and show your contribution to knowledge in person to the examiners. It is rarely a requirement for undergraduate research, and is occasionally required for postgraduate dissertations, but is usually the norm for M.Phil. and Ph.D. students.

However, undergraduates may have to present a project report as part of the assessment process. And industry too, often requires formal presentation of commercial research. Saunders et al. (2009) suggest that the skills required for an oral presentation are different to those involved with writing. As well as the planning, you need to consider the preparation of visual aids and the skills required in presenting. Your organisation should have advice available on presentation preparation and delivery which you can access, but additional suggestions are made at the end of the chapter.

Peer-reviewed journal

If you are an undergraduate, it is unlikely that you will publish your study in an academic journal. But there are specialist undergraduate journals, produced by some universities (such as the multi-disciplinary journal *Diffusion* from the University of Central Lancashire in England), which may welcome a paper on your research. Some universities are also encouraging the publication of student research online, so ask your tutor if this is the case at your institution, if you are interested in publishing in this way. Alternatively, some undergraduate research can be rewritten by a tutor and submitted by them to peer-reviewed journals (see Chapter 1). It is a good ethical practice to include the student's name in the submission. The order of names usually depends on the amount of the contribution of each of the parties (but sometimes it may be necessary to have the most prestigious name given first!). Whichever format you would like to submit in, it is essential that you follow the submission requirements exactly. These may well vary from your dissertation requirements; so many minor formatting amendments can be required. You should only submit a polished article, not a draft. However, some editors welcome an abstract, to confirm whether the study is of interest to the journal, which can save a lot of wasted time making amendments to meet a 'house style' unnecessarily. You can look online to find the publishers' guidelines on the preparation of a journal article for submission. The *Journal of Convention and Event Tourism* published by the Taylor & Francis Group (www.tandfonline.com/action/author-Submission?journalCode=wcet20&page=instructions) gives a number of detailed directions to authors before they submit their manuscripts, for example:

> All parts of the manuscript should be typewritten, double-spaced, with margins of at least one inch on all sides. Number manuscript pages consecutively throughout the paper. Authors should also supply a shortened version of the title suitable for the running head, not exceeding 50 character spaces. Each article should be summarized in an abstract of not more than 100 words. Avoid abbreviations, diagrams, and reference to the text in the abstract.

Professional or commercial report

Much of the advice given above is also relevant when writing an industry report. However, note that these reports begin with an executive summary rather than an abstract. It also tends to be set out using bullet points rather than the prose of an academic abstract, but contains the same key information. Unlike an academic dissertation or journal article, research written for commercial reasons makes little reference to theory or the application of theory.

Event research in action

As part of the legacy of the London Olympic Games, the Commission for a Sustainable London 2012 (2012) produced a post-games report, titled *London 2012: From Vision to Reality*. The report begins with an executive summary; followed by a thematic assurance overview; then eight sections, each dedicated to a theme; a section on each of the Olympic venues; and the appendices.

The executive summary starts by reminding the reader that London 2012 set out to deliver 'the most sustainable Games ever' (page 2). It then provides a summary of the findings, including for example that 'Free drinking water was available at every venue, another Olympic first. There were some problems with shortage of supply and virtually no signposting but in general, this initiative is to be commended'.

The thematic assurance overview sets out in effect what were the methods used to compile the report. The purpose of assurance was 'to assure the delivery of key Games-time sustainability objectives, targets and aspirations' (page 5). The

(Continued)

Event research in action (continued)

researchers used the process of work flow assurance, for example, following the food supply chain from beginning to end. First they identified eight themes and then the key assessment criteria, e.g. 'Does the process deliver the required outcome?' followed by the key dimensions, e.g. 'Size and scope of the operation'. Finally this section of the report identified the type of people the researchers spoke to (namely, the spectators, London 2012 staff and volunteers, sponsors and contractors at the venues), and that they used their own observations in compiling the report where appropriate. The next sections discuss each of the themes identified in detail using the theme name as the headings of the subsequent sections:

1   Food, including hospitality
2   Waste
3   Energy, including cooling
4   Logistics
5   Environmentally sensitive materials (HFC, PVC, timber)
6   Look and feel, including diversity and volunteers
7   Accessibility/transport
8   The 'last mile' on approach to venues.

To make the report accessible to a wider audience the style of writing, as can be seen from the quote given above, is specifically designed to be neither academic nor technical. Also, each section on a theme begins by identifying the sample using images and numbers.

Other information is presented in text boxes or by using bullet points, again for ease of reading and images; for example, a photograph of a menu board at a 'Live Site' is included. Each of these sections concluded with 'Lessons for the future'. With reference to the provision of free water, the report stated

> The London Games has shown that the public want to be able to access free drinking water. The experience also acts as a powerful behaviour change driver for consumers of bottled water. Future events would do well to follow LOCOG's lead – albeit with a comprehensive approach to providing sufficient and well-signed free water supplies.
>
> (page 13)

The final sections of the report assessed each of the venues, for example, the Olympic Park and Village and the Mall (the start and finish points for the marathon races), beginning each section with a half-page photograph and description of the venue.

In the appendices, detailed lists, of who was interviewed in respect of each theme and venue, are given, followed by a list of footnotes giving some detailed additional information or a web page address.

Professional publication

This was discussed in Chapter 1, and like a report the research is not theoretically underpinned. The style of writing can be quite different to academic writing, adopting instead a journalistic style. Again, precise directions are given to authors that they need to comply with before they submit their manuscript.

Conference presentation

A conference presentation is a good first step to publication and can not only help promote your research, but also enhance your reputation for the future. Again, there are now undergraduate conferences, which may be more accessible (and enjoyable) to a student than a mainstream academic conference. If you are interested in presenting your research, the first person to approach is your tutor for guidance. They may also be interested in presenting a joint paper on a similar basis as a peer-reviewed journal article, discussed above.

The organisers of conferences invite abstracts relating to the themes of the conference and state the key dates well in advance, by which the abstracts must be submitted. They then select which proposals they wish to be presented and notify the authors that they have been successful. After this full papers or occasionally extended abstracts are requested, which are published in the conference proceedings. Often authors of outstanding papers are invited to submit to a special edition of a related journal.

For example, the themes for the International Conference on Events (ICE2013) and 10th AEME Forum, titled 'Making Waves' which was held in a coastal resort, at Bournemouth University, on the 3rd to the 5th of July 2013, were:

- *Making waves* – transformational power; mega and major events; social media and technology; employment and careers; ISO20121
- *Riding the waves* – Experiential events, learning and research; hyperreal experiences; festivity; rituals and rules
- *Challenging the waves* – policy and practice; creativity and design; discourses and narrative; imagination and dreamscapes
- *Working the waves* – Business events; professionalisation; the revised purple guide; security; knowledge transfer; imagery, symbols and semiotics.

At the conference delegates present their papers, often using Microsoft PowerPoint (see Aimee's opening slide earlier in the chapter) or Prezi, a cloud-based presentation software. The conference organisers will set out the amount of time available to each delegate in the programme, and this is usually strictly adhered to. If need be the chair of the session might give a 5-minute or 1-minute warning, but the strict ones will cut off a presenter in mid-speech if they talk for too long!

An alternative to a full presentation at a conference is a poster presentation (see Chapter 1). Free poster templates can be downloaded at sites such as Poster Session. com and advice on creating a poster can be found in Miller (2007).

This chapter ends where the book began in Chapter 1, that is, with the finished output of the research. Remember, research always builds on what has been found before, so if feasible and appropriate, ensure that your study reaches as wide an audience as possible, whether academics, the public, event stakeholders or policy makers. Even then you may have to take further action if you want your research to have any influence on future events. This could involve raising awareness with the public or debate with politicians or industry leaders. Other means of intervention include use of the media, both traditional and web-based, and the action of pressure groups. These may be particularly effective for community groups.

Whether you intended to change the world or purely to achieve academic success, we hope that the outcome that you sought from your research has been achieved.

Scenario

Your research project is complete and you wish to ensure that as many people as possible of aware of it.

- List *all* the parties who might be interested in the various parts of your research.
- Go through, chapter by chapter, and identify which aspect would be of most interest to them.
- State why that aspect would be of interest to them.
- Consider what would be the best means of disseminating the information to them.

Summary

Chapter 13 has highlighted:

- Why it is important for research to be evaluated.
- The reliability and validity of quantitative research.
- The trustworthiness of qualitative research.
- How to organise the content of your output.
- The language appropriate to different forms of output.
- The specific requirements of different academic and industry outputs.

Further reading

Journals

Miller, J. (2007) 'Preparing and presenting effective research posters'. *Health Services Research*, 42: 311–328. This explores many of the issues involved in creating and presenting a research poster at a conference.

Books

Bazeley, P. (2013) *Qualitative Data Analysis*. London: Sage Publications. Chapters 12 and 13 offer comprehensive help for qualitative research projects.

Saunders, M., Lewis, P. and Thornhill, A. (2009) *Research Methods for Business Students*, 5th edn. Harlow: Prentice Hall. Chapter 14 provides some useful guidance on the preparation and delivery of an oral report.

Web links

A useful web page that discusses reliability and validity can be found at Writing@CSU (undated).colostate.edu/guides/research/relval/index.cfm (accessed 20 June 2013). See the end of the commentary section for an interesting study of bad research and its consequences.

Oxford University Press provides advice on good grammar when writing and the use of punctuation for abbreviations, in Oxford University Press (2013) 'Punctuation in abbreviations'. Online. Available HTTP: http://oxforddictionaries.com/words/punctuation-in-abbreviations (accessed 20 June 2013).

The report cited can be found at the Commission for a Sustainable London 2012 (2012) *London 2012 – From Vision to Reality*. Online. Available HTTP: www.cslondon.org/wp-content/uploads/downloads/2012/11/CSL_Post%20Games%20Report_Final.pdf (accessed 20 June 2013).

Hazel Burke has produced a useful guide to putting on an exhibition to disseminate your research, which 'covers budgets, choosing a venue, designing and producing the exhibition content, writing materials, and publicising your exhibition'. Burke, H. (2008) 'Putting on an exhibition about your research'. Online. Available HTTP: www.socialsciences.manchester.ac.uk/morgancentre/realities/toolkits/exhibition/2008-07-toolkit-exhibition.pdf (accessed 20 June 2013).

Video links

This video explains the mechanics of writing paragraphs: *Writing Structured Paragraphs* (28.39 minutes). Online. Available HTTP: www.youtube.com/watch?v=w183qB0KDFg&feature=relmfu (accessed 20 June 2013).

Whilst this one helps you with writing your thesis: *Writing a Thesis* (19.50 minutes). Online. Available HTTP: www.youtube.com/watch?v=vHHtfO-Bu1M&feature=relmfu (accessed 20 June 2013).

Glossary

Abductive research aims to provide an understanding of the social world of a person or organisation, which can help provide a more systematic explanation of their actions.

Abstract A summary of an article, book or research project report, which gives the reader a quick but accurate insight into the research.

Action research A method by which research findings are collected and then re-applied directly back into the environments being studied.

Applied research seeks to provide a solution to a real problem.

Basic research (sometimes referred to as pure research) seeks to expand knowledge about a phenomenon without an immediate practical application.

Case study Research that involves the intensive study of one particular case.

Categorical (or nominal data) As the name indicates, this is data belonging to one or another category, for example categories of male or female.

Causality (sometimes called causation) that is, one phenomenon causes another to happen.

Coding is a process in which raw data is transformed into a standard form which can be processed and analysed by a computer.

Comparative design compares two or more groups in relation to a variable or characteristic.

Conceptual framework identifies the concepts to be used in a study, describes them and their relationship to each other and how they are to be measured.

Constructivism has as its basis that people construct their own views of reality.

Covert observation When the researcher is not known to those in a particular setting as engaging in active data collection.

Critical realism A philosophical approach that uses theory to describe structures and mechanisms in society which we cannot directly observe and therefore measure, but whose effect we can observe.

Cross-sectional research The study of a phenomenon at a single point in time.

Deductive research entails the development of an idea from existing theory, which is tested by gathering data.

Descriptive research This describes an existing or previous phenomenon.

E-research (can also be written as eResearch) is the use of information technology to support research.

Empirical research   A form of research that is evidence-based rather than just theorising.

Epistemology   The philosophical study of how knowledge is acquired (how and what can we know about it).

Ethnographic   Concerning the description of individual human societies.

Ethnography   is a qualitative approach that has its roots grounded in anthropological studies.

Explanatory research   This seeks to show what causes a phenomenon.

Exploratory research   This form of research is used when very little is known or written about the subject.

Focus group and panels   are types of group interview where a number of people are interviewed together on a particular theme.

Grounded theory   is a method in which the data helps to develop a theory, as opposed to inform or test existing theories.

Group interviews   are similar to focus groups, yet usually have members with some association to one another, e.g. families.

Hermeneutics   has its roots in the study of meaning found in texts. It has, however, evolved recently to include the analysis of other forms such as visual objects (art and photography) and that of speech, e.g. conversation.

Human capital   The skills, knowledge and experience available.

Hypothesis   A predicted result, based on the findings of previous studies, which is tested.

Inductive research   This is an approach which begins with the collection of data from which generalisations are derived using 'inductive' logic to develop a theory or model.

Informed consent   This is consent given by a participant in a research project when they have a full understanding of the nature of their participation in the study.

Interpretivism   A philosophical approach that tends to be qualitative and subjective, because the researcher recognises that the social world (or context) of the participants cannot be separated from the research itself.

Literature review   The output from identifying, evaluating and critically reviewing what has already been published on the research topic.

Longitudinal research   A study, often of a single case, which is repeated either once or over a number of times and used where the aim of the research is to examine change over time.

Macrostructure   The overall scheme of organisation of the research output.

Mixed methods research   Using both qualitative and quantitative methods in the same study.

Netnography   Ethnographic research conducted in the social arena of the internet.

Nominal   (or categorical data) This is data belonging to one or another category, for example categories of male or female.

Non-parametric   tests are statistical tests used where there is no assumption about the distribution of the population from which the data was sampled.

Non-participant observation   When a researcher does not actively become immersed into a setting but rather observes the setting outside of active participation.

Null hypothesis   This suggests that there is no relationship between two variables.

Observation   The act of using human faculties such as sight and sound to capture data in a research setting.

Ontology   The study of the philosophy of knowledge (what is it that we want to know about).

Ordinal variable   One which, as its name implies indicates an ordering of the responses.

Outcome   The consequence of producing an output from research, e.g. a change in policy.

Output   The product created from research, e.g. a report.

Overt observation   When the researcher is known to those in a setting as engaging in active data collection.

Parametric tests   are statistical tests that assume that the sample data comes from a population with a normal distribution.

Participant observation   A researcher is intentionally integrated into a scene in order to actively experience and/or observe elements of it.

Phenomenology   A qualitative research approach whereby findings are grounded in the reflections of experience that are reported by the subjects under study.

Plagiarism   The use of someone else's work and presenting it as though it is one's own.

Positivism   A philosophical approach that understands knowledge as having only one 'true' form.

Post-positivism   A philosophical approach that is empirical, moving from theory to observation and measurement, and seeks to be as objective as possible.

Primary data   is data that is collected specifically for analysis in a particular study.

Primary research   generally refers to research that involves the statistical or other analysis of data for the first time.

Primary source   Information that is being presented by the original producer.

Probability sampling   (or random sampling) gives every respondent an equal chance of being selected from the whole population.

Pure research   (sometimes referred to as basic research) seeks to expand knowledge about a phenomenon without an immediate practical application.

Qualitative research   uses non-numerical data, usually in the form of words, but could also be images for example. Its aim is to describe, understand or obtain meaning and the research is therefore more subjective than quantitative research.

Quantitative research   is interested in information that can be assessed and used numerically and to examine the relationship between variables, and is often associated with hypothesis testing. It is usually more objective than qualitative research.

Random sampling   (or probability sampling) gives every respondent an equal chance of being selected from the whole population.

Reference   A source consulted and referred to in a study.

Reliability   The degree to which a scale produces consistent results if repeated measurements are made of the characteristics.

Research   A process of investigation which is systematic and increases knowledge.

Research aim   A general statement of the specific outcome that the research is intended to accomplish.

Research objectives   Specific statements that identify the individual stages that will be achieved which together accomplish the research aim.

Research proposal   A brief document setting out the plan of the research, including the topic, aim and objectives, key literature and proposed methodology, including timescale and financial aspects.

Research questions   explore the relationships between the elements of the research context.

Response rate   The percentage of people who responded to a survey; this can be calculated by taking the number of people who completed the survey, dividing it by the number of people contacted and multiplying by 100.

Retroductive research   This seeks to reveal the underlying structure or mechanism which is responsible for producing some observed occurrence.

Sampling   The process of selecting subjects or objects from the population of interest.

Secondary data   has been obtained by you or someone else for a purpose other than the current research, but is to be analysed or re-analysed in the current research.

Secondary research   usually relates to the whole or part of a study where information is retrieved and presented logically but not formally analysed.

Secondary source   Information that is not the original production but has been collated from another source.

Semi-structured interview   A type of interview that follows a set interview schedule yet has flexibility to add questions to probe participants further.

Snowball   A type of data gathering that rapidly grows by being passed from potential participant to potential participant. For example, asking friends to complete a questionnaire and to then pass it on to all of their friends.

Social constructivism   A philosophical approach based on the assumption that knowledge is constructed by social scientists rather than 'out there' to be observed and measured as in post-positivism.

Structured interview   An interview that has a set interview schedule that is followed without deviating from it.

Theoretical research   A form of research that generally analyses existing theory and explanations to develop new ideas.

Theory   A formal idea which seeks to explain something.

Unstructured interview   A type of interview that doesn't follow a set interview schedule as such, yet encourages discussion to flow more freely using topics as 'prompts'.

Bibliography

ActiveCampaign (2009) *Validity in Research Design*. Online. Available HTTP: www.activecampaign.com/blog/validity-in-research-design/ (accessed 18 October 2013).

Adler, P. A. and Adler, P. (1994) 'Observational techniques', in N. Denzin and Y. Lincoln (eds), *Handbook of Qualitative Research*. London: Sage Publications.

Adler, P. A. and Adler, P. (1998) 'Observation techniques', in N. Denzin and Y. S. Lincoln (eds), *Collecting and Interpreting Qualitative Materials*. London: Sage Publications.

Allen, J. (2000) *Event Planning*. Ontario, Canada: John Wiley and Sons.

Andrews, D., Pedersen, P. and McEvoy, C. (2011) *Research Methods and Design in Sport Management*. Champaign, IL: Human Kinetics.

Andrews, H. (2013) *Events and the Social Sciences*. Abingdon: Routledge.

Baines, P. R., Brennan, R., Gill, M. and Mortimore, R. (2009) 'Examining the academic/commercial divide in marketing research'. *European Journal of Marketing*, 43: 1289–1299.

Baker, S. E. and Edwards, R. (undated) 'How many qualitative interviews is enough?' National Centre for Research Methods. Online. Available HTTP: http://eprints.ncrm.ac.uk/2273/4/how_many_interviews.pdf (accessed 11 August 2013).

Banks, M. (1995) *Visual Methods in Social Research*. Guildford: University of Surrey. Online. Available HTTP: http://sru.soc.surrey.ac.uk/SRU11/SRU11.html (accessed 14 August 2013).

Banks, M. (2008) *Using Visual Data in Qualitative Research*. London: Sage Publications.

Barrett, S. (2009) *Anthropology: A Student's Guide to Theory and Method*, 2nd edn. Toronto: Toronto University Press.

Barthes, R. (1996) *Camera Lucida: Reflections on Photography*. New York: Hill & Wang.

Bateson G. and Mead, M. (1942) *Balinese Character: A Photographic Analysis*, vol. 2. New York: New York Academy of Sciences.

Bazeley, P. (2013) *Qualitative Data Analysis*. London: Sage Publications.

Berg, B. L. (2007) *Qualitative Research Methods for the Social Sciences*, 6th edn. London: Pearson.

Bernard, H. R. and Ryan, G. W. (2010) *Analyzing Qualitative Data: Systematic Approaches*. London: Sage Publications.

Bladen, C., Kennell, J., Abson, E. and Wilde, N. (2012) *Events Management: An Introduction*. Abingdon: Routledge.

Blaikie, N. (2000) *Designing Social Research*. Cambridge: Polity Press.

Bowdin, G., Allen, J., O'Toole, W., Harris, R. and McDonnell, I. (2011) *Events Management*, 3rd edn. Oxford: Elsevier Butterworth-Heinemann.

Bristol Online Surveys (2007) 'How do I pilot a survey?' Online. Available HTTP: www.survey.bris.ac.uk/support/faq/surveys/how-do-i-pilot-a-survey (accessed 12 August 2013).

Bryman, A. (2004) *Social Research Methods*, 2nd edn. Oxford: Oxford University Press.

Bryman, A. (2008) *Social Research Methods*, 3rd edn. Oxford: Oxford University Press.

Bryman, A. and Bell, E. (2007) *Business Research Methods*, 2nd edn. Oxford: Oxford University Press.

Burke, H. (2008) 'Putting on an exhibition about your research'. Online. Available HTTP: www.socialsciences.manchester.ac.uk/morgancentre/realities/toolkits/exhibition/2008-07-toolkit-exhibition.pdf (accessed 20 June 2013).

Cardiff Business School (2012) 'Learning to think like an expert management researcher'. Online. Available HTTP: www.restore.ac.uk/logicofenquiry/logicofenquiry/Pages/Home.html (accessed 7 April 2013).

Carmines, E. G. and Zeller, R. A. (1991) *Reliability and Validity Assessment*. Newbury Park, CA: Sage Publications.

Carroll, J. and Ryan, J. (2005) *Teaching International Students: Improving Learning for All*. London: Routledge.

Charmaz, K. (2006) *Constructing Grounded Theory: A Practical Guide through Qualitative Analysis*. London: Sage Publications.

Choi, J. and Almanza, B. (2012) 'An assessment of food safety risk at fairs and festivals: A comparison of health inspection violations between fairs and festivals and restaurants'. *Event Management*, 16: 295–303.

Clough, P. and Nutbrown, C. (2012) *A Student's Guide to Methodology*, 3rd edn. London: Sage Publications.

Commission for a Sustainable London 2012 (2012) *London 2012 – From Vision to Reality*. Online. Available HTTP: www.cslondon.org/wp-content/uploads/downloads/2012/11/CSL_Post%20Games%20Report_Final.pdf. (accessed 20 June 2013).

Copeland, M. J. and Schuster, C. P. (2008) 'Cultural theory in use: The intersection of business structure, process and communication in business practice'. *Journal of Public Affairs*, 8: 261–280.

Creswell, J. W., Clark, V. L. P., Gutmann, M. L. and Hanson, W. E. (2003) 'Advanced mixed methods research designs', in A. Tashakkori and C. Teddlie (eds), *Handbook of Mixed Methods in Social and Behavioural Research*. London: Sage Publications.

Crotty, M. (1998) *Foundations in Social Research, Meaning and Perspective in the Research Process*. London: Sage Publications.

Crowther, P. (2010) 'Strategic application of events'. *International Journal of Hospitality Management*, 29: 227–235.

Dahlberg, L. and McCaig, C. (2010) *Practical Research and Evaluation*. London: Sage Publications.

Denscombe, M. (2002) *Ground Rules for Good Research: A Ten-point Guide for Social Researchers*. Buckinghamshire: Open University Press.

Denscombe, M (2003) *The Good Research Guide for Small-scale Social Research Projects*, 2nd edn. Buckinghamshire: Open University Press.

Denzin, N. and Lincoln, Y. (2000) 'Introduction: The discipline and practice of qualitative research', in N. Denzin and Y. Lincoln (eds), *Handbook of Qualitative Research*, 2nd edn. London: Sage Publications.

Derrett, R. (2003) 'Making sense of how festivals demonstrate a community sense of place'. *Event Management*, 8: 49–58.

Dickson, C. and Arcodia, C. (2010) 'Promoting sustainable event practice: The role of professional associations'. *International Journal of Hospitality Management*, 29: 236–244.

Dillman, D., Phelps, G., Tortora, R., Swift, K., Kohrell, J., Berck, J. and Messer, B. (2009) 'Response rate and measurement difference in mixed-mode surveys using mail, telephone, interactive voice response (IVR) and internet'. *Social Science Research*, 38: 1–18.

DJS Research Ltd (2011) 'Definition of market research'. Online. Available HTTP: www.marketresearchworld.net/index.php?option=com_content&task=view&id=14&Itemid=38 (accessed 13 August 2012).

Easton, V. J. and McColl, J. H. (1997) 'Statistics glossary'. Online. Available HTTP: www.stats.gla.ac.uk/steps/glossary/hypothesis_testing.html#hypothtest (accessed 4 August 2013).

Edwards, D., Foley, C. and Schenker, K. (2011) 'Beyond tourism benefits'. Sydney: University of Technology. Online. Available HTTP www.businesseventssydney.com.au/fms/About%20us/Publications%20and%20resources/Documents/Beyond%20Tourism%20Benefits%20Measuring%20the%20social%20legacy%20of%20business%20events.pdf (accessed 15 August 2013).

Elliott, R. and Jankel-Elliott, N. (2003) 'Using ethnography in strategic consumer research'. *Qualitative Market Research: An International Journal*, 6: 215–223.

ESOMAR (2012) 'Codes and guidelines'. Online. Available HTTP: www.esomar.org/knowledge-and-standards/codes-and-guidelines.php (accessed 10 April 2013).

Feinstein, A. R. (2001) *Principles of Medical Statistics*. Florida, USA: Chapman and Hall/CRC.

Field, A. (2005) *Discovering Statistics Using SPSS*, 2nd edn. London: Sage Publications.

Field, A. (2009) *Discovering Statistics Using SPSS*, 3rd edn. London: Sage Publications.

Fink, A. (1995) *How to Measure Survey Reliability and Validity*.Thousand Oaks, CA: Sage Publications.

Fisher, C. (2007) *Researching and Writing a Dissertation: A Guidebook for Business Students*, 2nd edn. Harlow: Pearson Education.

Fletcher, M. (2005) 'Live issue O2: All the world's a stage'. UK: *Event Magazine*. Online. Available HTTP: www.eventmagazine.co.uk/news/search/517762/Live-Issue-O2-worlds-stage/ (accessed 24 November 2008).

Flick, U. (2006) *An Introduction to Qualitative Research*. London: Sage Publications.

Flick, U. (2008) *Designing Qualitative Research*. London: Sage Publications.

Flick, U. (2009) *An Introduction to Qualitative Research*, 4th edn. London: Sage Publications.

Flick, U. (2011) *Introducing Research Methodology: A Beginner's Guide to Doing a Research Project*. London: Sage Publications.

Food and Drug Administration (2009) 'FDA Food Code 2009: Chapter 1 – Purpose and definitions'. Online. Available HTTP: www.fda.gov/Food/FoodSafety/RetailFoodProtection/FoodCode/FoodCode2009/ucm186464.htm (accessed 14 March 2013).

Forza, C. (2002) 'Survey research in operations management: A process-based perspective'. *International Journal of Operations and Production Management*, 22: 152–194.

Foucault, M. (1980) *Power/knowledge: Selected Interviews and Other Writings 1972–1977*. Hassocks, Sussex: Harvester.

Fox, D. (2012) 'Urban-proximate nature as a resource for events and festivals: A SWOT analysis', paper presented at 6th International Conference on Monitoring and Management of Visitors in Recreational and Protected Areas, Stockholm, Sweden, 21–24 August 2012.

Fox, D. and Edwards, J. R. (2009) 'A preliminary analysis of the market for small, medium and large horticultural shows in England'. *Event Management*, 12: 199–208.

Fox, D. and Johnston, N. (2009) 'The contribution of an events programme to sustainable heritage conservation: a study of the National Trust in England', paper presented at International Event Management Summit, Gold Coast, Queensland, Australia, 6–7 July 2009.

Fox, D. and Morrison, P. (2010) 'The introduction of a learning innovation to enhance the employability of event management students: An action research study', paper presented at Global Events Congress IV: Events and Festivals Research, Leeds, England,14–16 July 2010.

Gaiser, T. J. and Schreiner, A. E. (2009) *A Guide to Conducting Online Research*. London: Sage Publications.

Galt, K. (2008) 'An introduction to mixed methods research'. Online. Available HTTP: http://spahp2.creighton.edu/OfficeOfResearch/share/sharedfiles/UserFiles/file/Galt_MM_slides_CU_092309.pdf (accessed 14 August 2013).

Garson, D. (2012) 'Sampling'. Online. Available HTTP: www.statisticalassociates.com/ (accessed 4 September 2012).

Gaur, A. S. and Gaur, S. S. (2009) *Statistical Methods for Practice and Research*, 2nd edn. London: Sage Publications. Online. Available HTTP: www.scribd.com/doc/30873720/Guide-to-Data-Analysis-Using-SPSS#page=133 (accessed 4 August 2013).

Getz, D. (2012 [2007]) *Event Studies: Theory, Research and Policy for Planned Events*, 2nd edn. Abingdon: Routledge.

Getz, D. and Cheyne, J. (2002) 'Special event motives and behaviour', in C. Ryan (ed.), *The Tourist Experience*, 2nd edn. London: Continuum.

Glaser, B. (1978) *Theoretical Sensitivity: Advances in the Methodology of Grounded Theory*. Mill Valley, CA: Sociology Press.

Glaser, B. (1992) *Emergence vs Forcing: Basics of Grounded Theory Analysis*. Mill Valley, CA: Sociology Press.

Glaser, B. and Strauss, A. (1967) *The Discovery of Grounded Theory: Strategies for Qualitative Research*. Chicago: Aldine.

Grant, J. (2006) *The Brand Innovation Manifesto: How to Build Brands, Redefine Markets and Defy Conventions*. Chichester: John Wiley & Sons Ltd.

GraphPad Software (2013) 'Ordinal, interval and ratio variables'. Online. Available HTTP: www.graphpad.com/guides/prism/6/statistics/index.htm?the_different_kinds_of_variabl.htm (accessed 10 August 2013).

Gratton, C. and Jones, I. (2010) *Research Methods for Sports Studies*, 2nd edn. Abingdon: Routledge.

Greetham, B. (2009) *How to Write Your Undergraduate Dissertation*. Basingstoke: Palgrave Macmillan.

Greig, A. D., Taylor, J. and MacKay, T. (2012) *Doing Research with Children: A Practical Guide*, 3rd edn. London: Sage Publications.

Grix, J. (2010) *The Foundations of Research*, 2nd edn. Basingstoke: Palgrave Macmillan.

Groves, R. M. and Couper, M. P. (1996) 'Contact-level influences on cooperation in face-to-face surveys'. *Journal of Official Statistics*, 12: 63–83.

Grunwell, S., Ha, I. and Martin, B. (2008) 'A comparative analysis of attendee profiles at two urban festivals'. *Journal of Convention Event Tourism*, 9: 1–14.

Gupta, S. (2003) 'Event marketing: Issues and challenges'. *IIMB Management Review*, 15: 87–96.

Hannon, P. (2000) *Reflecting on Literacy in Education*. London: RoutledgeFalmer.

Harper, D. (2000) 'Reimagining visual methods: Galileo to Neuromancer', in N. Denzin and Y. S. Lincoln (eds), *Handbook of Qualitative Research*, 2nd edn. London: Sage Publications.

Hart, C. (1998) *Doing a Literature Review*. London: Sage Publications.

Hede, A. (2007) 'Managing special events in the new era of the triple bottom line'. *Event Management*, 11: 13–22.

Hofstede, G. (2001) *Culture's Consequences*, 2nd edn. London: Sage Publications.

Husserl, E. (1931) *Ideas: General Introduction to Pure Phenomenology*. London: George Allen & Unwin.

Hvenegaard, G. T. (2011) 'Potential conservation benefits of wildlife festivals'. *Event Management*, 15: 373–386.

Institute of Risk Management, The (2002) 'A risk management standard'. Online. Available HTTP: www.theirm.org/publications/documents/ARMS_2002_IRM.pdf (accessed 13 August 2013).

Iran Daily (2009) 'Rose festival in Kashan' .Available HTTP: www.iran-daily.com/1392/2/8/MainPaper/4492/Page/6/Index.htm (accessed 18 October 2013).

Jamilly, D. and Cohen, T. (2010) *Secret Millionaire David Jamilly's Party People: How We Make Millions from Having Fun*. Brighton: Indepenpress Publishing.

Jennings, G. R. (2005) 'Interviewing: A focus on qualitative techniques', in B. Ritchie, P. Burns, and C. Palmer (eds), *Tourism Research Methods: Integrating Theory with Practice*. Wallingford: CAB International.

Johnson, R. B. and Onwuegbuzie, A. J. (2004) 'Mixed methods research: A research paradigm whose time has come'. *Educational Researcher*, 33: 14–26. Online. Available HTTP: www.tc.umn.edu/~dillon/CI%208148%20Qual%20Research/Session%2014/Johnson%20&%20Onwuegbuzie%20PDF.pdf (accessed 14 August 2013).

Jones, B., Scott, D. and Khaled, H. A. (2006) 'Implications of climate change for outdoor event planning: A case study of three special events in Canada's national capital region'. *Event Management*, 10: 63–76.

Knoblauch, H. (2004) 'Video-Interaktionsanalyse'. *Sozialer Sinn*, 1: 123–139.

Laybourn, P. (2004) 'Risk and decision-making in events management', in I. Yeoman, M. Robertson and J. Ali-Knight (eds), *Festivals and Event Management*. Oxford: Butterworth-Heinemann.

Lee, I. S., Lee, T. J. and Arcodia, C. (2013) 'The effect of community attachment on cultural festival visitors' satisfaction and future intentions'. *Current Issues in Tourism* (in press). DOI: 10.1080/13683500.2013.770450.

Legard, R. Keegan, K. and Ward, K. (2003) 'In-depth interviews', in J. Ritchie and J. Lewis (eds), *Qualitative Research Practice*. London: Sage Publications.

Mackellar, J. (2013) 'Participant observation at events: Theory, practice, and potential'. *International Journal of Event and Festival Management*, 4: 56–65.

Mahoe, R. (2013) 'Reflections on the dissertation process and the use of secondary data'. Online. Available HTTP: www.hawaii.edu/edper/pdf/Vol37Iss2/Reflections.pdf (accessed 10 August 2013).

Malhotra, N. and Birks, D. F. (2006) *Marketing Research: An Applied Approach*, 3rd edn. Harlow: Prentice Hall.

Maude, B. (2011) *Managing Cross-cultural Communication: Principles and Practice*. Basingstoke: Palgrave Macmillan.

McKercher, B., Mei, W. and Tse, T. (2006) 'Are short duration festivals tourist attractions?' *Journal of Sustainable Tourism*, 14: 55–66.

Meho, L. I. (2006) 'E-Mail interviewing in qualitative research: A methodological discussion'. *Journal of the American Society for Information Science and Technology*, 57: 1284–1295.

Miles, M. B. and Huberman A. M. (1994) *Qualitative Data Analysis*, 2nd edn. London: Sage Publications.

Miller, J. (2007) 'Preparing and presenting effective research posters'. *Health Services Research*, 42: 311–328.

Mintel International Group Ltd (2007) 'Telecoms retailing – UK – May 2007'. UK: Mintel International Group Ltd. Online. Available HTTP: http://academic.mintel.com/sinatra/oxygen_academic/search_results/show&/display/id=220262/displaytables/id=220262/display/?id=276065 (accessed 27 November 2008).

Morgan, M. (2008) 'What makes a good festival? Understanding the event experience'. *Event Management*, 12: 81–93.

Murphy, P. E. and Carmichael, B. (1991) 'Assessing the tourism benefits of an open access sports tournament: The 1989 B.C. Winter Games'. *Journal of Travel Research*, 29: 32–36.

Myers, M. (2013) *Qualitative Research in Business and Management*, 2nd edn. London: Sage Publications.

Neirotti, L. D., Bosetti, H. A. and Teed, K. C. (2001) 'Motivation to attend the 1996 Summer Olympic Games'. *Journal of Travel Research*, 39: 327–331.

NME (2012a) 'Example: "It's no surprise the UK festival circuit is struggling"'. Online. Available HTTP: www.nme.com/news/example/63029 (accessed 10 August 2013).

NME (2012b) 'Album sales down for the seventh year in a row'. Online. Available HTTP: www.nme.com/news/adele/61214 (accessed 10 August 2013).

Novelli, M. (2004) 'Wine tourism events: Apulia, Italy', in I. Yeoman, M. Robertson, J. Ali-Knight, S. Drummond and U. McMahon-Beattie (eds), *Festival and Events Management: An International Arts and Culture Perspective*. Oxford: Butterworth-Heinemann.

Nutbrown, C. and Hannon, P. (2003) 'Children's perspectives on family literacy: Methodological issues, findings and implications for practice'. *Journal of Early Childhood Literacy*, 3: 115–145.

Oberg, K. (1960) 'Cultural shock: Adjustment to new cultural environments'. *Practical Anthropology*, 7: 177–182.

Oliver, P. (2010) *The Student's Guide to Research Ethics*, 2nd edn. Maidenhead: Open University Press.

Onwuegbuzi, A. J. and Collins, K. M. T. (2007) 'A typology of mixed methods sampling designs in social science research'. *The Qualitative Report*, 12: 281–316.

Owen, J. and Holliday, P. (1993) *Confer in Confidence: An Organiser's Dossier*. Broadway: Meetings Industry Association.

Oxford University Press (2013) 'Punctuation in abbreviations'. Online. Available HTTP: http://oxforddictionaries.com/words/punctuation-in-abbreviations (accessed 20 June 2013).

Page, S. and Connell, J. (2011) *The Routledge Handbook of Events*. Abingdon: Routledge.

Pallant, J. (2010) *SPSS Survival Manual*, 4th edn. Maidenhead: Open University Press.

Patton, M. Q. (2002) *Qualitative Evaluation and Research Methods*, 3rd edn. London: Sage Publications.

Peat, J., Mellis, C., Williams, K. and Xuan, W. (2002) *Health Science Research: A Handbook of Quantitative Methods*. London: Sage Publications.

Perth and Kinross Council (ca. 2003) 'Events strategy and action plan for 2006–2011'. Online. Available HTTP: www.pkc.gov.uk/NR/rdonlyres/05399CFE-0CB4-4BA5-8DE7-C51BA9D434C5/0/EventsStrategy20062011.pdf (accessed 13 August 2012).

Pieters, R., Wedel, M. and Batra, R. (2010) 'The stopping power of advertising: Measures and effects of visual complexity'. *Journal of Marketing*, 74: 48–60.

Pink, S. (2001) *Doing Visual Ethnography: Images, Media and Representation in Research*. London: Sage Publications.

Pink, S. (2004) 'Visual methods', in C. Seale, G. Gobo, J. Gubrium and D. Silverman (eds), *Qualitative Research Practice*. London: Sage Publications.

Punch, K. F. (2000) *Developing Effective Research Proposals*. London: Sage Publications.

Punch, K. F. (2005) *Introduction to Social Research: Quantitative and Qualitative Approaches*, 2nd edn. London: Sage Publications.

Quinn, B. (2013) *Key Concepts in Special Events Management*. London: Sage Publications.

Raj, R., Walters, P. and Rashid, T. (2013). *Events Management*, 2nd edn. London: Sage Publications.

Ravald, A. and Gronoos, C. (1996) 'The value concept and relationship marketing'. *European Journal of Marketing*, 30: 19–30.

Reichertz, J. (2004) 'Objective hermeneutics and hermeneutic sociology of knowledge', in U. Flick, E. V. Kardorff and I. Steinke (eds), *A Companion to Qualitative Research*. London: Sage Publications.

Richards, L. (2009) *Handling Qualitative Data*, 2nd edn. London: Sage Publications.

Rihova, I., Buhalis, D., Moital, M. and Gouthro, M-B. (2013) 'Practice-theoretical approach in the study of C2C co-creation at festivals'. Paper presented at Making Waves: International Conference on Events, Bournemouth, July.

Ritchie, B. W., Shipway, R. and Cleeve, B. (2009) 'Resident perceptions of mega-sporting events: A non-host city perspective of the 2012 London Olympic Games'. *Journal of Sport and Tourism*, 14: 143–167.

Rittichainuwat, B. and Mair, J. (2012) 'Motivations for attending consumer shows'. *Tourism Management*, 33: 1236–1244.

Robbins, D., Dickinson, J. and Calver, S. (2007) 'Planning transport for special events: A conceptual framework and future agenda for research'. *International Journal of Tourism Research*, 9: 303–314.

Robson, C. (2002) *Real World Research*, 2nd edn. Oxford: Blackwell.

Roe, N. (2012) 'Portugal's secret city: A true capital of culture'. *The Times*, 21 January, 24–25 a–e.

Rose, G. (2001) *Visual Methodologies: An Introduction to the Interpretation of Visual Materials*. London: Sage Publications.

Rose, H. (1991) 'Case studies', in G. Allan and C. Skinner (eds), *Handbook for Research Students in the Social Sciences*. London: Falmer Press.

Rudestam, K. E. and Newton, R. R. (1992) *Surviving Your Dissertation*. London: Sage Publications.

Ryan, C. (1995) *Researching Tourist Satisfaction: Issues, Concepts, Problems*. New York: Routledge.

Sadd, D. (2010) 'What is event-led regeneration? Are we confusing terminology or will London 2012 be the first games to truly benefit the local existing population?' *Event Management*, 13: 265–275.

Saldaña, J. (2009) *The Coding Manual for Qualitative Researchers*. London: Sage Publications.

Sarantakos, S. (2005) *Social Research*, 3rd edn. Basingstoke: Palgrave Macmillan.

Saunders, M., Lewis, P. and Thornhill, A. (2007) *Research Methods for Business Students*, 4th edn. Harlow: Pearson Education.

Saunders, M., Lewis, P. and Thornhill, A. (2009) *Research Methods for Business Students*, 5th edn. Harlow: Prentice Hall.

Schulenkorf, N., Thomson, A. and Schlenker, K. (2011) 'Intercommunity sport events: Vehicles and catalysts for social capital in divided societies'. *Event Management*, 15: 105–119.

Seale, C. (ed.) (2004) *Researching Society and Culture*, 2nd edn. London: Sage Publications.

Sharples, M., Davison, L., Thomas, G. and Rudman, P. (2003) 'Children as photographers: An analysis of children's photographic behaviour and intentions at three age levels'. *Visual Communication*, 2: 303–330.

Shaw, C., Brady, L. and Davey, C. (2011) 'Guidelines for research with children and young people'. London: NCB Research Centre. Online. Available HTTP: www.ncb.org.uk/media/434791/guidelines_for_research_with_cyp.pdf (accessed 18 July 2013).

Shone, A. and Parry, B. (2010) *Successful Event Management*, 3rd edn. Andover: Cengage Learning.

Silverman, D. (2010) *Doing Qualitative Research*, 3rd edn. London: Sage Publications.

Skinner, J. and Edwards, A. (2012) *Qualitative Research in Sport Management*. Burlington, MA: Elsevier.

Spradley, J. P. (1979) *The Ethnographic Interview*. New York: Holt, Rinehart & Winston.

Spradley, J. P. (1980) *Participant Observation*. New York: Holt, Rinehart & Winston.

SQW Limited (2006) 'Culture 10 evaluation'. Online: Available HTTP: www.tourism northeast.co.uk (accessed 10 March 2012).

Stadler, R., Reid, S. and Fullagar, S. (2013) 'An ethnographic exploration of knowledge practices within the Queensland Music Festival'. *International Journal of Event and Festival Management*. Online. Available HTTP: www.emeraldinsight.com/journals. htm?articleid=17085034&show=abstract (accessed 7 April 2013).

Stebbins, R. (2006) *Serious Leisure: A Perspective for Our Time*. London: Transaction Publishers.

Strauss, A. (1987) *Qualitative Analysis For Social Scientists*. Cambridge: Cambridge University Press.

Strauss, A. and Corbin, J. (1990) *Basics of Qualitative Research, Grounded Theory Procedures and Techniques*. London: Sage Publications.

Sutton, R. I. and Shaw, B. M. (1995) 'What theory is not'. *Administrative Science Quarterly*, 40: 371–384.

Tashakkori, A. and Teddlie, C. (eds) (2003) *Handbook of Mixed Methods in Social and Behavioural Research*. London: Sage Publications.

Tayeb, M. (2003) *International Management*. Harlow: Prentice Hall.

The Idea Works (2011) 'Peer review emulator'. Online: Available HTTP: www.ideaworks. com/mt/peer_review.html (accessed 6 February 2012).

The Institute of Risk Management (2002) *A Risk Management Standard*. London: The Institute of Risk Management. Available HTTP: www.theirm.org/publications/documents/ARMS_2002_IRM.pdf (accessed 18 October 2013).

The National Trust (2009) *The National Trust*. Online. Available HTTP: www.nationaltrust. org.uk/main/ (accessed 25 March 2009).

The Times (2012) 'Deconstructing the medal table'. *The Times*, 11 August, 13a–e.

Tools4Dev (2013) 'How to pretest and pilot a survey questionnaire'. Online. Available HTTP: www.tools4dev.org/resources/how-to-pretest-and-pilot-a-survey-questionnaire/ (accessed 12 August 2013).

Tribe, J. (2006) 'The truth about tourism'. *Annals of Tourism Research*, 33: 360–381.

Trochim, W. M. K. (2006) 'Sampling'. *Research Methods Knowledge Base*. Online. Available HTTP: www.socialresearchmethods.net/kb/sampling.php (accessed 18 July 2013).

Tum, J., Norton, P. and Wright, J. N. (2006) *Management of Event Operations*. Oxford: Butterworth-Heinemann.

UsingMindMaps.com (2013) 'How to mind map a text book'. Online. Available HTTP: www. usingmindmaps.com/how-to-mind-map-a-text-book.html (accessed 10 June 2013).

Van der Wagen, L. (2007) *Human Resource Management for Events: Managing the Event Workforce*. Oxford: Elsevier.

Veal, A. J. (2011) *Research Methods for Leisure and Tourism: A Practical Guide*, 4th edn. Harlow: Prentice Hall.

Warnes, M. (2004) 'Heidegger and the festival of being: from the bridal festival to the round dance'. Online. Available HTTP: https://circle.ubc.ca/bitstream/handle/2429/43841/ubc_2013_spring_warnes_mathias.pdf?sequence=12 (accessed 13 August 2013).

Warren, C. A. B. and Karner, T. X. (2005) *Discovering Qualitative Methods: Field Research, Interviews, and Analysis*. Los Angeles, CA: Roxbury.

Wengraf, T. (2001) *Qualitative Research Interviewing: Biographic Narrative and Semi-Structured Methods*. London: Sage Publications.

Werner, O. and Campbell, D. T. (1973) 'Translating, working through interpreters: The problem of decentering', in R. Naroll and R. Cohen (eds), *A Handbook of Method in Cultural Anthropology*. New York: Columbia University Press.

Williams, M. (2010) *Are Music Festivals Offline Versions of Online Communities?* Online. Available HTTP: http://ideaction.co/are-music-festivals-offline-versions-of-online-communities/ (accessed 18 October 2013).

Wilson, J. (2010) *Essentials of Business Research: A Guide to Doing Your Research Project*. London: Sage Publications.

Wisker, G. (2009) *The Undergraduate Research Handbook*. Basingstoke: Palgrave Macmillan.

Witt, S. F., Sykes, A. M. and Dartus, M. (1995) 'Forecasting international conference attendance'. *Tourism Management*, 16: 559–570.

Wood, E. (2004) 'Marketing information for the events industry', in I. Yeoman, M. Robertson, J. Ali-Knight, S. Drummond and U. McMahon-Beattie (eds), *Festival and Events Management: An International Arts and Culture Perspective*. Oxford: Butterworth-Heinemann.

Writing@CSU (2013) 'Reliability and validity'. Online. Available HTTP: http://writing.colostate.edu/guides/research/relval/index.cfm (accessed 20 June 2013).

Xu, F. and Fox, D. (2012) 'Anthropocentric or ecocentric attitudes to nature and their influence on attitudes to sustainable tourism development in national parks: A cross cultural comparison of British and Chinese visitors'. Second Advances in Hospitality and Tourism Marketing and Management Conference, 31 May–3 June 2012, Corfu, Greece.

Yamane, T. (1967) *Statistics: An Introductory Analysis*, 2nd edn. London: Harper and Row.

Yates, S. J. (2004) *Doing Social Science Research*. London: Sage Publications.

Yeoman, I., Robertson, M., Ali-Knight, J., Drummond, S. and McMahan-Beattie, U. (2004) *Festivals and Events Management: An International Arts and Culture Perspective*. London: Elsevier.

Yin, R. (2009) *Case Study Research: Design and Methods*, 4th edn. London: Sage Publications.

Youngs, I. (2010) 'Festivals thrive in concert boom'. Online. Available HTTP: http://news.bbc.co.uk/2/hi/entertainment/8681763.stm (accessed 14 August 2013).

Index